All My Own Words

All My Own Words

The Sportswriter who was author of his downfall

Neil Harman

pitch

First published by Pitch Publishing, 2022

Pitch Publishing
9 Donnington Park,
85 Birdham Road,
Chichester,
West Sussex,
PO20 7AJ
www.pitchpublishing.co.uk
info@pitchpublishing.co.uk

A CIP catalogue record is available for this book
from the British Library.

ISBN 978 1 80150 378 5

Typesetting and origination by Pitch Publishing

Printed and bound in Great Britain by TJ Books, Padstow

Contents

Preface 7
1. The Beginning and the End 11
2. The Paper Round. 19
3. I'm a Sports Reporter 31
4. Birmingham 64
5. Laurie Cunningham 81
6. Young Neil Harman 89
7. Manchester .109
8. A Brave New World 152
9. The Football Job 181
10. The FA Premier League 212
11. A Little Light Turbulence 221
12. Did We Not Like That? 227
13. Musical Chairs 235
14. Coming Home and Playing Away 246
15. A Sunday Man 274
16. *The Times* Comes Calling 280
17. Goodbye JP. 290
18. The Davis Cup 296
19. The Making of Andy Murray 313
20. Courting Popularity 327
21. Murray's Wimbledon 350
22. Trouble Ahead 357
23. Unemployment 364
24. Yeah, I'm a Wanderer. 371
25. Epitaph 378

Preface

WHERE THE written word is employed, is there a more horrible term than plagiarist? Google 'Neil Harman' eight years after my journalistic demise and the word is here, there and everywhere (yes, I know these are Lennon and McCartney's lyrics).

There is barely a day goes by when I don't think on the 'P' word. It's the nature of the beast I suppose. I was guilty of it not once but many times, and I'm offended by the thought of using another person's work passed off as my own regardless of it being sloppy oversight rather than malicious act.

I had led a gilded existence if truth be told, so I suppose there would be a tripping up somewhere along the way. It was just that I didn't expect the fall to be quite so resounding.

You would think that covering sport at the levels I attained prepared you for anything in life, but it doesn't always work out that way. I've read of those suddenly unemployed in their 50s and 60s who've been so depressed they have taken their own lives. I know a little of how these poor souls tried to process such an upheaval.

In work, I did have a wonderful time of it. My own seat at the old Wembley, Old Trafford, Anfield, Highbury, Maine Road, St James' Park, on Centre Court at Wimbledon, in New York, Paris and Melbourne, perched with notebook in hand behind the 18th green at the Old Course, St Andrews, in the press box at Roots Hall (Southend United's home ground for the uninitiated), largely unfettered access to share confidences and intimacies with some of the greatest athletes of the last 50 years. I've seen some stuff.

Oh for a few more of those moments when you stare at an empty screen or a virgin piece of paper and wonder what the heck you're going to say with only half an hour to say it. And then the pride when the next morning's paper popped through the letterbox and there were my words, good, bad or indifferent.

There are people I seriously need to thank, not least the newspaper editors and sports editors who had faith that I could do the job as they required it. They are too many to mention all by name, but David Williams at the *Southend Evening Echo*, Leon Hickman at the *Birmingham Evening Mail*, Bryan Webster at the *Daily Mail* in Manchester, Len Gould at *Today* and the *Mail*, David English (*Mail* editor supreme), Colin Gibson at the *Sunday Telegraph* and Keith Blackmore and David Chappell at *The Times* were cornerstones at critical moments in my journalistic development. Some of those named have gone to that great back bench in the sky, as have too many of the colleagues and work-mates I made along the way.

In putting the book together I spoke to old pals Bob 'Scoop' Downing and Peter White on the *Evening Mail*, Rob Shepherd, my former sidekick at the *Daily Mail*, and Colin Gibson with whom I travelled extensively as two chief football writers and then worked for at the *Sunday Telegraph* who all helped massage my memory. I chatted with David Platt about England football trips together and Ivan Lendl about our tennis experiences. I'm honoured to call them friends.

I should like to thank the current *Daily Mail* head of sport Mark Padgett for letting me back into the office to check some files and sportsdesk secretary Nicole Wilmshurst for making the system work for me! My desk is still there, as is Jeff Powell, now an incredibly sprightly 80-year-old. He remains the best football match reporter in my experience and from whom I learned so much. Jeff, Shep and I were an exceptional team back in the day.

This is my third book since being kicked into 'retirement'. Harry Findlay, an extraordinary character and legendary gambler, was the subject of the first and remains a great mate, as do all those who helped steer me through capturing the 2019/20 season at Wycombe Wanderers, one of the most astonishing periods of my entire writing career. They didn't know me from Adam the day I first pitched up at Adams Park those three summers ago and now they're extended family.

Talking of pitch, I need to thank Jane Camillin at Pitch Publishing for her support of my little project, Duncan Olner for his artistic impression on the front cover and Gareth Davis, a former sports editor himself, for lending his expertise to the task of subbing the copy into presentable form.

She won't like me saying it but since my life was upended, my wife Maureen has been a resolute rock. While I was licking my wounds, she picked up the pieces and is a successful golf club manager, not for the first time deriving profit from loss. We're 33 years wed in 2022. She deserves multiple medals.

My daughters Elizabeth and Kathleen were always there with loving and positive emotions when they sensed I was feeling low, which was quite often. I love them all immensely.

You do learn a lot about yourself and others when you're in a period of adversity. Mostly that you're dropped like a stone. Only a few remain steadfast and even those fall away with time. But there is always a hand to be offered. My Christian faith has been a bulwark against what was said about me and I probably wouldn't be in the choir at Corpus Christi Catholic Church in Wokingham if I was still a full-time journalist, so life offers many consolations.

The media landscape has changed so much since the days of hot metal, typewriters, notebooks, pens, being content to kill to find a telephone that worked and then dictating copy, often to a disinterested voice at the other end of the line. From standing around in club car parks to catch an eye and a quote or being invited into a footballer's home without hesitation, it is now a question of myriad press officers, formal interviews, contrived set pieces, controlled access. The current crop is welcome to it.

What did strike me when I returned to the *Mail* for my research was how few reporters were in the place. We used to live for being in the office, and I tell a few of those stories as well, to give you a sense of what it was like back in the day. I don't suppose I'll ever stop missing it.

Neil Harman
October 2022

1

The Beginning and the End

IN EARLY spring 1964 I had turned seven years old and attended class nine at the Fairways junior school in cosy Leigh-on-Sea, Essex. 'Rag Doll' by Frankie Valli and the Four Seasons topped the UK charts, you could feed the birds for tuppence a bag with Mary Poppins and I was addicted to television programmes as widely diverse as *Crackerjack!* and *Z Cars* where Fancy Smith and Jock Weir led the fight against crime under the fearsome leadership of Detective Inspector Charlie Barlow.

I wanted to be a policeman when I grew up and the previous Christmas my parents had bought me a PC 49 uniform from the popular fictional character on the *BBC Light Programme*. It came complete with whistle and chain, helmet and truncheon and through sheer embarrassment I wore it only as far as our front gate.

That May, West Ham United beat Preston North End 3-2 in the FA Cup Final at Wembley, a match to which I was able to hitch a ride thanks to my father's latter-life conversion to London's East End and forever bubble-blowing. I was dressed for the occasion as if I was going to Sunday school: clean white shirt, jacket, smart tie, pressed pants.

The last of the country's steam engines had been phased out two years earlier, so the trains on the London Fenchurch Street line – if not as awe-inspiring as the locomotives – felt clean and elegant. The passengers boarding at Leigh station clambered into compartments that extended the train's width to squeeze together on either of the long, facing seats. The thrill was almost too much to bear.

When we arrived on Wembley Way thanks to a ride on something called the underground, I'd never seen so many people in such an overwhelming space. The stadium itself with its two turret-like towers appeared to touch the sky. Most of the men wore suits and ties and though there was no pushing or shoving, Dad clasped my hand tightly to guide me to our seats.

A lot of the fans of Preston were wearing peculiar round hats made of card with the club's name on the sides, which I'd have been embarrassed to wear to a kid's birthday party and certainly not out in full view of the public.

They didn't seem to mind being pointed out and laughed at. In fact everyone that afternoon seemed deliriously happy with life. My dad especially, as he had managed from meagre earnings to afford the tickets for us on a corner to the left of the Royal Box about halfway up the first tier. I was asked quite a few times if I could see over the bodies in front of me (I was a bit of a tiddler). Football crowds were very different way back when.

An upright defender with short-cropped blond hair named Bobby Moore stood out on the pitch and I appreciated fully that football could be played in all the colours of the rainbow rather than the fuzzy black-and-white of our 12in living-room corner Rediffusion.

West Ham – looking so fresh and neat in their claret and blue shirts – won with a late goal by Ronnie Boyce at the opposite end of the ground to our seats, and though I couldn't see at all then I didn't particularly care. I just jumped up and down like everyone else going mental around me.

Dad went on and on about Bobby Moore. Who would have thought that a good deal later in life I would befriend four of that cup-winning side – the wonderful Bobby included – and the most talked-about player in the Preston team that day, 17-year-old Howard Kendall? And that I'd have a seat with my name on it at Wembley for seven extraordinary years?

My school report in that awakening summer of 1964, when Peter and Gordon's 'A World Without Love' and Billy J. Kramer and the Dakotas with 'Little Children' were the British pop rage, marked me as 'excellent' in English Language, Spelling Comprehension, Handwriting, as well as Mathematical tables and Mental Arithmetic.

Form teacher Peter Hemmings's assessment presaged my future career as if he was a clairvoyant, 'Neil maintains an excellent standard in all subjects and takes pains to produce work done to the very best of his ability. However, on some occasions, a desire to be "first to finish" has resulted in careless work; care must not be sacrificed for speed.'

* * *

The room was small and anaemic. I recalled thinking that if this was to be the end, what an ignominious place it was to go out, an office so markedly lacking in spirit it was probably home to the obituaries' editor.

Four decades from a callow 16-year-old to nearing 60 were spent inside newspaper offices and press boxes of theatrical atmosphere, overflowing with frenetic, fractious hubbub, noisy equipment, noisier people, unrestrained emotion, shouting matches, surges of adrenalin and that thumping in the head that accompanied the on-rush of a deadline with an empty notebook on your desk. Was it really to finish in this nondescript cubicle with these strangers?

I was sitting across from two women I knew only by name and who had neither a clue about me, my career and my life nor remotely cared. I had worked with incredible zeal and a decent degree of success for *The Times* – which I considered the doyen of British newspapers – for a dozen years and now for the second occasion in my career I was dispensable.

Six months earlier I had been highly commended as a specialist correspondent at the Sports Journalists' Association (SJA) awards. *The Times* won Sports Team of the Year at the British Press Awards and retained its Newspaper of the Year title. As an individual and as a team we were flying. But the fallout from a News International inquiry into my use of other writers' work in books to promote the Wimbledon tennis championship without the proper acknowledgement needed clearing up.

The paper's deputy editor Emma Tucker, whom I'd met briefly when clinging to the hope that she might offer me a reprieve, shuffled her papers and said it was over. There was to be no coming back.

Thankfully I didn't have a desk in the office otherwise I'd have probably been asked to empty it before being frogmarched off the premises by a couple of muscly security attendants. That's what happened to offending journalists.

I was dismayed that editor John Witherow hadn't the balls to condemn me in person. He had moved 18 months earlier from the *Sunday Times* to *The Times* and I was among several members of staff he invited to his home in Fulham in the spring for a few drinks to get to know each other.

According to his company profile, Witherow had been sent on the aircraft carrier HMS *Invincible* to cover the Falklands War for *The Times* in the early 1980s. It said he survived Exocet attacks that destroyed HMS *Sheffield* and was put ashore at Port Stanley, the islands' capital, with the 5th Infantry Brigade.

He came under bomb attack while on an ammunition ship and was 'close by' when Argentine aircraft struck RFA *Sir Galahad*, killing 48 servicemen, the biggest single loss of the war. He was clearly a brave bastard.

It didn't, therefore, require exceptional courage to come and tell a man for whom I thought he had some degree of professional admiration that he was now unemployed. This was one bullet he needn't have dodged.

The two previous editors I served at *The Times*, Robert Thomson and James Harding, would have met me face to face and perhaps found the means not to have sacrificed me at all. I had enormous respect for them.

The other figure present on judgement day was NI's director of human resources, Amy Graham. When her eyes met mine, I just knew she wanted shot of me. What a ghastly job it had to be that required the occupant to show not a jot of human empathy. Harman out. Box ticked.

Tucker asked if I needed assistance – in the orienteering sense – to find my way out of a building I'd only been in the one time after the report on my two hearings at the old *Times* office in Wapping landed across her desk.

Instead of politely thanking her and being escorted away, I blurted, 'I know my way out, thank you,' which was absolute bloody rubbish because I had to ask three different people how to operate the doors and someone else to press the buttons that worked the lift. They all possessed shiny lanyards. My 'guest' pass was singularly useless and come to think of it, who had ever been invited to be a guest at their own funeral?

Sucking in gulps of fresh air, I stepped on to the draughty concourse across from London Bridge station. I remember my legs felt as if they had frozen. The famed red double-deckers were forming an orderly queue as black cabs patiently waited for custom. All else was typical London hustle and bustle near a major terminus and here was I, completely motionless.

I looked up to where I estimated *The Times*'s editorial floor was housed – I never got to see it after the paper's recent relocation – and supposed I might catch someone's eye. There was to be no thank you note, no leaving party, no reaching out, no nothing. All those bloody wasted years.

My timing was shit too.

NI was obsessed with keeping its noses clean in the light of the phone-hacking trauma that cast a deep shadow across the company and the industry as a whole. It had closed down the mega-successful *News of the World*, and its sister paper *The Sun* was front and centre of a still unfolding drama. I suppose, in a sense, I was collateral damage.

The reigning Wimbledon tennis champion Andy Murray had asked me only a few months earlier if I had been taught how to hack a phone. 'Come on, Neil, you must know how it's done,' he said, and for a minute I couldn't tell if he was being serious or not. That was the kind of poison pervading our profession.

I had once been invited into Rupert Murdoch's office in New York where we talked for half an hour about tennis and his love for the sport, especially Roger Federer. He said he really liked my work and to 'keep going, mate'. I walked back along Fifth Avenue with a real spring in my step. Now, despite requests to ask if he would intervene in my case, all efforts at communication went unanswered.

The All England Lawn Tennis and Croquet Club, aka Wimbledon, whose own leadership at the time was, in my opinion, both charmless and hubristic, didn't want me back into the grounds in a working capacity as I had sullied their well-crafted image.

I once really liked the place and worked in harmony with people who saw their role in running the tournament as a joyful opportunity to do good. This wasn't the same club where I made good friends and respect appeared mutual. It would always look nice from the outside but so did the Houses of Parliament.

For two such mighty establishments, the sacking of a sports hack was a necessary convenience. This time care had been sacrificed for speed to crushing effect.

The single consolation I held on to was that neither of my parents had lived to see this happen.

* * *

Could any journalist with four decades on the clock say hand on heart they hadn't at one time snitched a line or two, an idea or two or piggybacked someone else's initiative? I doubted it. As my fate registered, what nagged was how I'd been so naive after all my years in the business.

There was nothing to gain – Wimbledon were chipping away at the author's fee year after year – and a good deal more to lose as I crunched the editorial buried beneath a swathe of printed reports and quote sheets, trying to disseminate the best bits.

How difficult would it have been in the context of extracting three paragraphs from a match report in *The Guardian* to write, 'As reported in *The Guardian*'? Would anyone reading it have felt less of me as a writer? Why didn't something in my head click? The book was a rush job but another hour or two spent assembling an acknowledgement page was not beyond my capabilities. I let too much slide.

The sorry misadventure was exposed on a US-based website called Slate, described by Wikipedia as 'a liberal, progressive online magazine known for publishing contrarian pieces'. There was nothing contrarian in its piece about me, headlined 'Unforced Errors'.

The writer was a ferociously ambitious freelance from New York named Ben Rothenberg who was inordinately keen to nail me to a cross. Rothenberg called when I was changing trains at Gatwick Airport on my way to cover the 2014 LTA County Cup Group One finals in Eastbourne, which would become my final outing.

I was being snared into answering questions I should have blanked. More naivety. It's funny how things spring to mind but when I was stumbling around Devonshire Park trying to concentrate that day, Colin Beecher, a coach I'd known for years, asked, 'Are you OK, Neil, you don't seem your usual self?' I muttered something about being fine.

When the Slate article was published, I was on my way to dust. Rothenberg quoted me saying, 'There's a quick turnaround for the book and after [the] Andy Murray [Wimbledon victory] especially, emotions were all over the place.

'I lock myself into a room to try and get my mind back to writing again when that's the last thing you feel like doing. The book is the club book, it's not my book. They've trusted me to do something and clearly, on occasions, I've not done it properly.'

I had interviewed Rothenberg in the US Open's main interview room for my book on the 2012 tennis season, *Court Confidential*, but hadn't used any of his words as they added nothing to the text. Maybe he had the hump about that though I'd found him an unctuous individual which didn't make him unique in the annals of tennis reporting.

I wrote to the leaders of the International Tennis Writers' Association, of which I was a founding father in 1999, to resign my membership, an email sent on the proviso that its content remained between us until I said otherwise but silly of me to ask a group of journalists not to tell anyone anything.

What was a mystery was who had tipped off Wimbledon about these misdemeanours and had both the time or inclination to pore through the pages of the annual and hold them up to the light?

2

The Paper Round

THE RADIO alarm in my matchbox bedroom tuned to the BBC World Service and its distinctive 'Lillibulero' theme would sound at 5am and I was scrubbed, teeth brushed, hair combed and alert behind the newsagent's counter by half past.

There were 200 yards between 181 Eastwood Road North, Leigh-on-Sea and Milligan's at Coombes Corner, and a quick wash (we didn't have a shower) before pulling a light-grey tunic over my morning threads and dashing down the street rarely required having to be shaken awake by my parents.

The anticipation never waned as I awaited the sound of the engine of the white van that pulled up in the pitch black, whose back doors were swung open and the treasures therein were carried into the shop and deposited on to the counter.

Harry Milligan, bespectacled, hunched and always in a white flat cricket umpire's cap, slashed at the binding and separated *Daily Mail* from *Daily Sketch*, *Daily Telegraph* from *The Sun*, *Morning Star* – there were commies in Leigh?! – from *Sporting Life*, weeklies from the periodicals and passed them across to me for the marking process to begin.

The smell of printer's ink was the 1970 version of Costa Coffee. I'd hold the papers up to my nose, inhale deeply and then get down to making sure the numbers written on the top right-hand corners matched those in Mr Milligan's master book.

By six o'clock the first of half a dozen paper boys would be loading their bags and mingling with bleary-eyed commuters grabbing for their paper or gesturing towards their favoured cigarettes before catching the 23A to Leigh-on-Sea station and an hour pressed sardine-like on the Fenchurch Street train. I served as I marked.

As the boy in charge, I got first dibs on the shop's bicycle, which was just as well as my parents couldn't afford to buy my own. This was a black-framed masterpiece with a basket soldered to the front, so I didn't have to sling the bag across my shoulders and walk the entire round. I loved that old bike, which Mr Milligan kept in pristine condition.

That was more than could be said for the state of the papers when the good people of Leigh yanked them through the letterbox. Like any decent sports-mad kid, I thumbed through the pages from the back, picking up on the stories of the day and being attracted, always, to the names of the writers while drawing mental images of the lives they must lead.

My mum fretted about me having to push the bike across eight lanes of the Southend Arterial Road dual carriageway (A127) in the half-light of a morning for one stop at 10 Hazelwood Grove that took the *Sketch*. I'd often take these crossings dreaming I was Frank McGhee, Brian James or Peter Lorenzo.

On one dismal, misty morning, Mum was stirred by a knock at the front door, which was alarming given it was before 7am. Dad had departed for his commute into the City of London and Mum supposed he might have forgotten his pipe and tin of St Bruno Flake for the first time. Then again, he never misplaced his keys.

Opening the door to be greeted by two police constables who said they had some bad news, Mum let out a piercing scream that could have been heard in Shoeburyness and collapsed at their feet on the front step.

The coppers helped her to her feet and informed her that her brother, my beloved uncle Charlie, had passed away in London, no one could find our telephone number and they were sorry to be the bearers of such sad tidings.

When I dashed back down the front path a few minutes later to change into my school clothes, Mum opened the door and almost squeezed the breath out of me.

* * *

Though my enthusiasm for the work never waned, Mr Milligan's maudlin character was wearing and I was elated to discover that the much bigger shop at the other end of the road – Belfairs Newsagents – had been taken over by a couple from out of the area who were looking for a young assistant. I went to see them and was given the job.

Phil and Helen Brown hailed from Preston. I told them I'd been at Wembley for the 1964 FA Cup Final which helped break any ice. Their Lancashire dialect was broad, and disconcerting as I had to concentrate hard to catch all they said, especially if Phil had forgotten to put his teeth in at 5.30am.

Phil was a stocky bugger with a full head of greased black hair and a fetish for hard labour. Helen, bless her, was round-faced and unceasingly kind, pampering me rotten much to Phil's little-hidden disdain. 'Stop fussing over the lad,' I'd hear him say when she had disappeared into the kitchen area at the back of the shop to make me some more tea. They hadn't had children of their own.

I marked the papers there and though he'd never say it, Phil grudgingly liked the fact that I was always on time, never shirked a shift and would gladly take the bus from school two stops past the one nearest home so I could work behind the counter until closing time at six. Phil paid 30p an hour and I could earn over £5 a week if I put my shoulder into it.

There was something regal about helping to run a newsagent's shop. As boys of my age enjoyed a crafty one behind the scout hut, I was a purveyor of all they craved, be it No.6 (a packet of ten set you back 9p), Embassy, Silk Cut, Nelson (Mum's brand) or, for the suave who liked menthol mixed with their nicotine, Consulate.

In the time before machines did all the work, the totals were calculated using mental arithmetic and pencil scrawl on top of a confectionary bag, the till was awfully like Arkwright's killer contraption in *Open All Hours* and you measured the change counting backwards into the customer's hand. Glory days.

Phil was fastidious about the sweet jars being in alphabetical order – aniseed balls first, barley sugar, cola drops, etc. – and neatness on the magazine display where just a hint of one title should be exposed from behind its neighbour on the shelf. There wasn't a great deal of respite between this desire for smartness and serving the customers but any time we paused for breath he'd regale me with stories about his love for Lancashire County Cricket Club, of which he was a life member.

He would wax lyrical about Frank Hayes and Jackie Bond, Jack Simmons and Clive Lloyd so I'd counter with Essex's finest, J.K. Lever, Brian 'Tonker' Taylor and Robin Hobbs and if I really wanted to wind him up (which wasn't easy) I'd mention what a great cricketer Keith Fletcher was. If Phil had his teeth in he ground them and, if not, he sucked hard on his gums.

My father was much more into his cricket than football if truth be told. He was born in 1910 in Ealing, west London, and when the country was getting back to its wearied feet after the Great War and people went out to play again, Dad was mesmerised by the sporting exploits of a local boy.

Patsy Hendren was a thunderous batsman for both Middlesex and England and between these red ball heroics he managed to fit in 399 appearances for Brentford between 1911 and 1927, scoring 69 goals in the process. If not quite in the C.B. Fry class, Hendren was an incredibly powerful, charismatic all-rounder.

Dad's infatuation with Hendren was such that – though he was christened Eric John – he was known to all as Pat, for Patsy. I never once heard him called Eric, either by his elder brothers Maurice and Reg or anyone who worked with or for him.

My introduction to live cricket was every bit as astonishing as the first time I saw real football. Dad said we were in for a treat as we caught the bus – he wouldn't pass his driving test until well into his 50s and couldn't afford a car when he did – and after a half-hour journey to Southchurch Park we leapt from the conductor's platform to join those jostling to pay two shillings, or sixpence for juniors, to get in.

The Essex cricket team were in town and the opposition was from a world-away land called Australia. It was August 1964.

Dad rented a deckchair for himself and had brought a blanket for me to place as close to the boundary rope as possible. We found a spot sideways to the pitch, looking west towards the pavilion and I pulled out the scorer's book he'd bought for the occasion. The weather was idyllic summer Southend-on-Sea in one of the UK's five driest years of the 20th century.

On the opening day of three – Saturday, 22 August – Essex won the toss and proceeded to dominate with the bat in a manner few in the sun-kissed crowd could have believed against mythical opposition. Southchurch Park had a reputation for a flat track that favoured the batting side but this was beyond the wildest local imaginations.

Gordon Barker, methodical and circumspect by reputation, and Fletcher, more youthful but generally unspectacular, joined forces with the score at 42/2 and against an attack led by Graham McKenzie and Alan Connolly took great delight in dispensing them to all corners of the park. Dot balls were a rarity.

At the close of an uninterrupted day's play, Essex were 425/6 and promptly declared. Barker had made 123 and Fletcher 125 before both men played tired shots, had their stumps rattled and were cheered all the way to the pavilion. Dad and I were back to see the Aussies skittled out for 218 in their first innings and hanging on at 78/1 when the stumps were drawn on the second.

Essex would eventually win by six wickets and I joined the throng racing across the pitch at the end of the match simply to gaze up at and touch as many of Australia's players as possible to confirm they weren't make-believe.

These were the sporting zeniths of a blissfully contented early youth. My parents scrimped for all we had but I didn't know that at the time or cared. They saved up so we could holiday in Cornwall, the Channel Islands and abroad for the first time in 1968 to Lloret de Mar – flying British Eagle to Girona – on Spain's Costa Brava.

Carlos, the head waiter at the Excelsior Hotel, was to become one of my first sporting heroes. He was in his early 30s and, not only built like the wrestler Mark 'Rollerball' Rocco, he took on all comers in bouts on the beach and forced submissions from much younger opponents one after another.

I was first down in the restaurant at the crack of dawn and he'd constantly fuss over me. He asked one day if he could take me to a local bullfight. Mum was dead against it but there I was, at 11 years of age, surrounded by screaming Spaniards forced to watch some poor animal ritually murdered.

Carlos knew everyone ringside, was the loudest bloke in the place and paraded me around as his important little *amigo* from England. I won't say it didn't make me feel special for a day or so but I never went to a bullfight again. Nor have I ever returned to Lloret de Mar.

* * *

I ran a mean cross-country, swam, played football in the local parks, was a Cub Scout, a Boy Scout and took many a sixpenny bus ride into Leigh-on-Sea to walk the surrounding hills, then skipped down the steep steps of Church Hill to the old town to watch the fishermen bring the cockle catch in to the stalls run by the famed Osborne brothers.

Old Leigh had one narrow street that housed tiny homes, fishing tackle shops, three pubs, emporia full of local knick-knacks, spinning kites on sticks and candy floss. In the salty air hung a mixture of fish, vinegar and beer and the street was full of frolicking kids and grown-ups with smart, collared shirts and long trousers heading to the few square yards of Bell Wharf beach at the end furthest from the railway station.

The younger of the Osbornes, Cyril, took a real shine to Mum, though that was understandable as she was a striking-looking woman. Our small plates would be piled high with winkles and a second carton of jellied eels arrived even if we hadn't asked for more.

Cyril would wink at Mum as he served us and all of this gentle flirting took place while Dad was in the Crooked Billet buying the family Guinness – the only alcohol I saw him take.

I was my father's lone offspring. He was 47 when I popped into the world and he often said at his age he thought he'd missed out on having children, let alone a son. My birth date of 9 April 1957 was the same as Severiano Ballesteros, who I would interview 22 years later when he was on the cusp of becoming the electrifying superstar of world golf.

Mum had had two children from a previous marriage to an American serviceman she'd met during the war years and who I never met. Kenny, my half-brother, and Wendy, my half-sister, and I lived in an unpretentious semi-detached with Mum and Dad. I was the youngest by nine years so we didn't spend a great deal of time doing the same things.

Then, in an early teen blur, I was exposed to a very different concept of life. I suppose you could call it an encounter of the erotic kind. Wendy – stunningly attractive and in her early 20s – had a ton of young men vying for her attention, quite a few of whom passed though 181 and thought that befriending me might smooth their path to her.

One such was named Renato, a handsome *amante* from Rome who arrived on the doorstep one day and it began to feel very serious. He drove a Maserati and to impress he swept me up Eastwood Road

North, accelerating away from the dawdling Austin Minors and Vauxhall Vivas with a daredevil air of someone who lived the fast life. I thought he'd be a great catch. Just as it seemed to be getting very serious, Renato vanished in a similar screech of tyre on asphalt that signalled many an arrival.

Why all of this just-about-keeping-it-in-their-pants attention to Wendy? Well, she was a leading fashion model for an agency owned and run by Gavin Robinson, whose offices in Old Bond Street were at the throbbing heartbeat of London's Swinging Sixties.

Wendy would take me on an assignment, placing me on the edge of the catwalk dressed in a suede cowboy jacket like the one Jon Voight wore in *Midnight Cowboy* (purchased from one of Carnaby Street's finest) and watch my brain try to compute as the loveliest women I was ever likely to see sashayed back and forth.

She was chic and glamorous and I was as proud as punch to be her toyboy brother and be taken into the dressing room for the changeovers. The models bustled around, often in a state of severe undress and never took offence at this kid in his early teens trying not to stare at them. A few of the girls happily shook their boobs in my face just to witness my reaction. Where else was I to look?

Being a sought-after fashion model would bring you into contact with the stars of the time. Buddy Greco, the American jazz pianist and crooner, had met Wendy after a show and duly arrived at 181 one weekend. Greco was a regular at the newly refurbished Talk of the Town on Charing Cross Road and shared the spotlight with such luminaries as Shirley Bassey, Sandie Shaw, Paul Anka, Lena Horne and Eartha Kitt.

The venue became synonymous with the finest in nightclub entertainment, with shows produced by two of the country's leading impresarios, Bernard (later Lord) Delfont and Robert Nesbitt. Our lounge was pinhead small by comparison to the massive stage and dining floor at TOTT but here was Buddy, all teeth and tan, wooing and wowing us at the same time.

We bought all his LPs but if we hoped Wendy was to become Mrs Greco – even if he was twice her age – it didn't happen. Buddy retained his love for Essex and lived a few years of his later life in Westcliff-on-Sea, the next town along from Leigh. There's Vegas, there's Palm Springs and there's Essex by the sea. Who'd want to live anywhere else?

Wendy was in her pomp when she married a Tottenham season ticket holder named John Hall who, seeking to worm his way to my affection, presented me with an impressive-looking menu card from a 1968 boxing night at London's Anglo-Sporting Club and stood back awaiting a response.

I had never heard of any of the food on the menu and then reached the back cover where the treasure was found. It was replete with autographs of famous footballers – Terry Venables, Joe Kinnear, Alan Mullery, George Cohen and, unbelievably, the Bobby Moore I'd fallen in love with four years earlier, an affair consummated when he led England to World Cup victory in 1966.

Bobby had signed the card 'Best wishes to Neil'. I was totally bowled over.

Hall had worked surreptitious magic on an 11-year-old but as the years went by and the marriage ended our family learned that this hugely powerful man with a barrel-chest and broad shoulders was a complete fucking arsehole who hung around footballers like a bad smell and treated my sister abominably.

He had his comeuppance from some strong-armed characters in north London and ended up with only a few of his ribs not caved in. Certain folk who knew certain folk didn't take too kindly to men who were ungentlemanly to their women.

* * *

A summons to the teachers' common room at Westcliff High School for Boys was not something to be undertaken without a sense of impending doom, like a visit to the dentist where they removed teeth with a barbaric instrument which looked like a giant pair of pliers having attempted to gas you first.

It usually meant verbal admonishment or perhaps something more gruesome, like the sharp upward tug of whatever bit of a sideburn you had developed by your mid-teens which was the particularly sadistic form of punishment doled out by 'Tosser' Day, the school's infamous head of history.

Though he wore the same swirling cape that was the grammar school garb of that period, careers master John Roberts was one of the more pleasing members of staff and an invitation to meet him rarely involved physical discomfort.

It was October 1973. I had passed only four of the eight O levels taken the previous summer, a disappointment in many ways but as I was not a gifted academic it was probably as well as I could have expected. I did feel terribly as if I'd let the side down. My parents weren't the admonishing type but I could tell they were a bit crushed.

I passed English Language, English Literature, French and Maths – the last to my amazement and only because I had in Jim Harrison from the third year a teacher who was both inspirational in the classroom and played hooker for the Old Westcliffians first XV well into his late 30s and so was something of a local sports phenom.

In my rare appearances for the school XV, I also played hooker though Nick Mitchell, a tough-nut blond, was the number one choice in that position because he had that little bit more energy and verve and didn't seem to mind being bent double in the rucks and mauls. That wasn't really my scene.

I did 'score' one try on the lower field, under the posts in front of the dining hall with dad watching from the sidelines. I was being hauled up from the mud by the back of the shirt when referee Dougie Mason, a maths teacher built like a brick shithouse, whistled and said I'd knocked the ball forward. I just about got out 'but, but sir' when he gave me a look to kill and I lost my voice.

I resat the failed O levels and chose to stay on in the sixth form at Westcliff, taking A level English, English Literature and Economics. The first two choices were understandable for a would-be writer but choosing economics would continue to baffle me through the obligatory chore of attempting to balance my expenses against fiscal reality for the next 40 years.

It was two months into term when Mr Roberts ushered me to the masters' table on which an assortment of newspapers was spread. 'Have you seen this, Harman?' he asked, pointing at an advertisement deep in the pages of the *Southend Standard*, the town's weekly journal.

The message was three inches square and stood out from the small ads in a section I'd not normally take the blindest bit of notice of. It was headed 'Do You Want To Make Sport Your Career?' under which was outlined the opportunity to join the *Evening Echo*, our five-night-a-week local, as a junior sports reporter.

I told Mr Roberts during a careers lesson about my dream of working in newspapers and thankfully he remembered or the ad that changed my life would have remained a total mystery to me. 'This is right up your street, my boy,' he said, cutting it from the paper and pressing it into my hand. 'What are you waiting for?'

A letter answering the *Echo*'s call was swiftly despatched and a few days later I grabbed at an envelope with my name on the front and a distinctive green John H. Burrows Ltd franking in the top-left corner.

A stock reply said that due to the number of respondents, the powers that be decided to set a competition for the candidates to write a report of a maximum of 500 words on a specified match from the following weekend's *Match of the Day* and from those a shortlist would be drawn.

For the life of me I remember neither the match nor what I wrote but the upshot was the arrival of a second letter asking me to arrange an interview at the paper's main office in Basildon. I had to find my way there by bus.

The essence of my contribution that day was that I wanted to be a sportswriter more than life itself. The *Echo*'s editor, David Williams, told me later that he was startled when he called me Mr Harman and I called him David. When a third letter from the *Echo* arrived, it came sprinkled with magic dust.

David offered me the job – four months shy of my 17th birthday.

3

I'm a Sports Reporter

TO WALK into a newspaper office for the first time was akin to sexual arousal – though my experience of that amounted to no more than being backstage at fashion shows where some stunning models jiggled their beautiful breasts in my face.

The girls from the *Echo* advertising department who preferred reaching their desks by means of passing the editorial floor did emit a certain allure beyond the sensual comprehension of a 16-year-old, but it wasn't to them I was drawn.

All I could take in was the sheer crazy heaving activity of a mass of reporters, raised voices shouting orders, waving of paper, the clatter of typewriter key upon ribbon, a glorious maelstrom of insanity from which somehow contrived to appear a hugely successful local newspaper that sold over 60,000 copies a night, five nights a week.

The *Echo*'s main office was an imposing building – to a naive kid most buildings were imposing – at the junction of Chester Hall Lane and Luckyn Lane on the Pipps Hill industrial estate in Basildon, one of the 'new towns' built to accommodate overspill from London, whose reconstruction after the war years failed to keep pace with a boom in population and housing demand.

The initial protest from the Essex locals who thought their rural idyll would disappear beneath ugly slabs of concrete subsided greatly when major industries like Ford motors located to the area, delivering wealth and enhanced links – both of road and rail – to the capital.

Basildon was 25 miles from the centre of London to the west and ten to Southend-on-Sea to the east. My parents had been among many couples from the capital who decided spending their later years by the seaside afforded many advantages for health and welfare after the lingering deprivation of six years of conflict.

Mum and Dad had met at work in the City in the mid-1950s. Dad was high up in the management echelons at London Inland Telegraphs and Mum – christened Peggy – worked in a clerical role on a different floor Dad would pass on his way to the smarter offices. Their eyes met across a crowded workroom.

They could not have been more markedly different. Dad – 16 years Mum's elder – was fastidious, quiet, undemonstrative, a pipe and slipper man once home. You could set your watch by him. I only really saw him angry if Mum forgot herself once in a while and poured gravy over his favourite plain boiled potatoes.

The family would wait on Saturday evening for the comical moment when Dad, who regularly dozed off early with pipe dangling from his lips, jerked awake immediately he heard the theme tune to *Match of the Day* and managed to re-clench the pipe without having to use his hands.

Mum was as happy to be a housewife as she had been in her life, especially somewhere she could really call home. The war years had been tough on an outgoing girl from Bethnal Green – a true-life Cockney sparrow – whose teenage years had been basically destroyed.

She recalled with tears in her eyes the day she heard an air-raid siren as the bombs were dropping on east London and escaped from her home – 8 Ravenscroft Buildings – only to be rocked by an ear-splitting detonation yards away that brought part of the building down, killing one of her closest friends.

Mum was an extrovert who had dreamed of being on the stage as a kid. She loved to sing – those genes passed from mother to son

– and was extremely house-proud which I presumed was a reaction to having lived so long in East End squalor.

Her father was Charles Cornelius Banfield and Mum said she had almost christened me Cornelius before Dad intervened and suggested an abbreviated Neil. Cornelius Harman? Bloody hell, what an escape that was.

For 30 years Grandad Charles owned a stall – Banfield's Fruit and Veg – on Brick Lane, which ran from Whitechapel to Bethnal Green, a haven for Jewish and Irish immigrants with its various temptations to squander the profits from the sale of Cox's and carrots. My uncle Charlie worked for his dad at the same time as earning a few shillings as a light-heavyweight boxer on the undercard at York Hall and other local venues.

Grandad drank and smoked his earnings away and pretty much made life hell for my grandma Catherine (Kate to her friends) and her kids. There was often very little on the table, which led to huge rows, much slamming of doors, blasphemy and all-night disappearing acts. Charles Cornelius once tried to push his son around only to regret it when Uncle Charlie knocked him out cold.

Mum let Grandad hold me once. He died when I was eight months old, leaving the family £163 in his will.

* * *

Dad was getting used to his new pride and joy Austin 1100 – its fourth gear remained something of a mystery to him – and was happy to drive me to my first day at the *Echo* and hang around a bit while I said a few hellos and introduced him to those I knew.

The *Echo*'s editorial floor was open-plan; there was enough breathing space between desks to relish our own environment while being close enough to other departments to eavesdrop on their business if so minded. The sports department was tucked between the frosted glass of the editor's office and a wall of windows offering an unfettered view of the delights of Basildon's concrete hinterland.

Sports editor John Tanner and his assistant Terry Poskitt had the best seats as their adjacent desks looked across the expanse of the news operation. Ahead and slightly to the left were the news subeditors charged with making sense of a reporter's copy, fitting it into the space allocated on one of 20 or so live broadsheet news pages and putting a headline to the story.

Chris Fowler was the chief sub who possessed a distinctly chippy attitude and given to sundry explosive outbursts. He wore flamboyant shirts with huge collars and lairy patterns that wouldn't have gone amiss in the backing group for Crosby, Stills and Nash (especially given the expanse of his own moustache). I found him particularly intimidating.

God knows how but Fowler and I were once in a gathering at the Fortune of War pub just off the A127 at Laindon having a lunchtime beer. As an ambulance raced by, he thumped me on the arm, 'What the fuck are you doing sitting there, go and chase it.'

By the time I realised he was serious, necked my drink, reached my Mini Cooper and crunched it into first gear, I couldn't hear the siren and had no way of knowing in which direction the vehicle had gone. Fowler disapproved with a particularly disdainful sneer.

At the newsdesk top table sat news editor Peter Owen, his deputy Keith Bartels, secretary Sue Webb and urbane chief photographer Ron Case, a lovely man with one remarkable claim to fame.

When working for the Keystone photographic agency in London in 1952, Ron was deputed to cover the funeral of King George VI and was in a prime spot as the veiled Queen Mary, Queen Elizabeth the Queen Mother and Queen Elizabeth II stood together, the only time that three Queens had been captured in a single image. A picture never bettered.

The news bosses barked orders to a dozen reporters, chief of whom was Del Flatley, a rotund, bespectacled figure in his late 50s with a magistrate's demeanour and legendary reporting status. Nothing happened in south Essex politics that Del didn't know about or pass an opinion on.

He gave his backrest a daily workout and because he raised his seat to full height he would type with his forearms at a steep downwards angle. You could hear him pound away his copy on the useless fat cats of Southend council wherever you happened to be in the building.

Across from Del sat Jo Weedon, a niece of the hit guitarist of the era, Bert Weedon. Jo's specialist task as a reporter was to deal with death. I could hardly imagine a more awful task to perform and yet I doubt anyone could have done it with a greater degree of dispassionate feeling.

Jo reached through the contraption she was holding and drew from relatives and friends of a traffic accident or fire victims both endearingly heart-rending testimonies and innermost secrets as if she was holding their hands. What a gal.

The features department was squeezed away to the left of sport and contained a sea of characters like Val Flatley, Del's wife, who was an agony aunt one minute, a fashion guru the next and could turn her hand to superbly touching interviews.

Ron Godfrey, dark goatee and wavy hair, wrote the most beautiful pieces; the urbane Roger Diss was the theatre critic while Tully Potter, bespectacled and bearded, specialised in colourful classical music reviews. The *Echo* was blessed with splendid talent and silly names.

* * *

The sports department was rich in quality and looked upon by others with a level of respect not usually afforded the 'games area', so christened by Sue Webb. If a paper's circulation success was based upon which editorial element was the most widely read and discussed, then *Echosport* was major points scorer.

Directly behind the desks of Tanner and Poskitt and across from each other sat senior football writers Nigel Fuller and Roy Collins. In the furthest corner crouched the menacing figure of Colin Price, the rugby writer who played scrum-half into his mid-30s. My desk was set apart from the others as if in my own little world. One day I wanted to be right in the thick of everything.

The *Echo* employed two copy runners, Frank and Harry, both of whom were 70-plus and had long since given up running for a bus. The process of transferring the reporter's finished article to the print works would regularly be extended because Frank liked to chat about the state of sport whereas Harry was going a little deaf and often ignored the cry of 'copy down!' from the subs' desk. When it was repeated, only louder by an irate Chris Fowler, Harry would mutter, 'I bloody heard you the first time.'

I used to get right on their nerves when the bell sounded to signal the first edition's arrival from downstairs. It was their task to drop a neatly folded copy on each desk but often the slowpokes were nowhere to be found and I couldn't resist dashing over to grab one from the top of the pile.

It is difficult to explain the sense of a first feel of an edition, hot off the presses. The ink had barely dried; in fact, the paper was slightly damp with the newness of it all. It had a distinctive smell of newspaper nectar, the same that roused my senses behind the newsagents' counter a couple of years earlier.

Tanner received his copy, leant back, unfolded it with a satisfied flourish and studied his handiwork. The boss was a diffident Welshman, studied and remote. He had a smartly trimmed thin beard, was pale of complexion and superior in manner, disconcertingly so for a new kid on the block. He possessed no sense of humour I could discern.

Tanner's deputy was the engaging if scatterbrained Poskitt, an East Ender who covered boxing and seemed in permanent pre-occupation as if he'd been on the end of the odd uppercut himself. Tanner and Poskitt tolerated each other but were from completely different stock. I got the sense Terry believed John was unsuited to the job (and that he'd be much better at it).

Price, another Welshman, was built like a small tank, had a permatan, a goatee and emitted an intimidating air largely because he always looked so intense. He hustled rather than walked and most of his colleagues were in professional and physical awe of him.

Fuller was the Southend United correspondent and covered Essex CCC, so as a local sportswriter he had no peer. I liked him straight away; the unkempt appearance (I doubted he owned a comb), ill-fitting jackets, suede shoes, bitten nails, touch-typing, straight-talking, no nonsense attitude – especially to the sports editor and his deputy – were endearing.

Nigel would pick up the phone to Arthur Rowley, Southend's manager at the time, and show neither the slightest deference nor acceptance of bullshit. I see him now, finger to ear, probing at an unenthusiastic interviewee. He asked direct questions and wanted straight answers. His match reports were to the point and never written as if he was draped in a Shrimpers scarf. He was fair when he had to be and harsh if the team had played like shit (quite often).

Roy Collins was my hero. He wore leather jackets, often had his shirt unbuttoned, his hair was black and full, all the Fleet Street sportswriters were his mates, he was a stylish writer on London football, especially West Ham, and had a winning way with the girls.

If Roy asked me to join him for a lunchtime drink I was there, a panting puppy eager to soak up his craft and expertise – and not just as a writer. Nigel was teetotal and didn't often do lunch, Pricey wanted to keep his physique and played squash between one and three most days, the bosses usually stayed back to check on the editions and so it was Roy and me. He was the writer and person I yearned to be.

There was much to do for that aspiration to come to pass. I had to endure a period of indenture, the process by which a young writer was taught the often arduous but fundamentally imperative tricks of the trade.

If you didn't pass your proficiency certificate taken at the end of three years' experience on the job, you were not classed as a bonafide journalist. My task had extra pressure in that when I arrived at the

Echo I was one O level short of the stated requirement even to be a member of staff.

After three fretful months not knowing whether I'd be allowed to stay or be sent back to Westcliff High with tail between legs, I learned I'd passed two retakes – History and Biology in my case – and so here I was ready to set out into the big wide world. Well, Harlow.

In pursuit of verification as a journalist, I attended two 'block release' courses, living in the unremarkable new town for two months at a time, studying at the technical college subjects as numbing as Public Administration and Newspaper Law, while having to master Pitman shorthand to 100 words per minute to gain a pass grade from the National Council for the Training of Journalists (NCTJ).

Other than the depressing sensation that you'd only recently left school and were back behind a desk, what made this more arduous was that the NCTJ course was designed with the all-round news reporter in mind rather than someone designated as a specialist.

I needed to receive basic newsdesk grounding and was seconded to the branch office in Southend, just around the corner from the central railway station, where one floor and a single long room had an extended desk housing 20 reporters at the head of which sat Howard Southwood, chief of the operation and deputy news editor of the paper.

Howard was a Roots Hall regular as he freelanced on United for the *Daily Mirror* and so I presumed he might look kindly on someone who wasn't *au fait* with the whys and wherefores of news reporting.

On the contrary; he had me running around everywhere. One evening it was the wonders of Canewdon Parish Council, then a few days in the company of crown court reporter Tim Stout and his masterful shorthand, stopping people in the High Street to ask why they thought numbers were declining at Peter Pan's Playground or standing outside a church, gathering the attendees' names at the funeral of a local dignitary.

On my 18th birthday I had a planned party at Roots Hall in United's new nightclub – irresistibly named Fanny's. During the day I covered a fire brigade union meeting that promised disruption in the town if demands for increased safety on the job weren't met.

The meeting was volatile, the firemen proceeded to a vote and the majority signalled a desire for industrial action. This was front-page material. Potentially the lead. The newsdesk had been warned to expect an outcome around midday, as the first edition deadline loomed. A space was saved on the page, just in case. It was a reporter's task to make sure his copy was clean, readable and prompt.

All the phones in the station were either occupied with the men phoning relatives with news of the vote or being kept open for emergency calls. I scampered down the road looking for a red box. The first one was out of order, another had been vandalised and for the life of me, blood pumping, I couldn't find another one. Time ticked on. Something else had to be subbed into the space where my piece should have gone. I finally filed my story at 1.30pm. Deadline missed.

Howard was incandescent. 'I don't care what bloody day it is,' he said, referring to my partial coming of age. 'The next time you miss a deadline, you're fired. Knock on someone's door and demand to be let in.' A few hours later he was leaning against the bar at Fanny's wishing me many happy returns of the day as if nothing had happened.

There was another guest that night who had a bit more about him than Howard, in fact more about him than 99 per cent of the male population. Two of the three footballing Worthington brothers, Dave and Bob, played for Southend at the time, accepted an invitation to the party and asked if it would be OK if their other sibling tagged along.

Frank Worthington? At *my* 18th? Hell, yes. Frank duly arrived dressed like a rock star, leaned on a corner of the bar all night, toasted my good health and guaranteed that if I had wanted to consummate such a coming of age with something rather more potent than a bottle of Guinness, the likelihood was I'd have to drag one of the ladies away from his side and hope they may show me some pity. Suffice to say, there were no takers.

* * *

My passion for sports was all-encompassing and in the first few weeks at the *Echo* it needed to be. Everything that no one else cared too much about was thrown my way. My first by-line on a local paper in Essex was, therefore, a story on badminton from New Zealand.

The 1974 Commonwealth Games were being staged in that far-off land and a girl from Corringham named Nora Gardner – who would become Nora Perry – was enjoying a good deal of success. It definitely merited a mention and, asked to pick the best bits from agency reports, I pieced together a blockbusting five-paragraph story. John Tanner put my name on it.

My next half a dozen printed articles were on cyclo-cross, hockey, karate, diving, tennis (featuring one John Lloyd of Leigh-on-Sea) and table tennis before, on 22 February, I made my football debut about an English Schools Trophy quarter-final involving Basildon Boys and their pre-eminent player Paul Clark, who had been selected for England under-15s.

A week later my very first piece on Southend United appeared, all four paragraphs on Blues striker Kevin Johnson being loaned to Gillingham.

I had been a North Bank regular at Roots Hall – wearing Doc Martens a couple of times to Mum's head-shaking dismay – for five years. From that brilliant vantage point I watched our £3,000 signing from Northampton Town, Billy Best, in tandem with Gary Moore destroy non-league opposition King's Lynn (9-0) and Brentwood Town (10-1) in the first two rounds of the 1968 FA Cup. The blond Ian 'Chico' Hamilton was my idol though, spinning and crafting, in the number ten shirt. Sadly Chico passed away in February 2022 from a heart attack on a golf course in Florida.

Blues should have been promoted to the Third Division in 1967/68 but fell from contention when the goals dried up and we won one match in nine. Manager Ernie Shepherd would leave a season later but before he departed, he spent £100 on a young winger from Canvey Island named Peter Taylor.

What a signing that proved to be, a local player who dipped his shoulder, took on defenders and skipped past them with abandon. He was an absolute joy to watch.

Taylor was signed by Crystal Palace manager Malcolm Allison for £110,000 in October 1973 but remained living in Southend, coached a local team called Rocheway, and we'd often see each other on a Sunday lunchtime for a little lubrication. Peter, or 'Spud' as he was known, was my first real contact with superstardom as, I suppose, I perceived it.

Back at the *Echo*, Fuller and Collins took precedence writing about the Blues' first XI, so I sought to persuade Tanner that I should cover the reserve and youth teams in the Midweek and South-East Counties Leagues.

That would give me the opportunity to build a contact base among enough people at United to be a massive asset for the paper's needs. No one else had the time or inclination to report on the reserves and especially the youth teams. I'd endeavour to become their mate. After all, they were all my age.

The South-East Counties fixtures were played at Wellstead Gardens, a couple of roads along Southchurch Boulevard from Westcliff High School. The entrance to the field was hardly festooned with match advertisements; indeed, you did well to spot it at all, tucked inauspiciously behind a row of rather grand semi-detached homes.

The first United youth game for which I received a by-line was Southend v Reading in the spring of 1974. Initially standing on my own with notebook furtively concealed, I was drawn closer to a pair of vocal ladies on the touchline that I discovered were Pat Rafter and Cynthia Wellman, the mothers of goalkeeper Sean Rafter and right-back Peter Wellman.

I introduced myself and soon became a part of a regular Saturday morning coterie. I'd overhear the latest gossip about the workings at the club – parents could be rather indiscreet and very well informed – how their sons were coping with their games, their girlfriends, their lifestyles; you know, the juicy stuff.

Sean was someone I'd follow closely and not only because his mum was blessed with terrific antennae when it came to all matters SUFC. It did help that the Rafter home on Princes Avenue was open house, where any player and one fresh-faced reporter were allowed to knock and enter and be certain of a steady stream of coffee and confessional. I never took their hospitality for granted, though it did garner me a few back-page stories.

Reporting on a professional club at any level meant developing the best rapport possible with the manager and his coaching staff. At Roots Hall these were the boss Arthur Rowley, first-team trainer Jack Burkett, physiotherapist John Lattimer and the youth administrator Derek Hinchcliffe who was an oddball character, bald, a rasping voice (he smoked incessantly) and a moustache whose ends dropped vertically until they reached his chin. He possessed an unsettlingly clammy handshake.

For a kid who had just turned 17 and been entrusted with the responsibility to unearth the goings-on at a professional club – *his* professional club – the task would be made easier with a co-operative management. Rowley's latent mistrust of reporters, even those whose job it was to want to portray him in a flattering light, was evident from the start.

He did respond favourably to my request to write a 'Spotlight' feature on the club's progress towards building a reputable infrastructure for youth development, an article based on the fact that for a home match against Tranmere Rovers in October 1974 there was not a single homegrown player with a chance of selection.

The headline was 'A hunt for gold on the playing fields of Essex', by far the greatest projection of any piece I had written for the *Echo*, dominating an entire broadsheet page. The club had spent £40,000 in three years to develop a youth policy in the hope it may recoup that spend – and a good deal more besides – on the sale of players coached to a standard that made them potential assets.

Southend were proud of their efforts, especially in the face of opposition from the vast array of London clubs, many of whom had networks more populated and sophisticated than a rather remote town without much hope of rising beyond the Third Division.

I wrote, 'The aim is to avoid any hint of the shady dealings that have plagued schoolboy football – the cash and gifts to parents, the empty promises, the rosy futures invariably painted. What Southend have to show is that they give a young player a good chance of beating the obstacle course to professional football and the training to pick up the threads of another career if they don't make it.'

Rowley said he enjoyed the piece and thanked me for it. Hinchcliffe was all over me like a rash. The 15 apprentice pros were beside themselves with delight at the publicity, especially David 'Peanut' Keefe, a wire-haired winger who, though waif-like in appearance, was a sharp-witted, sharp-skilled lad who might be going places if he developed a bit more physically.

In time, almost all of them fell by the wayside. Chris Hutchings played for Chelsea, Sean for Leicester City and Orient and the rest weren't quite up to the demands made of them. Peanut became a security guard.

* * *

Arthur Rowley, born in the Black Country, had been utterly prolific in a playing career in England unmatched in its degree of productivity. He scored an English Football League record total of 434 goals from 619 games for West Bromwich Albion, Fulham, Leicester City and Shrewsbury Town, and managed both

Shrewsbury and Sheffield United before moving to Southend in 1970 when I was lining up the aniseed balls.

Two years later the club gained promotion to the Third Division as runners-up to Grimsby Town, though they struggled to make much of an impact and would be relegated in 1976. It was not an easy time to be the manager and Rowley was not an easy manager to deal with. I could sense his disquiet at being questioned by an upstart kid.

'Morning, Arthur, nice day,' I once ventured. 'Might be where you are,' he answered. I completely forgot my first question and there was an extended, embarrassed pause. I sensed Rowley rather enjoyed my silent excruciation.

As it turned out, having to deal with Rowley was the perfect initiation for future attempts to communicate with people who preferred not to talk. It certainly made me appreciate the value of a prepared follow-up question in case the first fell on stony ground.

Jack Burkett was a lovely man, soft-spoken but full of wisdom and solid insight. He had played at left-back for West Ham in my coming-of-age 1964 final against Preston. He didn't want to tread on Rowley's toes press-wise and most of what I learned from him was not for quoting, but a terrific exercise in picking the brains of a smart man who loved the job he was doing. His nuggets were invaluable when it came to piecing together either a match report or a feature.

By contrast to the calm authority of Burkett, John Lattimer spoke largely indecipherable Geordie at 100 miles an hour. It was a struggle to take in a word he uttered, especially when he was at his most endearingly enthusiastic – which was most of the time.

The players would take the piss behind Lattie's back at his exhortations either pre-match or at half-time when every other word was 'fook', as in, 'When the fook are we going to getting fookin' stuck in and fookin' win the fookin' ball?'

Southend played the vast majority of their home fixtures on a Friday night, freeing people in the area who supported West Ham or another London club to watch two matches inside a day. Fridays at Roots Hall meant I didn't miss a home game and spent Saturday reporting on the local clubs in the Essex Senior League.

The Southend press box was a three-row wooden-benched greenhouse in the spring and brass-monkeys icebox in winter at the back of the main stand, midway inside the southern half of the ground. The door didn't fit properly which allowed the wind to blow under the cracks and freeze your toes.

The seating plan was the same for every match. The one on the far right of the front row was empty, next to it sat Alf Smirk of the *Southend Standard* with me to his left between him and either Fuller or Collins – whoever was on duty – then Howard Southwood and on the far left the town's respected freelance John Marwood in trilby and smart coat.

The second row housed the opposition's reporters and, if the match was of significance, Jack Steggles often attended. It was like a royal patronage. Jack wrote the Third/Fourth Division scene column in the *Daily Mirror* each week and was a proper character. His coat was fur-lined and his moustache reeked of class. I tried to absorb his every word and action.

The only nose put out of joint if Jack arrived with his usual flourish was Howard's because he missed out on a freelance payment and could only charge the *Mirror* for the hire of his telephone, not a report on top of it. Howard would greet Jack through gritted, slightly yellowing teeth that had taken a firmer than usual grasp of his pipe stem.

Nigel freelanced for the *Daily Express*, John Marwood for the *Daily Telegraph* and assorted agencies and Alf covered for the *Daily Mail*, usually 100 and sometimes 200 words filed within 15 minutes of the final whistle. From out of nowhere one night as he unplugged his phone, Alf turned to me and said I'd work for the *Mail* one day. 'Yeah, of course, Alf,' I replied.

I had never before and never would again meet someone quite like Alfred Henry Smirk, known to one and all as 'Smirky'.

* * *

The seat in the far right of the Southend press box was empty because it offered only an obstructed view of the pitch (a boon when watching United, some might have said) and doubled as Smirky's ashtray and drink station.

There was rarely a time when a ciggie wasn't attached to Alf's lips. He smoked John Player King Size and usually got through the best part of a packet of 20 tipped in 90 minutes. Next to his fag packet nestled a gin and tonic with requisite ice and lemon for frequent re-lubrication.

Alf was born in Pershore, Worcestershire. He was a dashing right-winger for England schoolboys in the early 30s and had a short spell with Sheffield Wednesday before he was persuaded to the seaside in 1938 by Southend's most celebrated manager, the great David Jack.

After service in the Second World War, Alf signed a new contract in 1946, staying for two more years before moving to Gateshead. He always reckoned that had the war not come along, he would have won full international honours.

At the conclusion of his playing days, Smirky returned south and persuaded someone in the local newspaper industry – probably after a boozy session in the Railway Hotel – that he should write about sport. He was hired by the weekly *Standard*.

Smirky was 57 when we first met, standing around 5ft 9in – he'd have been taller were it not for his exaggerated bow legs – had slicked-back black hair with no parting, his cheeks were full of purple veins, he had arcus senilis (a halo around his irises) and coughed too much for it to be good for him.

To see him try to clamber to his spot in the press box was comic gold. He'd already been in the social club for a good hour on the booze, was usually last to arrive and had to reach the far corner, necessitating much holding on to our shoulders, passing around of his drink, balancing on the back of wooden seats and invariably ended with him missing his footing and a cascade of fucks. 'Smirk of Southend,' he'd say loudly into the telephone mouthpiece – usually followed by a profound belch – before receiving his word count from the *Mail*.

He jotted 100, 150 or on a good night 200 on the top corner of the notepad unfurled from his coat pocket and across which he'd spend many of the next 90 minutes brushing away cigarette ash to save it from catching fire.

The windows of the press box would require constant wiping free of condensation (my job) and I was also vital when it came to player identification, though it wasn't easy with Smirky's smoke engulfing you from one side and Southwood's pipe emittance swirling around from the other.

With no recall to replays and the constant chatter in the box, there was often much heated discussion as to whether it was actually Stuart Brace or Willie Coulson who had played the final ball to Chris Guthrie for a shot on goal.

What I thrilled at was all four of my fellow front-row occupants dictating copy at the same time. What craftsmanship to be able to deliver work so quickly and with such confidence.

* * *

Smirky had taken something of a shine to me, once saying he considered me the son he never had. He tried to take a shine to Mum too but having met him once when he was in a particular stupor, she would have nothing more to do with him and rather worried I spent too much time in his company.

Alf, Nigel Fuller and I would often make the journeys to away games together. Their banter was non-stop. We travelled as a threesome in February 1976 when the Blues reached the fifth round of the FA Cup, a privilege the club had not enjoyed for the best part of a quarter of a century.

We had been drawn at home four times in a row, taking full advantage with victories over Swansea, Dover, Brighton and Cardiff. Stuart Parker, a gangly centre-forward with a great personality, had been particularly productive with five goals, including an injury-time winner against Cardiff. The law of averages suggested an away tie in the fifth round and so it was, as Derby County's number was drawn first from the famous velvet bag.

Derby contained luminaries such as Roy McFarland, Colin Todd, Archie Gemmill, Bruce Rioch and Charlie George. There was much love for Southend's performance, quite properly for a match played on Valentine's Day. I can't recall a better showing from the side in all the times I watched them, and this on a tapioca pudding of a pitch.

The lads competed for absolutely everything. Arthur Rowley raged when Derby's 1-0 victory was secured by a goal from Rioch who got away with murderous tackling all afternoon. Ray Tinkler was a shockingly lenient referee. Rowley uttered the word 'cheat' which I had never heard him say before.

It felt like a long journey home and if I wasn't sure of the precise mileage from Derby to Southend, I'd never forget to the tenth of a mile how far Vale Park was from Roots Hall. Before setting off for an evening fixture at Port Vale, Alf and I struck a bet. He said the ground was more than 200 miles from Southend, I felt pretty certain it was less.

As we reached the outskirts of Burslem beyond Stoke-on-Trent, I swear Alf deliberately went past the ground, twice around a roundabout and missed a street that led directly to the car park before we pulled up with the mileage clock on 200.5. The bastard insisted it was the route he always took and shamelessly demanded my pound note.

Whatever the prevailing season, Alf was up to some trick or another. One late evening after a convivial few hours spent watching Essex play Glamorgan in the John Player Sunday League at Chalkwell Park, Smirky swayed back to his car, told me to get in and that we were heading off for another round of drinks somewhere.

He fell across the driver's seat, reached groggily to the passenger side glove compartment, opened it and at least 30 packets of JP cascaded around my ankles. Smirky never missed a chance to spend a sporting afternoon in the sponsor's tent and help himself to a few goodies.

If you ever had to locate Alf, the trail began at his favoured watering holes and, as the last resort, you tried the office. He never dwelt long in the *Standard*'s cosy corner on Nelson Mews and was either in the Railway Hotel opposite Southend Central station, the Airport Club on Aviation Way or probably at one of the local yacht clubs, regaling the admirals and ratings through rings of smoke.

To supplement my junior reporter's income – £14.39 a week was the going rate back then – I worked the occasional evening shift behind the bar at the Railway, with its tall ceilings and largely spotty and maladjusted clientele.

Smirky always asked to pour his own Guinness from a bottle (he never drank the draught variety). He called it a gin-i (the 'g' pronounced as in 'give'), demanding one from the cold shelf. He'd lick the traces of the head from across his lips but always missed a bit. The stories would flow, as would the alcohol.

One evening, a man I hadn't seen before was holding court. He was in his 70s and the spitting image of Walter Long, the American character actor who appeared in many cameo roles with Laurel and Hardy, most memorably in *Tough Guys*.

Alf told me I needed to meet this fellow because he was the hardest football player he knew. The man, thickset, gnarled of complexion and with a fixed scary-as-shit stare, held out a hand and proceeded to crush mine even though I prided myself on a decently firm handshake.

'This is Wilf,' Alf said. 'Wilf Copping.' When I got home, I read up on Mr Copping, who had been one of the Arsenal greats of the 1930s, always refused to shave before a match – not the accepted decorum of the 30s – but was never booked or sent off throughout a career of 363 league appearances, 20 England caps and several hundred tackles that both rattled bone and bent sinew.

He made Roy Keane look like a pantomime villain.

* * *

Smirky wrote a weekly column for the *Standard* on yachting, though what he knew about the sport he couldn't explain and neither did his copious jottings about a seafarer's way of life. I never did see him on a boat of any description.

The column consisted of a string of results with not a lot of comment in between. In effect, he typed out results that had been posted to him, stuck an intro on top, 'It was bright and breezy down by the esplanade this week at Southend Yacht Club', and called it 'Alf Smirk's Yachting Notes'. He was unbelievable.

The *Standard*'s sports operation was a three-man endeavour – Alf, sports editor Terry Waterman, bald, bookish and who kept himself to himself, and Roger Buxton who was the absolute opposite, a bright spark who seemed to know everyone in Southend whether they played sport or not.

The bearded Buxton breezed into all manner of gatherings 'whey-heying' his way around, thumping backs and garnering stories without requiring notebook or pen as backup. Roger's repartee in a group setting made me appreciate the imperative of social interaction that might entice people to part with important information.

I wasn't shy in the Harlow classroom. The block release courses fostered healthy competition among classmates and formed in my head the need to develop an inquisitive nature, sharpening both teamwork and individual skills and stressing the importance of being bold with opinions.

I hadn't imagined myself as a theatre critic before a group of us were sent to the local playhouse to review *Godspell.* The cast included a vivacious Barbara Rosenblat who took the part Julie Covington – of 'Don't Cry For Me Argentina' fame – performed in the original London cast recording. Rosenblat's rendition of 'Day By Day' blew me away, as did her physique.

The teenage reviewers were invited to join the crew for a post-performance drinks party at which copious plastic cups full of ghastly red plonk were handed around. I told Barbara at least a dozen times that she was wonderful as I staggered through the throng and she asked if I'd like to come back to the show as her guest.

I threw up copiously when I returned to my digs but went again the next night when her vibrant vocals worsened a shocking hangover. I wrote her a very flattering – sadly unpublished – review and latterly discovered she's still prominent in the artistic business. Her website describes her voice as being 'to audio books what Meryl Streep's acting is to film'.

It was possible we trainees took our studies at Harlow a little too lightly. Rather than heading to the Plume of Feathers pub to play bar billiards and drink too much Guinness most nights, I realised five decades too late I should have spent more time absorbing *Essential Law for Journalists*.

If a few imperatives about copyright rules didn't sink in as they ought, my report from the summer of 1976 was reassuringly positive. Tutor Tony Smith wrote, 'Neil was one of the most popular and brightest members of the group. The copy he turned out was never less than adequate which is a tribute to him in view of his limited experience where general news is concerned. One can only add that he has talent allied to the right personality for the job and the right attitude to it.'

* * *

Returning to the reporting ropes at the *Echo*, I was still required to spend time on the newsdesk to make sure I hadn't lapsed into any bad habits Howard Southwood needed to beat out of me – metaphorically speaking. One morning he offered me an irresistible assignment.

The Talk of the South club was going great guns under the management of Lou Manzi, a local entrepreneur who wanted to bring more pizzazz to Southend-on-Sea. The stars were lining up to perform at his venue and this particular week the top of the bill was one of the funniest men who ever lived, Tommy Cooper.

Manzi phoned the desk suggesting a feature with Tommy, who was happy to be interviewed. The comic needed a lift from his hotel to the Westcliff Leisure Centre on the seafront where he would pose for a picture and the reporter could have 20 minutes of his time.

With snapper Brian Parks in the back of my Datsun Cherry – I was going up in the world – we collected Tommy and set off for the rendezvous. There was a road in the middle of the town, Elmer Approach as I recall, which was a two-lane, one-way street. Tommy was squeezed into the passenger seat and as we approached a T-junction I was in the right-hand lane, preparing to turn right.

A car pulled up on our inside. Tommy wound down his window, reached across, tapped on the driver's window and, when the startled lady looked over, he performed his trademark shoulder-heaving cackle. The poor woman then recognised who it was, began to gasp for breath and promptly stalled her engine which caused a good deal of horn-hooting from behind. We just pissed ourselves.

Parks's photo of Manzi prostrate on a squash court with Tommy's foot on his stomach raising a racket to the skies was used on the front page.

When we returned Tommy to his hotel, he insisted Brian and I came in for a drink. We stayed far longer than we should but who would leave Tommy Cooper in full flow? The man was magic, in every sense.

* * *

My football remit for the *Echo* – covering the Midweek League and South East Counties League matches at Southend aside – concentrated on the lower semi-pro competitions, local high-profile schoolboy matches and, latterly, a column of random jottings called 'Inside Soccer'.

In my formative year of 1974, Basildon Boys had a particularly strong side, whose heartbeat was a darting, blond time bomb of a player named Paul Clark. He was a centre-back but loved to career into midfield, hunched and head down, bulldozing opponents aside.

Even with a limited discernment of who might make a player, I sensed Clark had what it took and wrote glowingly of him. He eventually made 311 appearances in two spells for Southend (he was the club's player-manager for a few months in the 1980s) and offered great service to both Gillingham and Brighton. Perhaps I was a decent judge of a footballer.

Weekends were divided between the exploits of Billericay Town, Basildon United, Bowers United and Canvey Island who produced football that, to a naive eye, was spirited and offered a considerable degree of quality. As months and matches went by, the boys from Billericay became a historic must-watch.

Billericay were founder members of the Essex Senior League in 1971 and won the championship two years later, establishing themselves as the most formidable club in the county by collecting back-to-back titles in 1975 and 1976.

At this time the Football Association was moving to scrap the distinction between amateur and professional which rendered obsolete the old FA Amateur Cup competition. It was replaced with a new glossy event, the FA Challenge Vase.

In the 128-club draw for the 1976 competition, Billericay were placed alongside Norton Woodseats, Slade Green Athletic and East Barnet Old Grammarians. In the first round the Essex side were drawn at Hatfield Town and by dint of some sticky and plucky performances reached the semi-finals where they would face Farnborough Town, regarded as the best side in the competition.

Even John Newman, Billericay's studious and well-connected manager, found it hard to imagine his side could win the two-legged affair against a club that paid many times more in fees and bonuses than his could possibly afford.

Newman had £100 to split between his squad after the routine of training on Tuesday and Thursday evenings and a match at the weekend. That worked out about six quid each so most of the boys were in negative equity by the time they'd talked a good game after

Tuesday training. A supporters' whip-round took care of post-match social requirements on Saturday afternoon.

Farnborough were ripping through the Athenian League Second Division but Newman trusted in the way he wanted his team to play. He was a ball boy at the transformative England 3 Hungary 6 international at Wembley in 1953 where he was so mesmerised by the fleet-footedness and exuberance of the Magyars, he routinely forgot to retrieve the ball when it bounced in his direction.

At 13 and filled with the notion of English supremacy, John was shaken to his core that evening as the players with three lions on their shirts were handed a lesson in international football they never forgot. 'I saw how immaculate the Hungarians were in everything they did down to the neatness of their shorts,' he recalled.

Billericay's success would become an extended offshoot of Hungary's, even if their players weren't aware of it at the time. 'On the training pitch, I constantly stressed pass and move,' Newman said. 'We had a big centre-forward, Geoff Aslett, who could be our get-out ball if we were in trouble but I wanted us to pass our way around the pitch. It wasn't always easy on the surfaces in those days.'

In a two-legged semi-final, Billericay won 2-1 at New Lodge and defended manfully for a goalless draw in Hampshire to earn a coveted place beneath Wembley's twin towers where the opposition would be Stamford of the United Counties League on 10 April, the day after my 19th birthday.

If Stamford were a step down in class from Farnborough, they provided rugged opposition and, in truth, Billericay struggled to stamp any authority on the game. There was no separating the sides after 90 minutes but nine minutes into the first period of extra time after a nimble build-up, Gary Smith fed Aslett who slipped one defender and guided the ball past the out-rushing goalkeeper. A goal in true Newman style. Sir Stanley Rous presented the trophy to the old man of the team, the perennially immaculate captain, Arthur Coughlan.

There was an obligatory open-top bus ride through the town, which took an age because the high street was heaving. Then came a rather more exotic journey. Billericay had received an invitation from the German club Baden-Baden to go and play them in an unofficial European amateur cup match. It would be my first professional journey abroad.

The Germans could not have been more accommodating hosts. Town's superiority on the field was evident and goals from indomitable forwards Aslett and Freddie Clayden secured a meritorious victory. That night the party were treated to a handful of chips to play at the Casino Baden-Baden, one of the most extraordinary pieces of architecture I'd seen, which was choc-a-bloc full of particularly chic people.

Goaded by the players, I sampled entirely too much schnapps and did remarkably well not to ruin the following day's happy flight home to Southend Airport by throwing up.

* * *

My first experience dealing with a genuine Fleet Street character arrived in 1976 when John Tanner left the sports editor's chair. The assumption – well certainly *his* assumption – was that Terry Poskitt would be promoted. We were told instead that Philip Osborn was to be our new boss.

Editor David Williams was a regular at Portman Road (he wrote the odd Ipswich piece on our pages) and Osborn covered the East Anglian beat for the *Sunday Express* and probably a few other outlets under an assumed name, I didn't wonder. Out of this particular blue, Osborn arrived. I didn't much take to him from the word go.

He lived in Cambridge and yet was taking charge of an evening paper 60-odd miles away. How could that work? He drove a maroon Jaguar X-Type he would regularly park across two spaces and strode to his desk with his driving gloves still on, munching on a Granny Smith apple. He only ever worked four out of our five production days.

Osborn had a nasally manner of speaking which I put down to his nose being flat to his face. His cheeks were almost as veined as Smirky's. His reputation among those on the street was that of a chancer. Given his looks, I decided that a few he had taken a chance with hadn't much appreciated it.

To be scrupulously fair, I learned a few tricks from him, none of which were particularly admirable. He liked to make mischief, see the negative in situations and generally antagonise for no reason. If Terry Poskitt thought John Tanner wasn't much of a sports editor, he positively seethed when Osborn would tell him what to do.

Osborn took an instant dislike to Paul Weaver, who had replaced Roy Collins on the desk and whose knowledge across many sports – notably cricket – brought added piquancy and flair to our output. For some reason – probably because he was so good with words and didn't push himself – Weavo was regularly scorned by the cage-rattling Osborn.

The pair clashed most days. Osborn sought any way to find fault, Weavo would give as good as he got and the boss didn't like that a bit. I lost count of the number of times he'd say that the next time Weaver argued with him, there would be consequences.

Fortunately, by the end of his first year Osborn was out of the door. He had found the lengthy travel and the lack of what he thought was sufficient remuneration too much of a labour and he left. We wouldn't particularly miss him.

This time Terry Poskitt wasn't overlooked. Howard Southwood came across from news to be his deputy.

* * *

When Osborn had chewed his last apple in the *Echo*'s employ, the sportsdesk setup was much the same as it had been when I joined almost three years earlier. Nigel and Paul headed me in the pecking order when it came to Southend's first team, the rest of the patch remained my responsibility but opportunities to write definitive pieces on league football were few and far between, however competent I knew I was to do them.

The departure of Arthur Rowley from the manager's chair at Roots Hall signalled both an opportunity to breathe fresh life into a squad that was labouring and offer me the chance to form a bond with a very different managerial kettle of fish.

Relegation to the Fourth Division was a descent too far for the Southend board. Arthur knew what was coming and appeared content to drift slowly into retirement to spend more time in his sports shop on Westcliff's Hamlet Court Road where his front-of-house etiquette was as lacking in warmth as he was when you probed for team selections.

I saw Arthur once more when sent to preview a testimonial staged for him at Roots Hall between Southend and one of his former clubs, Leicester. He still cut a formidable figure, built like a decent heavyweight, hair full, powerful handshake. We persuaded him to smile for a picture, which was a novelty.

He did say some profound things in the accompanying interview, 'When I played football you knew you were going to get kicked. You accepted the knocks, but the player who kicked you knew he'd probably get kicked back, and harder sometime later in the match. The players of today don't take the knocks as well as we used to. There's also an increasing gap between players and their respect for the referee.'

About his seven years at Southend, he reflected, 'In five of those years we made a profit and, in this day and age, that shows something. Everyone wants a successful team but I wanted to try to balance the books without greatly weakening the side. I think I succeeded in that respect. I've started to do some scouting for Spurs which is OK but I miss the pressures of winning and losing. I'm an outsider looking in.'

The two things you could never question were Arthur's commitment and his honesty. If he didn't want to talk, he didn't; if he didn't want to tell you his team, he wouldn't. He was the king of the short, sharp, biting response.

It brought to mind an incident at Blenheim Park when we persuaded him to represent the *Echo*'s cricket XI one spring evening. Arthur had clearly been a decent player in his time, he met ball on to his bat with defiance and occasional hostility but age had caught up with him where running between the wickets was concerned.

We took it in turns to umpire when not at the crease and I happened to be at square leg to determine that Arthur was well short of his ground while attempting a quick second. Up went the finger. 'How far was I out Neil?' he asked. 'Far enough, Arthur,' I replied.

As he trudged solemnly past me back to the pavilion, pads creaking, I distinctly heard him mutter, 'Ask a bloody silly question.'

* * *

Graham Taylor was developing a reputation as a young coach to follow at Lincoln City and it was clear he had become the preferred option to replace Rowley. Graham was in his early 30s, dynamic, highly regarded, and Blues chairman Bill Rubin believed he was persuadable.

Taylor was the only league manager in my experience who, when he couldn't take an initial phone call, messaged that he would get back as soon as he was free and kept his word. You never expected your phone to ring but in this instance it did. These small things resonated.

Graham's father, Tom, had been the local football man on the *Scunthorpe Evening Telegraph* and his son possessed a familial grasp of the importance of local newspapers to the fanbase and beyond. There were strong indications coming into our office that Taylor to Southend was a done deal.

We were never quite sure what happened to dissuade him – it wasn't as if Southend were institutionally stingy – but the move suddenly died a death and the man appointed was Dave Smith, who had steered Mansfield Town to promotion from the Fourth Division a couple of years earlier before falling out with his directors.

Dave, originally from Dundee, had coached at Sheffield Wednesday and at Newcastle United under Joe Harvey before Arsenal's Bertie Mee appointed him to take charge of the Gunners second team, so he arrived with enormous reserves of know-how.

In every respect, his appointment worked in my favour. I craved someone who would see me as a reporter, not just a kid reporter, who synthesised with my enthusiasm for the job but appreciated that I was a seeker of stories, not just his favour.

The savvy Smith enlisted Mick Buxton from Huddersfield to be assistant manager and, if we were cut from different cloths, I relished Mick's bullshit-free approach, readiness to converse and a keenness to embrace my desire to forge a different relationship from the one Nigel Fuller had with the management.

The two approaches both had merits. Nigel was not one to particularly cosy up to staff and players which was probably right in his senior position, whereas I believed that getting closer to them would provoke more in the way of stories a newspaper thrived upon.

Smith got to know my family, as I did his. My dad thought he was a smashing fellow and marvelled at how we got along. Dave would pop into my favourite pub, the Bull Inn at Hockley, for a chat and to charm the locals. He knew I visited the homes of certain players and didn't bollock either party. He called me 'Billericay Dicky' which I supposed was a form of flattery.

Smith recruited terrific lads: Colin Morris and Derrick Parker from Burnley, Micky Laverick from Mansfield and Alan Foggon with the experience of 61 appearances for Newcastle and 115 for Middlesbrough. All four shared the characteristic of hailing from the north-east – Morris from Blyth, Parker from Wallsend, Laverick from Castle Eden and Foggon from West Pelton. Football ran through their veins like blue in the finest stilton.

Southend could hardly have been further removed from their birthplaces than if they'd landed on the dark side of the moon, but all heeded Smith's call and would play significant parts in the resurgence the club desperately required.

I didn't know Foggon long enough to establish a bond but Morris, Parker and Laverick were different. We forged kinships strong enough for them to welcome me to their homes or for the odd beer where they would trust me enough to open up on the goings-on at Roots Hall knowing I wouldn't drop them in the shit.

I'm sure Smith knew what was going on and never blocked it. He was an astute manager, who was not always appreciated because he possessed a character that could move seamlessly from sarcasm to self-effacement such that players or journalists couldn't be sure exactly where they stood . He kept us all on our toes which was no bad thing.

Dave had a real go at me just once. I had written something about the first team he didn't like and called me to deliver a stern rebuke. For his notes in the next programme he wrote a piece headlined 'The Pen Is Mightier Than The Sword'. I knew exactly who he was referring to and never forgot the phrase.

* * *

Like many in our local world, Dave Smith found a measure of whimsy in that I was a qualified football referee. The idea of sitting the exams took root when I discovered that David Axcell, one of the *Echo*'s compositors, was a linesman on the Football League with pretensions to a highly prized place among the refereeing top flight.

Dave refereed matches in the Football Combination for the reserve sides of all the London and home counties clubs, was the senior official in the Essex Senior League and often brought those talents to the composing room where he bustled around officiously and got a kick out of putting cocky journalists in their place.

Only the sports editor or his deputy were generally allowed below stairs whereas in my curiosity to learn the production process I mooched about, getting in the way and making an arse of myself. I once touched the pasted copy with my bare hands and Dave threatened to lead a walkout.

Even if I was forever under Axcell's feet, I found his tales of refereeing exploits riveting and chose to take the plunge. From the moment I passed I was wedded to my Acme Thunderer and at the end of my second season was appointed to the middle for the Southend Thundermite League Under-17 Cup Final at Roots Hall. I was only 18 myself.

As a rule, I copped much nasty stuff in the middle and accepted more than I should. I was one of those who preferred to let the game flow and found that talking players around was better – and a whole lot less time-consuming – than pulling out my notebook which meant spending the weekend writing another set of reports.

Axcell was of the hang 'em and flog 'em type, a policy of discipline perfectly befitting an incredibly hirsute man who refused to wear long sleeves even in the bitterest of winters. He once asked one of his linesmen if he agreed that Dave was something of an Adonis.

He progressed to the Football League middle and became quite the local celebrity, not least when he flourished a red card at Tottenham's Graham Roberts at White Hart Lane as the central defender was being carried off on a stretcher. That got him some tasty headlines and plenty of ridicule.

I hadn't seen Dave for years when he was appointed senior linesman for the 1989 FA Cup semi-final between Liverpool and Nottingham Forest at Hillsborough. That was quite a testament to his abilities.

He was at the opposite end of the pitch to where the first semblance of that day's horrors began to unfold and realised from out of the corner of his eye something was going grievously wrong.

Referee Ray Lewis took the players off after six minutes and the officials left the ground in a state of numbed disbelief as the death toll rose steadily. 'People say that time is a healer but not for those of us who witnessed it first-hand,' Dave told the *Echo* on the 30th anniversary of the disaster. 'I shan't watch any of the coverage. It's too painful to be reminded of it again so graphically.'

* * *

Billericay Town retained the FA Vase in 1977. It was an even more extraordinary success than the previous year's endeavour, not least that they again clashed head-on with Farnborough in the semi-final and were two down after the first leg, away from home.

The return match in Essex was greeted by a ferocious snowstorm. The Farnborough team had arrived looking as if they were headed for a wedding, all dressed in same-coloured suits and ties, the smartest looking set of players imaginable

I clambered to the clubhouse roof to co-commentate for local hospital radio thinking that if I stayed too long, I'd be joining our listeners for treatment for frostbite rather than enjoying a couple of pints that evening to celebrate turning 20.

By half-time, Billericay had levelled the aggregate and then went on a remarkable rampage with four goals in the second half, including three in four minutes. Ricky McQueen scored a hat-trick, one direct from a corner. The Farnborough boys left looking rather dishevelled. Town were back beneath the twin towers to face Sheffield FC.

The day after the Vase final, Billericay were due to compete in the last throes of a competition to win a set of floodlights which would transform their humble ground. In five incredible days the Wembley final ended 1-1, John Newman's decision to leave Tony Wakefield out of his side was rewarded when Tony tore through several defences to land the floodlights and Billericay won the Vase replay 2-1 at the City Ground, Nottingham.

Geoff Aslett scored that evening with a raking left-footer from 25 yards, usually his standing leg. He was biggest among so many great characters. Newman would go on to become an official FA scout and work for both Glenn Hoddle and Peter Taylor in their spells with the England first team.

* * *

The *Echo* did Billericay Town proud with its dedication to their historic cause. It was a smashing broadsheet sports paper in so many respects with its sharp reporting edge, love for features and superb craftsmanship for which Terry Poskitt deserved enormous credit.

The pages were so clean and bright that at the 1977 Astroturf British Sports Journalism Awards, the *Echo* was recognised as the best regional sports pages for its 'writing, design and pictures'.

The judges were David Chipp, editor-in-chief of the Press Association, John Bromley, head of ITV Sport, and Leon Hickman, head of sport at the *Birmingham Post* and *Mail*. In a glowing judgement they said, 'It was obvious that the sports pages provided an excellent service to local sport, not only in the comprehensive nature of their coverage but also in the excellence of their sports writing.'

David Williams invited the boys to a seafront champagne celebration. The judges would also be there. A picture taken that night found me on the far right of the line-up with my arm across the shoulder of Mr Chipp as if he was a favourite uncle.

Such youthful bravado, probably fortified by a glass or two of something red and ripe, was further evidenced in that I buttonholed Mr Hickman and said what a privilege it would be to be considered for a job on one of his papers. A few months later, I was flying the parental coop and heading to the West Midlands.

4
Birmingham

DENNIS SHAW, the chief football writer on the *Birmingham Evening Mail*, had taken the bold and unusual step of quitting journalism to take up the post as commercial manager of Birmingham City, a veritable poacher to gamekeeper.

One man's shift of roles opened the way for others to climb the reporting ladder. It was to Shaw's enormous credit that his departure from the *Mail* offered a leg-up to more than one junior reporter with a gleam in his eye.

In the spring of 1978 I found myself in the lounge bar at the Imperial Hotel on New Street greeting John Richardson, who I had bumped into when he was carving a career at the *Brighton Argus* where the senior football man, John Vinicombe, was long-established and immoveable.

It was a case of 'what are you doing here?' to which we both replied, 'I'm joining the *Evening Mail*.' We drank to our good fortune, perhaps too liberally.

That first night, behaving like a pair of juvenile delinquents – which is what we were – we decided to pour water from our hotel windows on to the Brummie revellers below before hiding behind abruptly closed windows. Next morning, we were the ones in need of dousing as we clapped eyes on our new office on Colmore Circus, a landmark junction on a busy thoroughfare in the heart of the city.

The editorial floor of the *Post* and *Mail* was cavernous, one football pitch in size, housing the news, sports, features and subs departments of four papers, the *Post*, the *Mail*, the *Sunday Mercury* and the *Sports Argus*. I could hardly make sense of the heady emotions I felt, walking in the first time.

There were humans in various states of controlled disarray as far as the eye could see, a hum of industrious activity topped off by swishing noises made by cylindrical containers carrying the reporters' copy, being transported through a system of overhead zip-wires to the printing works.

Just as at the *Evening Echo*, no journalist was allowed to finger material in the production department. Unlike the *Echo*, I wasn't allowed in. The compositors defended their territory like it was Rorke's Drift. The subeditor on the stone (where the hot metal was bashed into shape) could merely point to where the copy or a headline should go. If a non-printing union finger touched metal, the entire workforce would down tools.

The timing of my move to Birmingham coincided with an increased tension between the Labour government of prime minister James Callaghan and the trade unions over a 'social contract' that had been negotiated to restrict union wage demands and help the government contend with rampant inflation.

The unions were becoming more aggressive, and the government pressed for them to stick to their word not to ask for anything more than five per cent pay increases to give the economy scope for re-balancing. There was a growing mood of discontent and in an industrial city like Birmingham where militancy was ardent, minds and positions hardened.

The ensuing industrial action didn't last long but the angst against those who chose to cross picket lines bubbled on for months, causing agonising rifts between friends. Those differences would surface again the following year when Margaret Thatcher's Tories mauled Labour at the general election and the emasculation of the trade unions became a slow and divisive process.

* * *

The *Evening Mail*'s sports subeditors' desk was H-shaped, with the senior editors amidships, the subs on either flank with the three-man team who produced the legendary Saturday pink paper, the *Sports Argus* – Ian 'Jonce' Johnson, Ken Lawrence and Peter White – at the right-hand bottom corner of the H.

The writers' desk, across which secretary Bridget in her firm Brummie tones kept watch, contained five workplaces. When I first walked, open-mouthed, into this cauldron, my new team-mates were the lead football writer Ray Matts, Dave Harrison, Chris Moore and cricket writer Chris Walder with 'Ricco' Richardson and me as the adolescent additions.

I sat opposite Mattsie who became both mentor and firmest of friends. I cannot stress enough what a bloody terrific reporter – and man – he was. In replacing Dennis Shaw at the helm of the *Mail*'s football coverage, Ray had huge shoes to fill as Dennis was a legend in Birmingham, a superb story-getter who wrote with firmness and authority against cascading deadlines and always on top of his brief.

Mattsie was a character unlike any I'd encountered besides Alf Smirk. He had a head full of brown curls, stood 5ft 8in and smoked too much, especially as deadlines approached of which there were two and sometimes three a day. He was improbably unsure of himself because he could write copy that needed no subeditor's interference.

Like Mattsie, Dave Harrison was Black Country to his boots and loved West Bromwich Albion, though he managed to hide his allegiance with understated brilliance. These two and the intrepid Welshman Moore were national-quality writers on a regional paper but the *Evening Mail* operated like a national and many considered it such in all but name.

The sports editor was an extraordinary character named Brian Sparks. He was in his late 50s, bespectacled, round-faced, had a spreading waist, was thinning on top but whose ginger hair often reached the tip of his collar. He smoked one cigarette after another and had quite the most appalling body odour.

His desk was the personification of tidiness, not a single item out of place. In front of him lay a carpet of layout pages, to the side of which were a slide rule, perfectly sharpened pencils (he spent hours crafting them), an ashtray, lighter and a cigarette often balanced on the edge of his desk with the ash pointing inwards so that any slight mishandling of a slide rule and his trousers were in danger of being set ablaze.

Sparky's page designs were half-sketched the previous evening and placed into his bottom drawer before his punctilious exit. It required something apocalyptic – Birmingham winning away let's say – for him to erase and re-draw anything. Once he had sculpted his page, the stories had to fit it, not the other way around.

There was the pinpoint accuracy of the draughtsman about his designs and I'd find myself marvelling at Brian's mastery of his slide rule when he would suddenly revert from drawing lines and use it as a back scratcher.

The framing of the pages and mechanical dexterity on the subs' desk was in vivid contrast to the mayhem and mess where the writers sat. For a start, each of us had a typewriter the size of a small boulder that took up three-quarters of the space on each desk. Trying to manoeuvre them placed inordinate strain on your back muscles.

These were mighty organs and when five were active at the same time – plus those from the newsdesk behind you – the din was constant and tremulous. The ability to concentrate on what you were writing while phones rang, copy flew through the chutes, shouting matches between news subs and the back bench were lurid and loud and someone was punching the coffee machine was a daily adrenalin surge but we always made it.

The rolls of copy paper were the exact size of the Kirkland Signature Premium Big Roll towel you can buy today at Costco, only five times as heavy. Having peeled away at an adhesive strip, you placed the roll on the typewriter carriage, threaded the open end under the bar and pulled it up so it leant against the rest of the roll and was perfectly aligned. Then you could start typing.

Keeping the roll balanced on the carriage wasn't an exact science. If it began to topple backwards, you would let it slip and come to rest with a thump behind the typewriter frame (giving the person opposite a mild heart seizure), continue to feed the paper through and type on. Occasionally, the bloody thing would lurch forwards, bounce against the keys and land with an agonising thud in your lap, requiring all manner of testicular reorganisation.

The roll contained four different-coloured sheets, linked by carbon paper. You would write three or four paragraphs, tear the four-layered sheet off, place it to one side and then type your next few pars and keep repeating the process until you were done.

The top sheet – white – went to the subeditors' desk and the second – yellow – was retained in case some dozy sub spilt coffee over the top one. The other copies were screwed up and tossed into a wastepaper basket. If you mangled your words and had to rewrite, you started the whole process again.

Such was the excess of carbon paper peeled from between the sheets, you often handed your copy to the subs with smudged fingerprints across it. That didn't go down well.

In the meantime, as smoke billowed across the top of Sparky's head, he was filling up his back page, piece by piece, line by line. The nearer to the first deadline of 1pm and the page still had empty spaces (Brian only cared about his beloved back page); he would become incredibly agitated.

I never saw his facial expressions as he had his back to me but the look on those of deputy sports editor John Lamb and number three Dave 'Stan' Stennett – who sat facing the writers – were masterpieces of the expectation of a lid blowing at any moment.

Ray Matts sensed it too. As the number one, he bore the brunt of Sparky's increasing discomfiture whenever he considered copy was running behind schedule. A cry of 'how's it coming, Ray?' from the desk behind him would provoke a few more puffs on Mattsie's cigarette and an exaggerated roll of his eyes.

'Soon, Brian, soon,' he'd reply, which really meant 'piss off and leave me alone'. Sparky would then indulge in one of his go-to catchphrases, 'They're crying out for it in the works,' (i.e. the printers downstairs wanted it now, which was simply a ruse for Brian to get his hands on the copy and settle his own nerves).

If that plea didn't provoke a reaction, Brian pushed his chair back and started to rise, very slowly. Ray would look at me and whisper, 'Is he coming over?' I nodded. Sparky squatted on his haunches at Mattsie's side, unleashing odour from his armpits as he splayed his elbows on the desk, looked up at Ray and said, 'When?'

In the absence of a response, Sparky would take it upon himself to rip the top sheet from his typewriter. We all sat rigid in our seats. Mattsie seethed. 'What the fucking hell did you do that for?' In the circumstances, his restraint was quite remarkable.

Any hint of insubordination would require Brian to impose his authority, which meant getting head of sport Leon Hickman to do it for him. Sparky's command of 'Right, over to see Lee' meant the pair marched past the subs' table to Hickman's glass-fronted office some ten yards away.

Ian Dowell, the chief sub whose feet were almost permanently perched on the desk as he leaned way back to a near-horizontal position in his chair, watched this regular routine with great glee. 'Off again, Mattsie?' he'd exclaim.

The two men would return a few moments later, Leon having done his politician's bit, Mattsie smirking, Sparky sweating and precious production minutes having been lost for the sake of nothing at all.

* * *

Each of the *Mail*'s football reporters bar Ray Matts had the weekly task of delivering a page devoted to the club for which they had responsibility to the *Sports Argus*. This pink-papered Bible had been a Brummie institution since its first issue in February 1897, a remarkable history of service to the West Midlands' sporting fanbase.

The *Argus* was a masterpiece in many ways. Getting it on the streets less than an hour after the end of the Saturday matches was a miracle of teamwork and craftsmanship.

Its small staff, like that of most publications, could not have been more different and was a fascination to watch at work. Ian Johnson, the editor, was a powerfully built man of the north-east, whose often stern features could suddenly dissolve into an ice-melting grin and deep guffaw.

The chief sub Ken Lawrence was a Scot with a head of blond tousled curls and was near enough my age to know a kindred spirit even if we were very different as people. We hit it off right away. Ken wasn't shy, possessed a chat-up line for every occasion and I sensed he was destined for the higher places in the industry he would very soon reach.

Peter White was the paper's standalone writer; blond and moustachioed, another charmer who used his terrific contacts – especially at Aston Villa – to bring the paper to life. This was a considerable trio bolstered by the decent backing group of the *Mail*'s team. Nothing beat seeing your name on the front page of the *Argus* on a Saturday night.

My initial remit was to report on West Bromwich Albion, a task that required filing two, sometimes three, feature stories – all of them as newsy as possible – and a ghostwritten player column every week.

As an introduction to an art form I grew to love, I could not have wished for a more professional, polished performer than Albion's stalwart centre-half and captain John Wile. I cannot recall a single time he wasn't at the end of a phone line at the agreed time and spoke with clarity and authority on the game.

The deadline to complete the *Argus* page was Friday midday but it was preferred – both by the subs and the writer – by the close of play on Thursday, to coincide with the opening of the Queens Head, the pub about 20 paces from the front entrance to the *Post* and *Mail* building on Steelhouse Lane.

The Queens, as we knew it, was a favourite mingling hole of journalists and lawyers, who took it in turns to be the noisier bunch. Ray, the pub's neatly attired owner, was a Birmingham City season ticket holder and Barry, his chief bartender who had mottled cheeks and untamed hair like Jeff Lynne of the Electric Light Orchestra, was a rabid Albion fan.

You can imagine how much fire and brimstone was generated in a couple of hours of alcoholically stoked debate. These well-into-the-evening sessions were enhanced by the presence of the two football writers for the *Birmingham Post*, the morning broadsheet which sold a good deal fewer copies than the *Mail* but had the greater challenge of competing for readership with the national dailies.

Ian Willars, aka the 'Duke', and Michael Gouge were the *Post*'s pair. Top, top blokes. Willars's profound pronouncements on the state of football were delivered after a seismic contracting of his nostrils, like a magistrate about to pass sentence. The Duke would draw extravagantly on his pipe, take a great gulp of Brew XI and opine widely.

Gouge possessed the most remarkable-shaped stomach I'd ever seen, which was in a daily contest with the lower buttons of his shirt to see which might burst first. Mike could knock back the pints and puffed constantly at a cigarette. Most of his teeth had disintegrated.

You didn't even have to cross the road from the office to be covered in ash and smell beer on people's breath. Two floors up from the editorial level was the Printer's Devil (imagine a newspaper office with a pub on the premises these days). The sporting centrepiece of the Devil was a majestic snooker table where Mattsie regularly demonstrated his skill with a cue.

I was bloody hapless, unable to form a bridge and thus having to fashion crazy attempts to lay cue ball on to a colour and hope it might move in the general direction of a pocket. Mattsie loved to wipe my arse, taking great relish at flicking his marker across the scoreboard on the wall whereas mine remained defiantly static.

What a joy this was though. A pint of Guinness and a frame or two of crap snooker without leaving the building, emboldened by a reporter's tendency to play fast and loose with the drink-driving laws.

Here was a chance to relate the day's investigations and irrelevances, replay Sparky's memorable meltdowns, mix with all sorts of reporters and listen to their experiences of sex and story-getting, much of it not fit to print.

If this was the life of a journalist, I didn't want it to stop.

* * *

My initiation at the *Mail* was intense and, when I reflect upon it, immensely fulfilling. I started at the paper on 26 May 1978 and if someone said that in precisely ten days I would have the front-page lead with a story of local, national and international importance, I'd have thought them stark-staring bonkers. But I was soon earning every penny of my sparkly new wage of £4,000 a year.

The 1978 World Cup finals in Argentina were in their opening throes when, in a startling development, Willie Johnston of Scotland failed a routine drug test after the 3-1 defeat to Peru. Not just Willie Johnston of Scotland, but Willie Johnston of West Bromwich Albion.

Had Johnston been playing for Stoke, Sheffield Wednesday or St Mirren, the story might have been squished into the Sports Lines column on the back page consisting of four or five one-sentence briefs. But he was a star at a First Division club in the hub of the *Mail*'s catchment area. I can only presume the senior lads were catching up on days off because the story was handed to me.

Footballers had their home numbers printed in telephone directories in those days and by a process of elimination I made contact with Johnston's wife Margaret in Sutton Coldfield and persuaded her to pose with a telephone pressed to her ear, to make out as if she was talking 'live' to her husband. When they had chatted for real, Margaret revealed that Willie said, 'I might be home early.' That quote formed the front-page headline.

Margaret also said that Willie 'sounded quiet and subdued but that [this] was his normal manner'. Their conversation was cut short by an Argentine telephone operator who said, 'No more talk.'

Johnston was a hay fever sufferer and had complained of an awful cold in a previous conversation from the Scottish camp. The next day I was on the front page again, in a joint by-line with Andrew Parker, one of the *Mail*'s noted news reporters. The headline was 'Albion Man: I've Given Him Pills'.

Roger Rimmer, one of Albion's four-man medical team, revealed that he prescribed Johnston a drug named Reactivan – 'but I hadn't given him any to take to Argentina' the doctor iterated. Johnston informed the national paper now paying thousands for his story that he had taken the drug but he was not alone among British players using it.

FIFA decided to ban Johnston for a year, which ultimately ended his international career. Helmut Käser, the secretary-general, said that the player had committed 'a flagrant breach of the rules'. The winger told a hearing he only took the pills 'when I was feeling low'. He was about to come home early, just as he told his wife he feared he would.

The Johnston affair was a bare-knuckle introduction to West Midlands football and helped establish my credentials to a man who would become a dominant influence on my reporting career for the next 25 years.

Ron Atkinson had been recruited by Albion that January. He had led Cambridge United to promotion from the Fourth Division the previous year, steering the club to the threshold of the Second Division when Albion made their move. Ron's was an impressive pedigree and the daring style with which his teams played marked him out as one of England's more progressive young bosses.

Atkinson and I had met briefly at Roots Hall in 1977, when, as player-manager, he strutted his stuff – and there was plenty of stuff to strut – for Cambridge's reserves in a Midweek League fixture in which he scored the only goal, a coruscating header at the far post at the North Bank end.

To catch as many people as possible for a quote, I stationed myself just inside the swing doors that led from the players' tunnel at one end to the main entrance at the other. Dave Smith's office was one side of the corridor and the secretary's with sliding windows like an old dentist's reception on the other.

Ron burst through the swing doors like John Wayne ready to take down the occupants of a particularly dastardly Wild West den. I was about to introduce myself when Smith's door opened with equal force. 'You're a bloody disgrace,' Smith shouted, which rather extracted the wind from Ron's sails. 'I've nothing more to say to you.' The door slammed shut.

Atkinson's response was along the lines of 'what the hell was all that about?' and before I could ask him what he thought it meant, he had flounced out of the main door, on to the team coach and away. My theory was that Smith was furious at the way Atkinson took Sean Rafter, Southend's reserve goalkeeper, out of the game with a roughhouse charge in the process of scoring the only goal.

A year or so later and here were Ron and I – the Roots Hall imbroglio still an unsolved mystery – becoming manager and local reporter ready to embark on a game-changing relationship for both of us.

My access to the manager and players at West Brom was never questioned. There was no such thing as a press officer to poke his nose in and ruin everything. If the players wanted to give me their home number or speak at the training ground, that was their prerogative. No one turned me down. I felt very blessed. The Albion team of the late 1970s was just about the most joyous to watch in the whole of English football.

* * *

Ron Atkinson was fiercely protective of Willie Johnston during his World Cup tribulations and, typically, took the fight to the opposition. He would not be forced into a position where he hung his player out to dry. I could sense that working with Atkinson would be both illuminating and adventurous.

When you dealt with Southend United, the interest from the national papers was minimal. Jack Steggles of the *Daily Mirror* moving into view on a Friday night was akin to the sighting of a journalistic superstar. In effect, you had the whole playing field to yourself.

On the *Evening Mail* the pressures were ramped up. This was no kid-in-a-candy store existence but bloody serious business. Well, sometimes. One early morning I rang Ron's home chasing the day's news. Twice it was engaged. I persevered. Maggie, his wife, answered and said Ron had been busy on the phone and might have something. Cue an exaggerated rustling of paper in the background.

'Hel…lo' was Ron's signature way of answering the phone. 'What do you want?' 'Anything about? I hear you might have been busy this morning.' 'Yep,' he replied. 'We're signing a top Dutch player. His first name is Rudi. Have a guess.'

Caught on the hop without coffee at eight in the morning, the only Rudi who sprang to mind was Ruud (Rudi) Krol, stalwart defender for Ajax of Amsterdam. That would be some signing. 'Rudi Krol?' 'Nope,' came the reply. Shit. I couldn't think of another Rudi. 'Give up?' Ron asked. 'Yes.'

'It's Rudi Wakening,' he said. 'I've never heard of him, who does he play for?' 'A Second Division club, Vas Dasleep.' 'What position does he play?'

I was beginning to flex my fingers to begin to type but the manager of West Bromwich Albion couldn't hold back any longer. 'It's a Rudi Wakening!' he said, bursting into laughter. 'Now get lost.' Maggie was pissing herself in the background.

The lads around the desk had eavesdropped my conversation, having been brought to attention when I said Rudi Krol so confidently. Now they needed to know why I'd turned a deepish shade of crimson and put the phone down.

My ignominy was all over the editorial floor by nine and much of the West Midlands by midday.

* * *

I can only think it was some kind of reward for surviving a baptism of fire with six major by-lines on the Willie Johnston affair that I was immediately despatched to Scotland, my first visit to the country. This story had nothing to do with footballers or drugs.

The only time I had been involved with golf – apart from trying to play the game properly, which remains an ambition – was when the *Evening Echo* hosted a pro-am at Boyce Hill GC in Benfleet. I caddied for former Ryder Cup international Bernard Hunt, who barely spoke a couple of words through the round and gave me a pound for lugging his clubs for four hours. Miserable sod.

Now I was on a train to Troon on the Ayrshire coast for the final instalment of the 1978 British Amateur Championship.

Boyce Hill was close to the sea and studded with picturesque holes but walking through a coastal town and on to a golf course in Scotland touched my soul in a manner hard to put into context. There was something in the architecture, the landscape, the scenery in which you could lose yourself. The office had found me a room at the South Beach hotel. I read something called *The Scotsman* and ate kippers for the first time.

Peter McEvoy from the Copt Heath club in Knowle was the defending amateur champion and he had reached the final to face Scotland's Paul McKellar. It was a level of assignment on a sport on which I knew nothing of the custom and practice that meant both learning and moving fast.

There weren't many writers around. David Davies of the *Birmingham Post* was there but he didn't take too kindly to competition, even from the same company. It was probably my nervousness, perhaps his gruff demeanour and maybe I misread him completely but Dai was an acquired taste and one that, despite initial misgivings, I would ultimately revel in.

Covering golf for an evening paper was like cross-country with a purpose. The imperative was to pick the moment to leave the action and dash back to the press tent to deliver copy with plenty of shot description and which kept as much pace as possible with the ongoing play.

A lot of stuff could occur between filing and slogging it back out on to the course to catch up with the players but there was no other means than my running (literally) reports by which anyone in Birmingham could know what the hell was happening.

My very first piece on the final had McEvoy two up after ten; for the second edition he was three up after 16. He had a nice lead heading into the second day of the 36-hole final and eventually retained his title, winning 4 and 3.

The office must have thought I'd done sufficiently well because the following month I returned to Scotland to cover the Open Championship where – like many thousands of others – I fell in love with an undulating expanse of God's green earth, namely the Old Course at St Andrews.

Walking into the press marquee at the Open was rather like the first day at the *Echo*; I stared open-mouthed and marvelled at the noises, colours and odours. Most of the reporters were dressed like golfers, the Americans especially looked as if they had each swallowed the pages of the latest Pringle catalogue.

I'd never seen so many gaily coloured shirts, jumpers and hats, the movement and chat were a blurred accompaniment to the clatter of sharp spikes on the steel walkways laid down in the press tent to save the grass beneath being ruined for weeks.

The British writers were more conservatively attired and gave off an air of authority and gravitas. I instantly recognised the *Daily Mail*'s Michael McDonnell from his picture by-line. He had a jacket tossed across his shoulders, which carried a little jangly thing that looked like a medal, hanging from the lapel.

This, I discovered, certified membership of the Association of Golf Writers. Michael looked terribly smart and significant especially when he spoke to what I presumed were his colleagues with one leg raised on to his seat.

I was a bit of an anorak when it came to fitting faces to by-lines and a dreamer as I imagined what it would be like to have a job of such importance. The rather aristocratic Michael Williams of the *Daily Telegraph* walked with a limp, Mark Wilson of the *Express* was suave, Pat Ward-Thomas of *The Guardian* reminded me of a schoolteacher, Ron Wills of the *Mirror* had a jumper thrown across his shoulders like McDonnell (a fashion I would try to copy) and you couldn't miss Renton Laidlaw of the *Standard* who had a voice like silk from the Stonehouse weavers. This was journalistic utopia for a kid like me.

At each alternate desk was a hooded, soundproofed booth into which you dictated copy that could not be overheard by your neighbour. The only problem was that my debut at the Open – the biggest event I'd covered in my life – coincided with a telecommunications strike in this neck of the Fife woods that rendered all telephones in the tent unusable.

This was really stressful, especially for someone who required constant access to a line for his running reports. Performing that task was exactly as it had been at Troon except that rather than two players in the field, there were bloody masses of them at the Open.

In the wake of the irrepressible John Oakley of the Press Association, I scampered the first five holes accompanying a threesome of note, scribbling down the scores and particular defining strokes, then set off back to the tent, dodging the flow of the hordes heading in the opposite direction while having to navigate the course from back to front, so to speak.

I'd do the same over again for the following edition with the next trio of players I hoped might figure at the top of the leaderboard. That was fine but how was I going to file four times a day from a press HQ where not a single phone worked?

I would become indebted to Jack Statter, the sportsdesk stone sub at *The Sun* who was released at certain periods of the year to double as the golf writer. He had a medal thingy too but his was attached to one of the belt loops on his trousers.

Jack, tall, grey-haired, bespectacled and an utterly charming character, had found a downstairs pay phone that worked, at a public house within a couple of hundred yards of the Old Course and, rather than keep it to *The Sun*, took pity on a 21-year-old wet-behind-the-ears lad and let me in on his secret.

Frank Clough, *The Sun*'s chief football writer, dabbled as the golf colour writer at the Open and was I grateful that – gruff as he seemed – he acceded to Jack's plan. The three of us would creep down the stairs (not easy in golf spikes), take it in turns to press button A, then button B, to fill our respective pages with the required word count and hotfoot it back to the course. Then repeat.

Had it not been for the lovely Jack and the accommodating Frank, I might have been sacked soon after my second coming of age as had been the threat at my first.

In total during my first Open, I had five back-page leads, starting with Japan's Isao Aoki bursting into an early lead on the first day; Arnold Palmer, after a break of 18 years playing at St Andrews, 'capturing golfing hearts with four birdies in his first seven holes' on day two; a surge from Britain's Peter Oosterhuis on the third day, and eventually the final round, when Jack Nicklaus had moved into a menacing position.

The *Sports Argus* had to be off the presses at 5.30pm so my final report was a non-committal, 'Jack Nicklaus, golf's Golden Bear, stole ahead of the field in a drama-packed final round of the Open at St Andrews today. With five holes left to play, the great American stood on six under par and looked set for a dramatic repeat of his 1970 victory at St Andrews.'

I was proudly spot on as Nicklaus won by two strokes from fellow Americans Tom Kite, Ben Crenshaw and Ray Floyd alongside New Zealander Simon Owen who, if he had kept his mind and legs together over the final four holes, may have become one of the championship's unlikeliest winners.

There was little time, though, to wallow in the glories of golfing superstardom. The First Division season of 1978/79 beckoned.

5

Laurie Cunningham

I HAD never met a black footballer until I introduced myself to Laurie Cunningham, Cyrille Regis and Brendon Batson at The Hawthorns when West Bromwich Albion returned for pre-season training in the summer of 1978.

On the rare occasions Dad took me to see West Ham when Mum didn't want to use her season ticket, I'd watched Clyde Best, Clive Charles and Ade Coker feature, and if Best bore the brunt of terrace ribaldry at Upton Park I had assumed it was more for his lack of a first touch than the colour of his skin.

To my recollection, Southend United hadn't a black player in their squad at any level and neither had Billericay Town. I can't recall a single black pupil at Westcliff High School for Boys in my five years there and there were none on my journalism courses. How far removed from the real world were we in seaside Essex in those days?

No self-respecting football writer of the time could have failed to marvel at the impact Laurie Cunningham, especially, had had on the game while at Leyton Orient where the skilled and patient guidance of manager George Petchey helped steer him towards a wider prominence. And it wasn't just in the manner of his freedom on the pitch that excited.

Laurie was once pictured in the newspapers standing in the centre circle at Brisbane Road dressed in a broad-lapelled, striped suit and ridiculously flared pants, wearing the widest tie you had set eyes on and with a trilby tilted flamboyantly to one side, like the coolest dude in the world, certainly in the East End.

This guy I needed to get to know. Laurie was beguiling. He had all the style a man could want and was possessed of a sensitive soul not entirely resolved with his surroundings and status. A veritable paradox. I suppose you could say we were kindred spirits in that respect (except that I had no style at all). From Finsbury Park to West Bromwich was quite a leap of fortune for him; as was mine from Leigh-on-Sea to Birmingham.

He had moved into a new company and so had I. He was the actor on the stage, I was the juvenile critic. He was 22, I was 21. I loved to watch him play football, I couldn't tell you for certain if he ever read a word I wrote and yet, remarkably, we gelled.

The contrast between the players who entered football folklore as The Three Degrees (named after the black women's pop group of the same name) was evident. Ron Atkinson inherited Regis and Cunningham because former manager Ronnie Allen had been open-minded to see beyond their skin colour and to know they could play. Batson was Atkinson's first Albion signing from his former club Cambridge, a right-back blessed with pace, positional sense and attacking awareness.

Brendon would never mind being third on the bill. Strikers took the lion's share of the kudos and headlines. Regis could illuminate a small village with his smile, and with the ball at his feet he combined a gauche power that came to him easily and a naivety about how good he was. His body was like a Rodin sculpture.

Laurie was more thoughtful about football and life. He craved the ball at his feet and knew how good he was with it but why did he seem reluctant to show off though it came naturally to him? He played as if in a state of levitation, which was useful those days on the pitches that could suck at your ankles like quicksand.

I was appointed to Albion's first away game that season, at Queens Park Rangers, whose defence performed in a state of permanent petrification. The surprise was that they conceded just one goal when Ernie Howe chipped his own goalkeeper Phil Parkes as Cunningham pursued the centre-half toward his own penalty area.

The Baggies' team at Loftus Road that night was: Godden, Batson, Statham, Cantello, Wile, Robertson, T. Brown, Robson, A. Brown, Regis, Cunningham. I doubt in the 44 years since that they've sent out one more accomplished and beloved. Inside four months as the Albion man 'my' boys were top of the First Division performing a brand of football that delighted their fans and paralysed the opposition.

The club had qualified the previous season for the UEFA Cup and played with great tactical awareness and self-control in the Istanbul cauldron of Turkish side Galatasaray – the force of nature that was Bryan Robson and Cunningham scored in both legs – then took out the Portuguese team Sporting de Braga in the second round.

The next test would be demonstrably tougher up against the Spanish side Valencia, spearheaded by their technically blessed, volatile striker Mario Kempes who had been the leading scorer in Argentina's success in the recent World Cup.

Rather than Kempes dominating the tie, it was Cunningham's time to shine. When he scored Albion's equaliser in the away leg, his body was at a peculiar angle and yet he regained his balance with an acrobat's grace, as if boogieing on the dance floors across which he moved with such an innate flair.

This was Laurie the absolute soul provider. When he was prolific in the second leg at The Hawthorns, the peseta had dropped among those clubs in Spain eager to provide their supporters with a player to illuminate stadiums and enrich fortunes.

He would be available in the close season. English clubs often allowed a player's contract to wind down on the assumption that, for a few hundred quid and a pat on the back, they'd tug their forelocks and gratefully re-sign. It was not to be the case where Laurie was concerned.

Every match he played added copiously to his reputation and thus value. Four days from the turn of the year, Albion played Manchester United at Old Trafford, an occasion etched in the hearts of those fortunate to be there – Dave Harrison had that privilege for the *Evening Mail* – and in the heads of the United directors the next time they were minded to change their manager.

The Baggies were irresistible that night, winning 5-3 in a match that ended in flurries of Manchester snow and was memorable for the exquisite flow and devastating finishing that transfixed those both straining for a decent view in the pens at the Stretford End and well beyond.

In that Albion side, the shrewdness of Tony and Ally Brown in link play was bolstered by cunning and invention from Robson and Len Cantello in the middle of the field, who in turn offered Regis and Cunningham the perfect platform on which to indulge their skills.

For the fifth goal, Laurie skipped 30 yards along a treacherous right touchline with United defenders snapping hopelessly at his heels. His pass to feet brought a quick swivel and clip with the outside of his right boot from Ally Brown into the path of Regis whose first-time right-footed thunderbolt drew from ITV's commentator Gerry Sinstadt the blistering one-liner, 'Oh, what a goal!'

In the first half, Sinstadt referred to the jeering of Albion's black players and how unperturbed they appeared to be by it. It was a watershed moment in commentary, a realisation that paying lip service to racism on the terraces was simply not good enough. It needed to be called out. It still does.

Albion's title ambitions were to be dealt a cruel blow by one of the wickedest winters in years. The surface at The Hawthorns – the highest above sea level in the four leagues but which did not have the benefit of undersoil heating – was like rock for the best part of two months.

A fixture pile-up mounted until Albion needed to play 25 matches in 12 weeks, an insurmountable burden for a side with a relatively thin squad. Liverpool, whose Anfield pitch was protected, went on to win the title again, Brian Clough's Nottingham Forest were second and Atkinson's boys a respectable but frustrating third.

* * *

Real Madrid were the behemoth of European football and as such their chequebook was well-thumbed. Now they wanted Laurie Cunningham to join to a cast of esteemed stars. It didn't take long for a deal to be agreed, as Real bid £950,000 which, with the odd attachment, took the fee beyond £1m. Albion couldn't keep any player worth that amount and certainly not one eager to spread his wings.

The contracts were signed in Lorenzo's restaurant in Digbeth – the go-to place to bump into a sporting celebrity in those days – and soon afterwards, an invitation landed for me to visit Laurie and his long-time girlfriend Nicky Brown in Madrid.

This was quite an exclusive for the *Evening Mail* to have first sight of how he was coming to terms with the unique demands of the club and its fanatical *Madridistas,* supporters for the team in all-white who were falling in love with a black man. He was their *El Negrito* and he was revelling in it.

I recall a conversation with his great friend and former Orient team-mate Bobby Fisher which shed a ton of light on the kind of person and player Laurie was. 'Fish' tried, as many had before, to pin labels on his pal but found it impossible. A couple of instances that occurred at Brisbane Road in those formative months took us to the heart of this carefree footballer.

'The boss, George Petchey, told us to expect a new lad to arrive who had been released by Arsenal,' Fisher said. 'We normally started to train at 10.30am by which time Laurie was nowhere to be seen. Eventually, at about ten to 11, he turned up, sauntered across the pitch and started to get changed.

'I thought to myself, "Right, let's teach this kid a lesson." We were going to be on opposite sides for the session, me at right-back and him on the left wing. He wasn't wearing protective pads so I told myself I'd give him one down the shin, just to let him know what professional defending was all about. The next thing I remember I was flat on my back looking up at the sky. He'd nutmegged me. I don't think I ever got close to him.

'At one home match we had a shot on goal, the goalkeeper got a touch, the ball landed on the roof of the net and stayed there. Usually one of the defenders or the keeper would knock it away to waste a bit of time.

'All of a sudden Laurie twisted his body into an overhead kick, launched the ball into the air, brought it down on his thigh and volleyed it to the corner flag, all in one movement. Just the look on everyone's face was: did that just really happen?'

Fisher would be foremost among the few people Laurie invited to Madrid when he needed reassurance, more about personal matters than anything on the field. He knew exactly what he was doing out there.

Fish recalled, 'Laurie told me before one match at the Bernabéu that the first corner he took he'd hit the crossbar. Not score mind you, hit the bar. Real got a corner on the left, he swung it in and it struck the bar though the ref said the goalkeeper got a slight touch.

'Laurie skipped across to the opposite corner flag, struck the next corner with the outside of his right foot, the ball swerved and dipped, hit the bar and bounced away. The first thing he said after the match was, "There, I told you."'

When the *Evening Mail*'s photographer Tony Flanagan and I landed in Madrid, Laurie and Nicky could not have been more hospitable. As a team they were incredible and more so when you considered that the sight of a black man and white woman holding hands in the 1970s both turned heads and enraged the haters. Theirs was a love driven initially by a shared devotion to the finest designer clothes and their moves on the dance floor. They were just so right together.

The pair invested £85,000 in a penthouse flat of a dozen rooms on Avenue Alberto Alcocer in a luxurious suburb. Real offered them a Spanish designer to kit the rooms out but Nicky said she would do it herself. 'I'm a mirror freak,' she said. 'We'll have loads of mirrors. We are tinting all over in gold and cream.'

Our series with them was called 'The Life of Laurie' and opened with a decree from the man himself that he was determined to play a major part in England's 1982 World Cup campaign and an insistence that Real would not prevent him from playing in qualifying matches as had been widely reported.

Laurie said, 'I've had a long chat with Mr [Ron] Greenwood and he fully appreciates my position. He knows what I can do if he calls on me. I am a better player for this move and intend to prove it. Frankly I've never been happier. I had seven years of football in England and by the end I just stopped learning. I've signed a five-year contract and expect to see it out.'

It didn't work out as he expected, but then life rarely does. Laurie was summoned by Greenwood for the qualifier against Norway but remained stuck on the substitutes' bench. He was a substitute again later against Romania and was never to appear for his country again. A shocking waste of talent.

His Madrid career stalled when injuries began to dog him, not least in 1980 as he endured a series of operations to try to repair torn knee ligaments. At the end of the 1980/81 season, Real somehow reached the final of the European Cup to play Liverpool in Paris.

Vujadin Boškov, the Real coach, was desperate to pick Laurie – whatever his lack of physical preparedness – believing that he would be inspired against English opposition. The plan would backfire; Laurie was nowhere near his optimum and Liverpool won with a late goal by Alan Kennedy, the man Boškov had expected Cunningham would run into the ground.

Laurie rejoined his old manager Ron Atkinson, now at Manchester United, on loan, then moved to Sporting Gijon in Spain, Marseille in France, to Leicester City, to Rayo Vallecano in Spain, to Charleroi in Belgium and to Wimbledon, where he came on as a second-half substitute in the club's astonishing 1988 FA Cup Final victory over Liverpool. He returned to Vallecano the following season where it was his goal that secured their promotion to the country's first division.

On the morning of 15 July 1989, Laurie was driving in Madrid, moved across lanes to pass a car that had broken down, then a front wheel clipped the pavement and his vehicle spun out of control and crashed. He was killed. When I heard the news, I wept.

We shall never know what Laurie Cunningham could have become. These 33 years on, conjecture is all we have. I asked his best pal Bobby Fisher who, together with Laurie, had once stood in the middle of the pitch at Millwall's Old Den and delivered a black power salute after a match in which they were racially abused from start to finish. How bloody brave was that?

'Laurie could have owned his own dance school or been a clothes designer or something in architecture. He could have been at the very top. Or at the very bottom. I don't think there would have been much middle ground,' Fish said.

'I hate to say it but I often wonder if he'd have been a happy adult. Even when I visited him in Madrid I saw an unhappy person. There was nothing behind his eyes. We were together every day and I never really knew him. There was a bond but not a normal bond because he always had a defence mechanism.

'He didn't want to allow people to see that he was a really vulnerable person.'

6

Young Neil Harman

IN JUNE 1979 I was sent to cover the Lada Golf Classic at the Brabazon course at The Belfry, two years after the hotel and golf centre on Birmingham's outskirts was unveiled to critical acclaim as the new home of the Professional Golfers' Association.

A zestful young Spaniard named Seve Ballesteros had stunned everyone by driving the 310-yard across-the-water par-four tenth the previous spring and promised to be a sparkling jewel in the sport. Oh to have had Seve's talent for a single day.

After two rounds of the Lada event, the 22-year-old and his fellow countryman José María Olazábal were struggling for touch and form. The former West Brom manager Ronnie Allen – who knew the pair from his time coaching Athletic Bilbao and was walking inside the ropes as their guest – thought the boys needed an infusion of something to remind them of home.

'I wondered if they were getting decent food at their hotel so I decided to make them a Spanish speciality,' Ronnie told me. He asked if I'd like to join them.

I sat chatting to Ballesteros in Allen's lounge. I told him we were born on the same day and he patted me on the shoulder. He said he did not know precisely what he could achieve in golf but there was fire in his eyes. He was a charming fellow, a free spirit whose approach to his sport was uninhibited as it was when Allen served a classic paella. We ate it with an uncomplicated relish.

Two days later a fortified Seve won the Belfry tournament and entered the upcoming Open Championship at Royal Lytham & St Annes with mind and digestive system in perfect harmony. I should have tipped him to win.

Instead I picked Isao Aoki to be the champion, recalling that the great South African Gary Player had said that from 50 yards from the green he had not seen better than Aoki, which was potentially critical in links golf. Entering the final round, there were seven players ahead of the Japanese on the leaderboard. One was Ballesteros, who was two shots behind the leader, American Hale Irwin.

The wind then howled in the north-west of England. Who could tame these archetypal conditions that sorted men from boys? Step forward Seve who missed almost every fairway on the back nine and yet produced a slew of amazing recovery shots – famously clubbing his ball back into play from a temporary car park on the 16th.

Golf would fall head over heels for this handsome swashbuckler who could win at a sport normally requiring a metronomic technique and a tendency for accuracy as the basis for enduring success. Seve was the only player at Lytham to finish 72 holes under par. Americans Jack Nicklaus and Ben Crenshaw tied for second and Aoki, my pick, was eight shots behind the new champion.

The following year the journey took us to Muirfield, home of the Honourable Company of Edinburgh Golfers and where two memories of my final Open for the *Evening Mail* stood out. The first was a masterclass by American Tom Watson whose third-round seven-under-par 64 meant he could almost stroll the final day.

The second was an invitation to share accommodation for the championship from 'Dai' Davies of the *Birmingham Post*. I thought it was extremely generous and looked forward to a cosy bedroom in a house ten minutes from the course vacated by the owners for the duration.

We were approaching Muirfield when Davies turned the car towards Dunbar and made for the coast. Ah, the scenic route. Instead we ended up on a beach where one of three caravans parked on the sand was to be our home for the week. Dai did make a decent bowl of porridge but I was kept awake most nights either by him snoring, or the bloody seagulls.

* * *

Some of the most noted productions in British television in the 1970s and 80s were filmed at the ATV Studios in Broad Street, Birmingham.

I was a devoted *Tiswas* fan – most lads in their early 20s had a massive crush on Sally James – and I loved *Spitting Image* but didn't watch a single edition of *Bullseye* or an episode of *Crossroads* even if the Tony Hatch theme tune was a constant backdrop to Birmingham life.

The main ATV studio was the setting for many sports occasions, notably the Midland Soccer Writers' annual prize-giving, the highlights of which were televised a couple of nights later on the local network. I had never hired a dress suit before but think I found one that fitted.

At the end of the 1979/80 season – when Nottingham Forest had wondrously retained the European Cup, West Bromwich Albion were still lauded and Aston Villa a club about to perform wonders under Ron Saunders – the studio was the only place in the city large enough to house everyone who required to be invited.

Summoned to the main auditorium for dinner, I scanned the table layout and realised I'd been sat with the Forest players, none of whom I had met before. This was going to be a special night even if I was nerve-wracked to have to introduce myself to a sea of faces I perfectly well recognised but who had no idea who I was.

I had said hello to a couple of the Forest lads and as my hands rested on the back of my chair, I felt a tap on the shoulder. Half turning, I was met by the uncompromising stare of Brian Clough.

'Who are you young man and what are you doing sitting with my players?'

'Er, I'm Neil Harman of the *Birmingham Evening Mail*, Mr Clough, and this is where I've been told to sit.'

'Well, Neil Harman of the *Birmingham Evening Mail*, you don't know me, I don't know you and you're not fucking sitting there.'

'Um, er, where should I sit then?'

'I'll tell you what, Neil Harman of the *Birmingham Evening Mail*, I'll sort it out and you can come and sit with me.'

That evening Brian was part compere, part analyst, giving a commentary on the award-winners and their contribution to the game. This meant his table was constantly monitored by cameras seeking his reaction to the pieces of football action being displayed on screen behind the stage.

The tables mostly sat ten or 12 guests whereas the one Clough led me towards was a deal more intimate. I recognised his assistant Peter Taylor and there were two other people he introduced as his lawyer and a friend, whose names I can't recall.

'Who's this?' Taylor asked, rather gruffly. 'This, Peter, is Neil Harman of the *Birmingham Evening Mail* and he's got more fucking right to be here than you have,' Clough said. Taylor grunted and didn't really engage much the entire evening. Brian could not have been more different.

'Now, young Neil Harman, we'll get along if you just make sure that this [he pointed to his wine glass] is always full and here's a cigar,' at which point he thrust a huge cigarillo between my fingers and lit it.

Only for someone like Brian Clough would I have feigned enjoyment drawing on a cigar that was frankly disgusting. I coughed the rest of the evening but Brian's glass was never less than replete with the best white wine the Midland Soccer Writers could afford.

* * *

Delivering Saturday match reports for the *Sports Argus* was a skill acquired as you went along. They didn't teach you how to write running copy at Harlow technical college.

These were a ball-by-ball, action-by-action account and therefore an open telephone line was imperative for a reporter to file to his designated copy taker in head office. Each of our local teams had its regular Saturday specialist (Val for Villa, Bob for the Albion etc.), fans who knew all the surnames and had often typed the teams before you'd reached number 11.

In general, each report would be around 800 words of free-flowing delivery. Ten minutes from time the reporter sent a three-paragraph intro to sit on top of their inside-page running copy, so the report was non-conclusive yet authoritative at the same time.

A minute or two before the final whistle, we composed a 100-word précis of the match together with the team's form rate and a choice of man of the match, which gave the front page a real sense of impact and command. Then you would offer a quick prayer that no one scored in the last few seconds or a rewrite was needed with no time to properly compose yourself and deliver it.

Back at base camp – though those of us in the field never saw it in operation – headlines were being written, the six front-page summings-up were placed in order of importance, the pictures chosen, with all the copy leaving the subs' desk in time for the paper to be off the presses 30 minutes after the final whistle.

The reporter had ten minutes to draw breath and then ad lib a report – between 500 and 700 words depending on the importance of the match or the circumstances of the result – to the company's Sunday paper, the *Mercury*, edited by the eternally jovial Barry James.

Once that was done you scurried down to the huddles in the car park for any quotable material needed for your report in Monday's *Mail*. Each weekend, therefore, you would write three pieces on the same match – *Argus*, *Mercury* and *Mail* – seeking new angles and storylines for each one. It was all a joyous blur.

It was while constructing a story to fill one of the slots in an *Argus* edition in January 1979 that I had another of what would become a kaleidoscope of encounters with Ron Atkinson, the only manager with whom I conducted an interview while he was stark-bollock naked lying on a sunbed in his own office.

West Brom had agreed to pay Middlesbrough £516,000 for striker David Mills, who would become the first footballer in Britain to fetch over half a million pounds. The player's terms had been negotiated and all was well with the deal.

I was chasing background material with a couple of directors to beef up my report. John Gordon tipped me the wink that when Big Ron told the board he was pursuing Mills, John had erroneously believed the manager was talking about Mick Mills of Ipswich and not David Mills of Middlesbrough.

It was remarkable that such a senior director hadn't asked for a player's verification before raising his hand when the vote was taken. I reported this prominently in the story.

At the Europa Lodge that evening an animated debate between a cabal of Midlands reporters with Atkinson was in full flow. I made my way over with a folded *Sports Argus* tucked beneath my arm which Ron yanked free and used to smack me across the back of the head.

The West Brom manager had not taken kindly to a suggestion that he blindsided his board by not explaining which Mills was which. Leon Hickman threatened legal consequences unless he apologised, especially as there were prominent journalistic witnesses present.

I said I didn't want to get involved in anything like that and the whole matter was dropped as quickly as you could say Rudi Wakening.

* * *

Perhaps it wasn't such a bad move when, in 1980, there was a shuffle of responsibilities and I was taken off Albion to become the Birmingham City writer for the *Argus*. Bob 'Scoop' Downing, once of the *Express and Star*, was a renowned Albion expert so it made perfect sense that he should stick with the Baggies.

Birmingham had been relegated to the Second Division the previous season but kept faith with manager Jim Smith and possessed a playing staff that was an enticing blend of young and quite a bit older. Smith, aka the Bald Eagle, was a smart operator whose teams played in a free-spirited manner that entirely matched his love of spirits.

Smith persuaded old-time internationals like Colin Todd, Archie Gemmill and Frank Worthington – my 18th birthday party guest – to buy into his plan for the resurgence of a club that played up to its reputation as the put-upon poor relation to their esteemed neighbours, Aston Villa and West Bromwich Albion.

In Kevin Dillon and Mark Dennis, Birmingham had a couple of talents raw and liable to rebellion. Dill and Den – as I labelled them – played both at home and away and not exceptionally when it came to football matches. They were a real pair of scallywags.

Guiding them in the team were sturdy pros like Republic of Ireland full-back Dave Langan and prodigious workers Alan Curbishley and Alan Ainscow. The captain Gemmill was my new ghosted columnist who, like John Wile, was always there at the appointed hour and spoke such compelling sense.

Archie was a consummate professional in every way, and far better judges than I ranked him among the best players of his ilk in the land. One such was employed as a columnist by the *Evening Mail* with whom Dave Harrison and I took it in turns to work. When it came to my debut for this particular task, I was shaking like a leaf. The columnist was Bill Shankly.

I don't know who at the *Mail* had the masterstroke of offering the legendary former Liverpool manager a weekly column but it kept football alive in him. He loved to talk, even to a lad like me who he'd never met. His wife Nessie always answered the phone.

'It's Neil Harman of the *Birmingham Mail*, Mrs Shankly,' I'd say, at which she'd call down the hall, 'Bill, it's Neil Harman from the *Birmingham Mail*.'

There was a distant cry of recognition, a shuffling of feet, a passing of the phone and Mr Shankly would say, 'Aye, Neil. What are we going to talk about?' There were times I was so flustered by the voice I struggled to take notes.

He was as sharp as a tack on any subject you wished to raise but would wax prodigiously when it came to Archie Gemmill. Indeed, whatever you may be chatting about, he'd manage to turn the conversation around to, 'How's wee Archie playing for Birmingham?' 'He's doing really well, Mr Shankly.' 'A great player. Give him my regards won't you, Neil.' 'I promise I will, Mr Shankly.'

* * *

It would have been unnatural for a kid sportswriter on one of the country's foremost regional evening papers not to harbour national paper aspirations. If you're in your early 20s and playing Championship football, it makes perfect sense to want to show your wares in the Premier League.

The *Daily Mail* and I had felt a natural match, not least because Alf Smirk told me I'd work for the paper one day. In autumn 1980 a vacancy arose in the *Mail*'s London office for a football writer and I was at the nearest postbox with my application before you could say West Bromwich Albion.

I received a reply asking me to attend an interview in early November with Tom Clarke, the sports editor, and Peter Moss, his sports news editor. I felt the meeting went well, despite my initial sense of intimidation at meeting two such senior journalists of national repute.

A few days later a letter arrived saying I'd lost out but because I knew I was a decent shout for the job, the rejection stiffened my resolve. I was disheartened but not dismayed.

Dear Neil,

We have decided to offer our vacancy to Harry Harris [then of the London Evening News] *rather than you. Your claim was a good one but we reasoned that we needed someone who would go directly into the news field of London football rather than a talented newcomer, no matter how enthusiastic he was.*

In other circumstances and with another set of people here, we might have moved in your direction but we think our decision is right for our particular demands. My thanks for your visit and my best wishes for your future.

Yours sincerely,
Tom Clarke
Sports Editor

* * *

Shortly before midday on Boxing Day 1980, a Rolls-Royce Silver Shadow II the shade of yellowish-brown purred into the car park of the Seaburn Hotel on the north-east coast, about a mile and a half from Roker Park, home of Sunderland.

Two Albion directors stepped from the car, John Gordon and the vehicle owner, Brian Boundy. They headed up the front steps of the hotel to where the team had travelled on Christmas Day and were now mingling in the lobby before lunch and a final debrief prior to kick-off at 3pm.

I had put my hand up to cover the match, a decision my parents were disappointed with but long accepted was part and parcel of a football writer's lot. A full league calendar was a 26 December tradition and if Sunderland v West Bromwich Albion wasn't the pick of the crop, the *Mail* needed someone there.

I arrived at Seaburn off the train just a few minutes before the directors pulled in and was sitting at a table in an alcove from where you could look out upon a particularly dark and frothy North Sea.

The Albion directors were a jovial, outgoing group. The chairman Bert Millichip needed to be rather more sober as befitted a leading solicitor and FA panjandrum, but his acolytes loved to have a natter and a beer. Gordon, who had taken Laurie Cunningham under his wing when he moved to Real Madrid, was a West Midlands impresario possessed of a jaunty spirit; likewise Syd Lucas, with his Mr Bumble sideburns; and Boundy was crinkly haired, open-faced and an implacable ally of Ron Atkinson.

Boundy came bounding over to my table, 'Neil, would you do me an enormous favour dear boy? The other directors and I want to go back on the team bus to play cards. Would you take the Roller to the ground and back to the Midlands? Here's my car park pass, here's the keys. Just park the car up later and leave these at reception at the Europa Lodge. I'm staying there tonight.'

Albion were playing Manchester United at home the next day, the kind of turnaround all too familiar into the 1980s but that would have turned Liverpool manager Jürgen Klopp into a gibbering idiot if it happened today.

Having to play football matches in successive days was child's play set against the challenge I'd just accepted. I'd never seen inside a Rolls-Royce let alone be let loose behind the wheel. Mr Boundy gave me a quick guide to turning it on and off and after I'd spent five minutes looking for a gearstick that didn't exist, he explained it rather drove itself. 'What does automatic mean?' I asked. 'You'll be fine,' he said, which was hardly calming reassurance.

When he tossed me the keys and I clocked the dimensions of the steering wheel – three times the size of mine – anxiety levels shot up. 'Don't go just yet,' he said.

Two smartly dressed kids came skipping over. I was introduced to Graham and Phillip Silk, the young sons of Tom Silk, the Albion vice-chairman who had been tragically killed with his wife Catherine in a light plane crash over France three months earlier. I was to be the twitchy driver of a shockingly expensive car and guardian angel rolled into one.

It shouldn't take ten minutes to reach Roker Park and when the boys had piled into the back, I started the engine, which made a pleasing low hum and the car glided forward. I was keen to keep the Albion coach in sight but just as I spotted the reassuring outline of the stadium, the Rolls was hemmed in by hundreds of people, very few of whom were sticking to the pavement.

Then the coach went one way and all I could do was turn another, trapped between growing numbers of fans and wary that if I pressed the hooter – if I could work out where it was – they might not respond obligingly.

The VIP parking lot at Roker Park was a horrendously tight squeeze and those gesturing through the driver's window were not stewards or fellow drivers. A posse of folk in red and white scarves were clearly not used to seeing a Silver Shadow II being driven by a 23-year-old who didn't appear to have a clue how to reverse it.

I made it into a gap not measured for a Rolls-Royce and once I'd extricated myself from the driver's side and gathered the Silk boys from the back, it was a case of getting from the car park to the directors' entrance and turning a deaf ear to the flying insults.

The insults were a mixture of ferocity and piss-taking, usually involving the words 'rich' and 'bastard'. I didn't see the point in stopping to engage because that would have generated worse harassment. What was I to say? That it wasn't my car or that I was actually a football reporter? Think of the shit I'd have got then.

Sunderland's stadium was one from the old school that throbbed with passion and drew astonishing crowds. That this was the holiday season served to steepen the levels of intensity on the terraces. The coastline was near enough for the wind to be at its most piercing, whistling through the wooden press box which occupied the first two rows of the main stand, turning your face deep red and your hands a shade of shocking purple. Holding a pen was a challenge especially as they were both still shaking from the first experience of trying to park a Roller.

After the pre-match adrenalin flow, an anti-climactic goalless draw duly followed and it was – thankfully – under cover of darkness that I collected Graham and Phillip and ushered them back to one yellow vehicle remaining in the car park. I thanked the Lord there wasn't a scratch on it.

Once I clocked the sign for 'A1 South' I felt a trifle safer, although the number of roundabouts on that single carriageway road between the north-east and wherever it was I got off was a bloody nightmare and at one stage I was nonplussed by a flurry of activity on the dashboard, first a red light, then a green.

I discovered later from Mr Boundy that these were warnings first sensing the formation of ice on the road followed by confirmation the tyres had, indeed, touched a frozen surface. I don't think I drove over 50mph and we arrived home without further incident in three hours and 25 minutes, the car having timed the journey for me which was very decent of it.

The young Silks thought it had been a terrific adventure and seemed sad when I turned off the engine. I was never happier to park a car, hand the boys over to a professional taxi driver, down a beer, find my own way home and slump into bed.

* * *

Word reached the sportsdesk that Willie Bell, the former boss of Birmingham City, was back in the city on a crusade offering infinitely more security than managing a football club. His mission was to bring the word of Jesus Christ to Britain in the company of a group of teenage disciples from the United States.

Bell had been among the school of hard footballers fostered by Don Revie at Leeds United at a time when to be described as uncompromising was regarded as a virtue. A left-back of Scottish descent, Bell played alongside Bobby Collins, Jack Charlton, Norman Hunter, Billy Bremner and Johnny Giles in a team distinct for its lack of angels. Hunter once said of him, 'Willie was one of the bravest men I've ever seen. He never blinked and never flinched.'

That was evident in the infamous 'Battle of Goodison' against Everton in 1964. Tackles flew in from the first minute, Bell had to be carried off on the shoulders of two team-mates after one nasty lunge at him, and the Everton bench screamed at Leeds trainer Les Cocker to 'find his own fucking stretcher'.

Bell ended up scoring the winning goal of a match that at one stage was stopped for ten minutes when the referee took the teams back to the dressing rooms in a bid to level tempers.

He was twice a member of the side that finished second in the First Division and played left-back in the 1965 FA Cup Final team when an extra-time winner from Ian St John secured victory for Liverpool. After 204 appearances for the Yorkshire club, Willie played over 40 times for both Leicester and Brighton before turning his hand to management.

His experience at Birmingham lasted for the best part of two years until the team lost their first four games of the 1977/78 season and he was replaced by Sir Alf Ramsey, one of the board of directors who took the decision to sack him.

Willie was appointed manager at Lincoln City but that was a sharp, unhappy experience. He sat down after that and sensed he was being called in a direction he would never question, giving his life totally to his Lord and saviour.

This exceptional journey would initially take him to a burgeoning American university that, over time, shaped the lives of many students and was exposed as an example of how the Christian right in the US played a role in determining American political discourse that was neither righteous nor acceptable.

The night I first met him at the Hall Green Baptist Church on the Stratford Road, Willie preached the gospel and his teenage entourage sang and shared the message with a small, jubilant congregation that was spiritually affirming. I couldn't recall having met anyone as contented as him.

His commitment to God was unshakeable. We shared Bible readings, prayed together and in autumn 1980 he invited me to stay with him, his wife Mary and their three children at his home in Lynchburg, Virginia, where he was the soccer coach at Liberty Baptist College.

It was an absolutely beautiful spot in a rural state where the colours were in mid-change and the entire place looked as if it was gold-embossed. Having flown into Washington, DC, the concluding part of the journey was on a hopper propeller plane taking in such stops as Shenandoah, Roanoke and finally into Lynchburg. I had never seen such scenery and certainly not from 10,000 feet into the sky. It really did feel as if you were looking down upon God's own country.

The Bell's wood and brick home was perched on the side of Liberty Mountain (think of *The Waltons* and you're more or less there) and filled each evening with polite and prayerful young men. It was clear the boys Willie coached saw him as more than someone who taught formations and styles of play. He taught styles for life.

The day before I departed the US, I kept an appointment with Jerry Falwell, the university's chancellor whose *Old-Time Gospel Hour* radio programme weekly reached millions of apostles. His was an avuncular delivery but with an overtly conservative message that in turn helped procure both him and the college huge sums of money and influence.

It was said that without the evangelical vote, spurred by the eloquence and tub-thumping of Falwell and other mainstream pastors on television and radio at the time, Ronald Reagan's 1980 US presidential election victory would not have arrived as decisively as it did.

Falwell's was an office fit for a king, a sprawling expanse with luxurious furniture that seemed to me to be about the size of the *Evening Echo*'s editorial floor. I couldn't remember ever having seen a tie tied with such perfection, a shirt quite so white or the waistcoat of a three-piece suit so amply filled. It really did feel as if I was sitting across from a deity. Falwell's voice boomed across the room.

'Since Bill Bell arrived a great excitement has lit up the campus,' he said. 'I feel that in time he will give this college a respect in soccer that will be known throughout the land. God has prepared a life for Bill and His grace and power shine through in him.'

The whole life-affirming experience seemed a million miles from the days at Elland Road when Leeds' fans chanted, 'Willie Bell, Willie Bell, will he run? Will he hell.'

* * *

At the turn of the year, Aston Villa were the talk of West Midlands football and if my involvement with the club was limited compared to others in the area, there was something about walking into Villa Park that was very special. In full voice, it matched any other ground in the land.

Villa trailed champions Liverpool on goal difference heading into 1981. Ipswich were third, a point behind with two games in hand. On 10 January, Villa defeated Liverpool 2-0 at Villa Park and the race was thrown wide open.

I had never particularly got along with Ron Saunders, Villa's manager, though I respected him enormously. Saunders liked his reputation as a disciplinarian, one that he did little to play down. His players would say that Saunders' team talks were nothing fancy, like the man himself. 'If you win your individual battles the match will take care of itself,' was one of his edicts.

He wasn't one for tactical wizardry; it was pretty basic 4-4-2 and take the game to the opposition. The last line of his match notes would always extol a demand for '110 per cent' from players and supporters alike.

A month before the end of the season, I put in a request to travel on the team bus with the boys to Sunderland (it was always Sunderland, it seemed). It felt like a good time to find out what made the team tick and Saunders, to my immense surprise, not only agreed with the proposal but seemed positively to welcome the idea.

When I arrived for the trip, Roy MacLaren, Saunders' number two, told me the boss was ill, wouldn't be travelling and that he was in charge. Part of me relaxed. I'm not sure whether MacLaren's unlikely role enhanced the story but I do remember Saunders was not best pleased when the *Evening Mail* on Monday contained a piece that was hugely complimentary of his assistant after a 3-1 victory at Roker Park.

The red phone on the writers' desk pinged into life. It was a special line to which few were privy to the number. For the most part, whoever rang wanted to speak to Ray Matts. This time, a recognisable voice asked for me and when I said, 'Hello, Ron,' he spent at least two minutes giving me a rollicking before the line went dead when I tried to answer.

The only other time Saunders and I spoke on that phone was after I sent off the brother of Gordon 'Sid' Cowans in a local Sunday league match. Cowans' father was a scout for Villa and Sid's younger sibling (I can't recall his first name) was a cocksure lad. He was giving me lip from the first minute and when the phrase 'cheating fucking bastard' was uttered, I pointed to the dressing room.

As I walked off after the match, young master Cowans decided to come back on to the pitch, punch the ball from my grasp and think himself tremendously amusing. More stuff to have to send in my report to the local FA.

Saunders was told about the incident and on Monday morning before training he couldn't contain himself. 'Get a thrill sending off boys, do you?' he asked when the red phone was passed to me. When I tried to reason and said he should listen to both sides of the story, the line went dead again.

Villa would win the title in May, an achievement for so many to savour, built on trusted teamwork, incredible endeavour, flashes of individual brilliance and self-belief rather than any Churchillian oratory. Saunders set the tone, yes, but the players had a drive from within that didn't require motivational speeches.

It wasn't a 'show us your caps' team because they hardly had one between them, it hadn't required foreign influence, there were no theatricals and no egomaniacs. The goalkeeper was huge, the defenders defended ably, the midfield engine room was well lubricated, the team had mercurial talents in Tony Morley and Gary

Shaw who could shred defences apart and a totemic striker in Peter Withe having the season of his life.

They were truly worthy champions. I wasn't at the heart of the club but appreciated what they had done and applauded from a distance. A distance that would soon grow.

I spent three remarkable years in the Second City, met and worked with incredible people and would depart with a degree of sorrow. I would never see Brian Sparks again, though the cry of 'Hormone Forward' when he demanded a conversation about the state of my copy would remain indelible.

When I asked my old Midlands pals Peter White and Bob Downing what they remembered most about my time on the paper, both recalled an incident that had nothing to do with writing ability or story-gathering.

The paper had run a competition along the lines of Spot the Ball and I was entrusted with the task of picking a winner. Drowning in a sea of entries, my thought processes were interrupted by Sparky shouting, 'Hormone, have you got a second?' to which my response was, 'Bloody hell, Brian, I haven't even got a first.'

* * *

Having come within a whisker of joining the *Daily Mail* in November 1980, I sensed another opportunity would come my way sooner or later to return to my roots in the south. Moving in the opposite direction hadn't really entered my head.

It was then that the lure of Manchester gathered irresistible momentum. Ronald Crowther, a bastion of story-getting in the *Mail*'s northern office for a couple of decades, was to retire and – as with Dennis Shaw's departure from the *Evening Mail* in 1978 – the search was on for a young reporter to join the team where everyone would get a leg-up.

I don't know if Tom Clarke had put a word in but Bryan Webster, the sports editor in Manchester, phoned to ask if we could meet. One thing led to another and a formal interview was arranged between the two of us and the *Mail*'s northern editor John Womersley.

The *Mail* building, though only four storeys high, was an intimidating deep brown in shade, which I took as a reflection of how long it had stood there and what power and influence it emitted down the decades. It hugged the corner of Deansgate and Hardman Street with a centrepiece that looked like a huge bell tower with a mast atop it.

Across the main entrance, the newspaper's masthead was simple and yet had a hypnotising effect. Before walking in that first day, I looked up, took a deep breath and said to myself, 'This is the place for me.'

Deansgate was usually choked from one end to the other, the direct extensions of which were Old Trafford football ground to the west and Strangeways prison to the east. It was a little like Fleet Street in respect of its congestion and proximity of the newspaper offices. The *Mail* was next door but one to the local *Manchester Evening News* and *The Guardian*'s editorial office could be reached by a series of criss-cross walkways and corridors, without having to go outside.

The main staircase was breathtakingly imposing and led to a long corridor which creaked and groaned when applying the lightest pressure to it. On either side of the corridor stood tall oak-panelled offices, the third on the left of which belonged to the editor. Bryan Webster escorted me in to meet his boss.

John Womersley had been a journalist of considerable influence at the *Mail* for a decade, after its merger with the *Daily Sketch* in 1971. Under the renowned editorship of David English, John was the initial news editor and then an assistant editor before heading up the New York bureau for five years. In 1979, he was recalled to Britain to lead the northern operation.

What struck one initially about Womersley was the fact that he stood 6ft 4in tall and – how to say this kindly – he possessed an extremely prominent nose and eyeballs that shook back and forth, a condition known as nystagmus. It meant that even if you didn't particularly want to, your eyes were drawn to the middle of his face and it felt as if he held you in a trance.

The three of us sat at one end of a massive table, a daunting experience made less tense because of the people in the room with me. I knew I could work well for John and Bryan if only they would give me the chance.

On 30 June 1981 I received a letter and immediately recalled Alf Smirk's words to me in the Southend press box six years earlier.

> *Dear Mr Harman,*
>
> *I am now very pleased to offer you a position as a sports reporter on the staff of the* Daily Mail *in Manchester. The position will be at a salary of £11,385 p.a. and this takes into account a 3.5% salary increase to* Daily Mail *journalists effective from July 1, 1981 under the current House agreement.*
>
> *In addition to this, there is a media allowance of £464 p.a. and the company will pay your telephone rental together with the cost of calls that you make on their behalf. I will also sanction for you to be placed on the authorised car users list.*
>
> *As I explained to you during your interview, there were many applications for this position and I have given great consideration to them. I was impressed by the manner in which you presented your case, your career background to date and your responsible attitude towards your profession.*
>
> *I am confident you will fulfil my belief that you will make an important contribution to the sports content and coverage of the* Daily Mail *with the emphasis we place upon results, quality and style.*
>
> *If this offer is acceptable to you please acknowledge it in writing, and I would like you to start with us at the earliest opportunity subject to your present commitments.*
>
> *Yours sincerely,*
> *John Womersley,*
> *Northern Editor*

When the letter arrived and it was safe to pluck me from the ceiling, the attention of most sporting enthusiasts in Britain was tuned to cricket and tennis. The first Test of the 1981 Ashes series had been won by Australia at Trent Bridge so we looked set for an agonising few weeks under the heel of the baggy greens.

In London, at the All England Club, an American left-handed tennis player with unruly curls randomly contained under a red headband was cursing British umpires and their fading competence. 'You cannot be serious,' he yelled and the Wimbledon crowd tittered as they were wont to do.

John McEnroe seemed a very complex character but not one ever likely to cross my path. I was 24 years old and heading into one of the great football cities of the world for an adventure that would fulfil me like no other.

7
Manchester

RON ATKINSON stopped in his tracks. 'What the hell are you doing here?' said the new manager of Manchester United. The location was the Midland Hotel in the city centre where a Football League tribunal which would decide how much United had to pay to sign Frank Stapleton from Arsenal continued its deliberations.

I'd been sent to doorstep the meeting for my first football assignment on the *Mail* and told Ron the news of my career advancement. 'You're stalking me,' he said. 'But I'm delighted for you. Now what do you want?'

A few quotes on United having to pay £900,000 for the Irish striker were safely gathered in and I put the story together that Stapleton was a brilliant signing who'd fit precisely with what Ron was seeking to achieve at his new club. The story led the back page in the northern editions.

The Stapleton latest was penned the week after my first by-line for the *Mail* appeared on 18 August on a story from the other Old Trafford, the home of Lancashire CCC. The cricket series that became immortalised as 'Botham's Ashes' had contained some incredible chapters with hardly a dull session in an enthralling two-month contest.

England sensed a series success and thanks to routing the Aussies for 103 in their second innings in Manchester had set the visitors 506 to avoid the ignominy of losing the Ashes with a Test left to play. Heading into the fifth day, they were 210/5 so needed to buckle down and bat with real defiance.

A day's play was attended by the cricket correspondent, in the *Mail*'s case the superbly connected Peter Smith, and someone to assist with peripheral stories and attend press conferences while the main writer produced his descriptive story of the day. Colin Wood, our Liverpool football beat writer, had been at Smith's side for a couple of days but cried off on the fifth. Bryan Webster despatched me in his stead.

Allan Border and Rodney Marsh – two belligerent buggers – were at the crease and added 86 on the last morning before Marsh edged a delivery from Bob Willis into the gloves of his fellow wicketkeeper Alan Knott.

Dennis Lillee kept life in the match for a while with a robust knock of 28 but the tail hardly laid bat on ball and Australia were 402 all out – 103 runs short. All hail another England Ashes triumph.

I dashed down the back steps of the press box to the pavilion where the captains, Mike Brearley of England and Australia's Kim Hughes, would speak to the media. Brearley was his usual unruffled, reflective self but when Hughes sat down for his turn, his features were ashen.

I reminded myself that Hughes was only three years older than me and here he was captaining his country to a horrible defeat. His voice cracked as he spoke. His bottom lip was trembling and there was a distinct redness around his eyes.

I made notes of what he said, took the steps up to Peter Smith in the press box two at a time and told him Hughes had been crying. This was a terrifically emotive piece in the offing. 'Brilliant,' Smith said. 'I'll take all that, you go and find something else.'

Something else? Bloody hell. I retreated back to the pavilion and luckily found Border, who had made a brilliant 123 not out in the second innings to try to preserve some Australian pride, willing to say a few words about his innings and the sting of defeat. Hughes and his tears were the back-page lead and tucked away to its right-hand side were my half a dozen paragraphs on Border. A small contribution maybe but a historic one for me. A back-page piece at the first time of asking.

Peter Smith asked Bryan Webster to relay his best wishes for a job well done and how professionally I'd responded after he'd snatched the story of the day from me. The sod.

* * *

Bryan Webster was the sixth sports editor I had worked for and by some margin the most sartorially blessed. Nothing about Bryan was out of place, not one of the hairs in his resplendent headful, not his perfectly tied ties and his desktop was on a par with Brian Sparks when it came to tidiness.

The minute he arrived for his shift, Bryan peeled off his jacket, hung it in his private office and pulled a regular buttoned cardigan over his shirt and tie to prevent unwanted damage to his finest threads when work got messier as the day progressed.

At lunchtime, Bryan – known as Webby, though I never called him that to his face – would regularly take himself a couple of hundred yards along Deansgate to Kendalls, Manchester's equivalent of Harvey Nichols, to replenish his already extensive wardrobe. God knows how many ties he owned. He loved the fact that the staff would regularly debate his clothes sense.

The *Mail* sportsdesk in Manchester was a cosy affair in comparison to the expansive clutter in Birmingham. The entire editorial floor was compacted into 40 yards square to either side of the wooden walkway that extended from the main offices where I'd been interviewed two months earlier.

Emerging from the passageway, the sports writers were seated immediately to the left at four desks soldered together. Ahead of this were two rectangular subs' desks with space for eight souls and a back bench for four department heads.

Webby was on the far right of the row, with deputy Tony Lanigan next to him, then assistant editor Alan Beesley with two associate editors, Jim Lord and Dave Bowman vying for the fourth spot. They made for a divergent team.

If Webby was a light-touch editor – not a criticism but a fact – Lanigan was more inclined to rattle a reporter's cage. The two often rubbed each other up the wrong way and my sense was Tony believed Bryan was too abiding of us. He would delight at his days in charge – every Friday and others besides – to edit the way he thought it should be done. I really liked him.

Tony and Bryan both fancied themselves as writers and were able to freelance at Saturday matches for the *People* and the *News of the World* respectively. If they were at the same match it was great fun to see them jousting, Tony always finishing first and bustling along to managers' press conferences while Bryan was often painstaking in his written work. Tony would get a kick out of how slow Bryan was and revelled in the fact he could get one up on him. It was exactly how they were in the office.

Alan 'Beezer' Beesley was an old-style charmer with crimson cheeks who loved being around the lads and edited in an open-hearted, collegiate manner that endeared him to everyone. On Beezer's days at the helm, lunchtime writers' meetings would often be held in our local, the Sir Ralph Abercromby, across Deansgate on Bootle Street.

It was amazing how much easier the stories fitted together when the page layouts were debated with a barmcake in one hand and a pint of Boddingtons in the other.

Jim Lord had been seconded from the newsdesk and it was clear from the word go that he neither knew nor cared much about sport. He was a rough-hewn character from Lancashire's hinterland with a straggly beard stained brown with nicotine from the non-tipped, full-strength cigarettes he lit one after another. His face would often disappear in a self-inflicted smog, lucky for us.

Dave Bowman was the dependable, secure, solid desk man every department needed, never outwardly flustered and with an eye for detail that covered his superiors' arses from time to time.

Dave dealt on a daily basis with the writers from the farther-flung reaches of the northern office's spread, the Scottish and Irish lads.

The circulation of the Manchester edition had steadily risen under Womersley's leadership. When I joined the *Mail* it sold two million copies nationwide, with 600,000 in our circulation area whose contours had seemingly been drawn by a nursery school kid let loose with a map of Britain and a biro.

There was a Scottish edition, an Irish edition, a northern first edition which went to the north-east, Cumbria, Merseyside and North Wales; a second edition to Yorkshire and a final which took in Manchester, its extensive suburbia and surrounding towns as far south as Stoke-on-Trent.

Brian Scott and Glenn Gibbons were our Scottish football writers; Adam Coates was based in Belfast and Dermot Gilleece in Dublin. The district men were Colin Wood on Merseyside, Bill Mallinson in Yorkshire and Doug Weatherall in the north-east. This was a powerful, experienced well-connected staff.

In the ranks of writing seniority at head office, Peter 'Jonno' Johnson was the number one with Derick 'Dino' Allsop his deputy. I was the new kid in town. The other writers based on Deansgate were feature writer John Roberts and rugby league correspondent Brian Batty.

Jonno was a superbly gifted writer, both on football and cricket. He was a touch introverted until he got to know you and then became a much-loved colleague and mentor. There was something about his prose that shone, neither a word out of place nor one that didn't carry gravitas. He made a report on Manchester City's team news read like an ode by Keats.

Derick Allsop was Dino to one and all, his given middle name a homage to Italian ancestry. Dino was a big fan of Manchester United and couldn't always disguise it in his writing. He was another consummate wordsmith, though, self-confident and sharp. You could tell he absolutely loved doing what he did.

On the extremes of our desk sat Roberts and Batty. John became JR after the main character in the vogue American TV series *Dallas* though he was hardly Cheadle Hulme's answer to the eldest Ewing brother. Everything about him was very predictable.

Roberts had been a lead sportswriter on both the *Express* and *Guardian* in Manchester before joining the *Mail,* not long before I did. He deliberated long and hard over his prose, which was first class, and we hit it off to an extent, though he could be maddening in his foibles and just-so mannerisms.

Though Webby was his boss on the spot, JR often circumvented his leadership to take his directions straight from Tom Clarke in London. Bryan never said as much but you could tell it gnawed away at him.

In the office, reporters' copy went through a vetting process overseen by Derek Marshall, the sports copy-taster, before it was despatched across the wires to London. JR would stamp his own work, walk it into the wire room and wait there until he knew it had reached Clarke's desk without the risk of being buried in Derek's out tray. Dear old Marshall used to get terribly narked.

John was set in his ways too when it came to eating arrangements. On days I was around for a sit-down meal, JR would let us know where he wanted to go, the Café Istanbul on Monday, the office canteen on Tuesday, an Italian on Deansgate on Wednesday and so on.

He'd get in a strop if you suggested an alternative venue – the Abercromby usually – and got his way because Webby didn't want a sourpuss looking at him for the rest of the day. JR always chose the same thing to eat, usually having studied the menu for 20 minutes.

I naively assumed rugby league writers would stand over six feet tall, were built like scaffolders, had squashed noses, shovels for hands and sounded like Eddie Waring. Batty was as quiet as a church mouse, you hardly knew he was in the office half the time.

I just couldn't imagine the smartly turned out Brian in among the roughness of rugby league, its blood and thunder, bump and thump, mixing it with the locals in Featherstone, Batley or Hunslet. But most nights he was out there amid the sweaty throng, getting mud and grime all over his nice clean shoes.

Poor Batty used to get the sharp end of the tongue of the subeditors, a couple in particular. When it came to characters, our office was overflowing with northern wit and not-so-gentle piss-taking. On the day I was first introduced to the subs, taken around to each one, shaking hands and engaging in small talk, Ian Ogden's first words of greeting were 'not a fucking southerner'.

Oggie was a Burnley lad, as Lancashire as they came, loud and proud. Jolly-faced and bespectacled, his phone conversations, especially the more private ones, could be heard right across the office.

In those days, subs would have a spike on which to pin unwanted copy and a jam jar of glue and requisite brush to paste the completed writer's work on to another sheet of paper on which the typeface was written before it was sent down to the works.

When a piece of copy landed on his desk, Oggie would look across to see who was sitting at the writers' desk. Knowing I was within hearing range, he'd announce, 'More Harman shite,' splodging my work into its place, laughing the while. Over time, I'd feel offended if he didn't take the piss out of my words as he subbed them.

Ian's associate-in-mischief was Jack Dunnill, the sports splash sub who lived up in the hills in Holmfirth where they filmed *Last of the Summer Wine.* How the hell the producers didn't stumble over Jack on location and offer him a lead role on the spot always baffled me.

Jack was a tremendous craftsman who could write the kind of brilliant headlines in a flash that were the absolute necessity for newspapers as the editions flew by. He could also match Oggie for caustic comments, delivered in a lower tone but exaggerated for maximum effect.

Whenever Batty's copy dropped, Jack pronounced 'it's out!' just loud enough for Brian (and the rest of the department) to catch it.

Jack chuckled to himself as Brian's face reddened. If Webby heard, he'd mutter 'you horrible little bastard', though this only made Jack chortle all the more devilishly.

The boss's friendship with Doug Weatherall, our man in the north-east, was also a subject of cynical joshing in the office. Doug and Bryan were from the same part of the world, had known each other for years, supported Sunderland, and wouldn't have a bad word said about the other.

Doug was something of a star in his native region, probably the best-known reporter around save for John Gibson, the sports editor of the *Newcastle Chronicle* whose writing was perfectly good enough for him to have earned a job on a national. It was fair to say that Doug revelled in his notoriety, which helped swell *Mail* sales in the region enormously.

He had a habit of typing with emphasis at the top of his copy 'Believed Exclusive, Not In Evenings' to make sure the office knew he (believed) he had a story to himself as it hadn't appeared in either the *Chronicle* or *Sunderland Echo*.

Jack and Oggie ribbed this self-promotion mercilessly. Webby took it as a personal affront and would often subtly rewrite Doug's copy to protect him from spike-happy subs. The next morning Bryan dealt with an affronted Doug by explaining that he was only seeking to improve the content.

It wasn't only the two jokers in the pack who made the *Mail*'s subbing department so professional and pride-swelling. We had talent wherever you looked. Ray Clarkin was not only a tip-top pro but doubled at weekends writing match reports for the *Sunday People,* often on the bigger games.

Gareth Williams, Dave Shaw, Lyn Callaghan, Peter Boyle and Peter Ferguson could all write perceptively across a range of sports and improved anything and everything written by the boys in the field. I had much to be thankful for.

For a single lad who liked to stick around the office late and watch the guys go to work, they were bloody superb company.

Whether they asked me or not, I'd often join their appointed evening break for a glass or two of something northern and nutritious with a firm foam on top.

* * *

Ron Atkinson was still secreted at the Midland Hotel in the midst of negotiations with Frank Stapleton to finalise his move from Arsenal when the pair of them were alarmed by a knock at the door.

The United manager answered it to Remi Moses, a Miles Platting lad he had brought to West Bromwich Albion in 1979 and who now, at the end of his Baggies contract, wanted to play for his former boss in his home city.

Atkinson gave Moses the key to his room a few doors down from where he was anxious to conclude wage negotiations with the player currently occupying his thoughts and United's chequebook. He'd get to Remi later. Four hours later as it turned out.

Remi hadn't budged an inch from where he had originally sat when Ron returned to his room. Stapleton was going to be a star attraction but Ron said that Remi was the first signing he made that gave United the requisite steel to move from their present position of overtly subservient to a good deal more assertive.

What made the Moses signing so compelling was that he arrived in a package that also included one Bryan Robson. In total, United paid Albion £2m for the pair and left the press to speculate how much each had cost. My suspicion was £1.75m for Robbo and £250,000 for Remi, give or take a thousand. Whatever the financial nods and winks, there was no mistaking the shrewdness of the deal and how important it would be to the direction of the club under Ron.

My debut back-page lead for the *Mail* (both in the northern and southern editions) was Atkinson's confirmation that the move for Robson was going ahead. A moment to treasure for United and certainly one that settled my nerves in office terms. It was a real 'biggie'. 'We signed pure gold,' Atkinson would later say. 'Robbo proved his worth over and over again.'

We didn't know it at the time – indeed I didn't discover this until Ron appeared on the *Old Spice Boys* podcast that my old pal John Richardson and I launched in 2021 – but the amount United paid to secure the bedrock of England's midfield would lead Sir Matt Busby to step down from his role as a club director.

There was no rancour, it was just that Sir Matt couldn't get his head around the money now changing hands for players, even Robson, and believed that it was better he recused himself from responsibility for such outrageous spending. 'Now,' said Ron on the podcast, 'there are substitutes at Manchester United who fetch £30m. What would Matt have made of that?'

The Robson deal was concluded with an on-the-pitch signing at Old Trafford, with Ron seated across from the club chairman Martin Edwards who probably couldn't believe what he and his board had done. The trio were glowing.

There was an obligation for United to play their football in a manner befitting the reputation from the astonishing era of the Busby Babes. Certain teams at certain times had come close to emulating the style of those wonderful young men, so many of whom were torn from life, their families and their club on 6 February 1958 at the Munich air disaster.

Ten years on, United lifted the European Cup they had sought with nation-unifying abandon in the 1950s. Busby had the cup he cherished and British football was awash with emotion as Bobby Charlton – a Munich survivor – Nobby Stiles, George Best and company swept Benfica aside at Wembley.

There had been the occasional domestic cup triumph since but nothing of comparable import. Might Ron Atkinson be able to deliver on the undoubted improvements he had made to both Cambridge United and West Bromwich Albion? Manchester United were an altogether more exhaustive challenge. He took it on with the relish of a man not daunted by the demands upon him.

Across at Maine Road it was a case of accepting that no two weeks were ever the same. Four months before I landed in the city, the light blues had reached the final of the FA Cup, losing in a replay to an extra-time goal by Ricardo Villa of Tottenham that remains one of the classiest individual acts to grace a Wembley finale.

One month into my 'new' career, City signed Trevor Francis, the Nottingham Forest and England striker, for £1.2m, a purchase that enraptured their support but caused rancour behind the scenes when Peter Swales, the club's chairman, said he might renege on such an expensive deal, which prompted manager John Bond to threaten that either Francis signed, or he left. Francis signed. Bond yearned for a relationship with Swales as he'd had at Norwich with Arthur South. It never quite happened.

I would quickly come to discover that this was run-of-the-mill turmoil at City, a club that lived an existence of fur coat and nae drawers. *Coronation Street*, filmed in the Granada Studios a couple of streets behind the *Mail*'s office, needed a slew of writers to manufacture incredulous storylines but at Maine Road they came along with the pies.

* * *

Covering United and City at any time would be a blessing for a 24-year-old third in the queue in the department. My dealings with these giants would be mostly as cover when Jonno and Dino were on their days off. I had best make my mark at the rest of the clubs in our formidable circulation area.

There were new folk to be acquainted with, those prominent in northern football and the characters who reported on them. The *Mail/Express* battle for mid-market superiority was as intense in Manchester as anywhere else and the number three on the *Express* in my new sphere of influence was one Jimmy Armfield.

This was a hopeless mismatch. Jimmy had captained England 15 times from his 42 caps, was a member of the 1966 World Cup-winning squad and remained an absolute legend at Blackpool, for whom he made 569 appearances in 17 years at his one and only club. I was a kid from Leigh-on-Sea who Ron Atkinson once smacked with a *Sports Argus*.

Armfield had moved into management in 1971 at Bolton and notably turned Leeds United around after the rancorous 44 days of Brian Clough's mismanagement of the club in 1974. Under Jimmy's guidance, Leeds reached the 1975 European Cup Final, which they lost to Bayern Munich in the face of some of the most fraudulent refereeing ever seen.

He left Leeds in 1978 in the highest regard, choosing to move into the journalistic world and joining the *Express* as a football reporter. Everyone in football, especially in the north of England, knew Jimmy. The area was flooded with Armfield contemporaries; George Mulhall at Bolton Wanderers, Bobby Saxton at Blackburn Rovers, Jimmy Frizzell at Oldham Athletic, Jim Iley at Bury, Brian Miller at Burnley, Jimmy McGuigan at Stockport County and Allan Brown at Blackpool.

Jimmy's frontline colleagues in the iconic *Express* building on Great Ancoats Street were Derek Potter and John Bean, both terrific reporters, backed by long-established feature writers Peter Thomas and Alan Thompson, the latter also known as Tommo, 'The Voice of the North'.

The football coverage in the *Express* was first-class with deep insider knowledge of everything at City and United, comment, critique and trusted writers pulled together by northern sports editor Mike Dempsey who wasn't afraid to let his men give full range to their talents. They were a truly formidable adversary.

The *Daily Mirror* had its own northern voice, Derek Wallis, a considerate man and quality writer who, like Peter Thomas of the *Express*, was afforded a silhouetted by-line with pipe in mouth. The Mirror's north-west team was Bob Russell, Alec Johnson and Keith Meadows, a trio of unforgettable personalities.

Peter Fitton, aka the 'Growler', was *The Sun*'s man in Manchester and if there were many reasons not to like his paper and what it stood for, Fitton was a master of his craft: short, sharp and to the point. He broke a ton of stories and was generous and great fun (when off duty). He would be joined in 1982 by young David Walker to forge as formidable a pairing as you could imagine.

The Star had a fascinating double act in Don Hardisty, a sage who seemed a mite highbrow for the newspaper he worked for, and Kevin Francis, always full of mischief and merry-making and who knew a story when it hit him.

These were but a few of the characters who enriched the next few years of my life. Many more would pop in and out of the story, one of whom, Howard Booth of the *Mirror*, was a real charm – dapper in appearance with his perfectly parted white hair and David Niven-like moustache.

It was Howard who coined the term 'reverse mileage'. His expenses would famously include charging his newspaper for backing out of the long drive of his home in Yorkshire. He got away with it for years.

* * *

Jimmy Armfield would never have contemplated anything so daring. Had a goodlier man walked the planet? Our reporting diaries clashed a lot of the time. I'd be in my seat in the box at Ewood Park, say, and up the steps came Jimmy – back-slapped by the diehards of the game who recognised him as much for his flat cap and pipe as anything else.

He would be cheerily waved in, sit in an adjacent seat, take out his notepaper and watch a match unfold in a state of discerning contentment. If a goal was scored and as near as mayhem was unleashed around him, Jimmy puffed on his pipe and made a small but significant note.

The only time I saw him flustered was in constructing his report. When faced with a blank sheet of paper at 9.15pm, he, like so many of we lesser mortals, found it exceedingly hard to express himself in the written word. Jimmy endlessly fretted about his work.

He didn't require the addition of a manager's quote that was an imperative for the majority of tabloid writers because he knew the game better than they could explain it. There was many a time when I'd settled on my intro, raced to the manager's office and returned to splice a few quotes into my text and Jimmy hadn't moved, troubled that he hadn't got his piece to say what he wanted it to say.

'Is this OK, Neil?' he asked, pushing his notepad across. Now think of any reporter showing his copy to another and asking for reassurance. Then imagine telling Jimmy Armfield of England you didn't think much of his piece. It would never happen. 'It's fine, Jimmy, it's fine,' I'd say, though he rarely seemed convinced.

The constant challenge to all of us was writing something that made sense and contained splashes of expertise, with one eye on the clock in the corner whose hands moved altogether far too quickly. My experiences on the *Argus* in Birmingham meant that I wasn't unduly unnerved by the prospect and – wouldn't you know – was often among the first to finish.

If Jimmy was labouring, he was nothing compared to Keith Meadows of the *Mirror*. Keith was a lovely chap though scarily wild in appearance. He, too, wore a flat cap to try to tame his Bobby Charlton-like, combed-across hair. He wore glasses, sported a *Viva Zapata!* moustache and, as he wrote with his right hand, he constantly rubbed his chin with his left and made a distracted murmuring sound.

He used green biro for handwriting as unruly as he was, great gouges, crossings-out, sprawls and indent marks. How the hell he managed to make sense of it to a copy taker I never knew. It was a regular toss-up between Keith and Jimmy as to whose turn it was to extinguish the press-box lights.

Getting the after-match quotes at Blackburn required a bit of stamina. The management and secretarial offices were housed on separate floors of the corner terraced house across from the ground on Nuttall Street. Press conferences were held in a small room at the top of the stairs.

One time in Jim Smith's reign at Ewood Park, Keith was heading towards the post-match inquest in his usual mist and knocked at one door down, startling the elderly residents who, being decent Blackburn folk, accommodated this stranger.

During Keith's running commentary as the football results clattered through on the *Grandstand* teleprinter, the lady of the house took pity on him and offered a cup of tea and a biscuit. More time passed and Keith asked the couple if it normally took this long for the rest of the press boys to arrive.

'Oh, you want next door, love,' the lady said. Keith thrust the teacup back into her hand, muttered his apologies and dashed out.

* * *

Ron Kennedy would have been upstairs next door when Keith arrived frantically that particular afternoon. Ron was Blackburn's freelance reporter covering news and sport, one of those real local diggers who could turn their hand to anything – council minutes and daylight robberies one day, Simon Garner hat-tricks the next.

Gap-toothed, bespectacled and jolly (except when Rovers were losing), he used to bring an old-fashioned timepiece to Ewood Park and place it with a loud thud on his desk. We didn't have to worry about checking the times of the goals, Ron's pale green alarm clock was sacrosanct. He chattered endlessly through matches and nobody ever minded.

The freelancer's treasure was their ownership of all the phones in a press box. It was the job of the sportsdesk secretary – in our case the delightful Jean Webb – to call ahead and make sure the freelance knew you were attending, so he could allocate you a phone that aligned with the seat you were designated in the box.

Some were nicer about handing out their wares than others. Eddie Booth (aka 'Booth of Denton') had the phone franchise at both Old Trafford and Maine Road. Eddie was a rottweiler with owl-like glasses, a pugilist's face and a miser's attitude.

You try to persuade Eddie that you needed a phone if you hadn't booked one and a deadline was nearing. He'd bloody laugh in your face.

Ron Kennedy was the more humane embodiment of freelancing. What a character. Once when summarising for local radio on Blackburn against Derby in early 1984, Ron was in the midst of his description of the fourth goal for the home side when the net bulged again, prompting him to inform the listeners, 'Fuck me, we've got a fifth!'

But Ron's major claim to fame went largely unrecognised, though millions across the world would become aware of his work. He was covering a routine town council meeting in the late 1960s when the state of the roads was addressed. His news report – sent out in normal manner to all the national papers – included the statistic that there were 4,000 potholes in Blackburn.

Reading the next day's *Daily Mail*, John Lennon of the Beatles found the paragraph at the bottom of one of the news pages. Something stirred in his head.

In 'A Day in the Life' from the *Sgt. Pepper's Lonely Hearts Club Band* album , the lyrics refer to the thousands of holes in Blackburn.

Ron Kennedy immortalised. I never did check with him if he received his freelancer's fee. He did hate Burnley though, that was a given. It was the way it was between the neighbouring towns. You were one or t'other.

I had no specific sentiment either way though there was an endearing quality to Burnley's story in that Brian Miller, the 1960 First Division title-winning captain and now club manager, also owned the corner sweet shop a couple of streets from the main entrance to Turf Moor.

Brian was charming, rugged, open-faced and devout in all things about his only club. It did seem remarkable to me that he had managed to remain sane having spent so much time having to work closely with Bob Lord, the club's infamously tyrannical owner.

The reporter on the local *Burnley Evening Star* was Keith McNee, aka the 'Prince of Darkness'. Remembering how Nigel Fuller at Southend would never allow his colours to show at work – you sometimes wondered if he cared if the Blues won or not – the same could not be said of Keith.

The outdoor press box at Turf Moor was positioned in the back two rows of the stand and if a visiting defender should lay an untimely boot on a home forward, McNee would spring to his feet and, his voice carrying across the heads of the home fans, scream 'you're a dirty bastard' to the guilty party.

Keith was a Burnley legend.

* * *

Once in a rare while, the opportunity came to work the Mersey beat. Colin Wood, a Devonian by birth, was our man there and, of all the football patches, it was the most ferociously protected by its local reporters. They were known as the 'Mersey Mafia' – Wood, John Keith of the *Express*, Chris James of the *Mirror*, Mike Ellis of *The Sun* and Matt D'Arcy of *The Star*.

Bryan Webster said one Thursday that 'Woody' was taking the following day off and I had to cover for him. This meant collecting John Keith who lived nearer Manchester than Liverpool and didn't drive, before gathering the team news from the two managers, Howard Kendall of Everton and Bob Paisley of Liverpool.

Howard had registered early in my memory for his gallant performance as a 17-year-old for Preston at Wembley in 1964. He was building something special at Goodison and relished the company of the press. He called me 'lad' and I was told he called people a lot older than me 'lad' so I wasn't to think he was belittling me for my inexperience.

I was nervous about meeting Bob Paisley, though I didn't know why. 'Bob's fine,' Keith assured me as we walked down the corridor towards his office. I got there first and took the seat nearest the fridge. 'That's where I sit,' said Chris James, who doled out the drinks and poured himself a mega gin, very little tonic, no ice. 'Colin sits over there,' he grumbled, pointing airily at no seat in particular.

Paisley, dressed in carpet slippers and the kind of cardigan you bought your grandad for a joke at Christmas, walked in and asked who I was. Keith performed the introductions.

Liverpool were playing Stoke at Anfield the next day, Paisley read out his prospective team, talked through the whys and wherefores and all was very convivial until I asked a question. 'Stoke are thinking of bringing back Mark Chamberlain tomorrow, Mr Paisley, do you have a view on that?'

There was a momentary pause. 'Well,' he said, 'he'll certainly bring a bit of colour to the occasion.'

* * *

Near the end of the 1981/82 football season, Bryan Webster sent a memo around to the writers asking if anyone would be keen to cover some tennis in the summer. The opportunity would amount to five consecutive weeks, culminating in working at Wimbledon. I said I'd be up for it.

The previous summer there had been a contretemps in the *Mail* camp. Harry Harris, seconded from football to shadow the very proper tennis correspondent Laurie Pignon, had demonstrated an eagerness to stick his nose into everything that moved in a manner that ruffled Laurie's feathers.

The ignition for this falling-out was the loss of John McEnroe's temper on No. 1 Court and his 'you cannot be serious' outburst against umpire Edward Janes. Harry wasn't used to being told how things were and weren't done in the tennis world. Such political niceties were anathema to a football news hound.

While tennis writers waited for Wimbledon's diplomatic wheels to turn in their own sweet time, Harry talked his way to the inner sanctum where only puffed-up folk with silly badges or lower ranks of royalty were allowed to tread without the guard dogs being unleashed.

Fred Hoyles, the tournament referee, was so stunned by an unexpected arrival at his office door that he stammered out a few remarks that Harry jotted down and included in a report sent to the office before anyone else knew he'd been there.

Laurie phoned the desk to tell them what he was going to write and discovered Harry had already filed it, but thanks anyway. The upshot was Pignon demanded someone other than 'that bloody nuisance' to work with him in 1982, hence the call to arms.

The tennis agenda amounted to reporting on three grass-court tournaments at Beckenham, Birmingham and Bristol before teaming up with Pignon, John Roberts and the wonderful Ian Wooldridge to cover the Championships. It sounded like an awful lot of fun and, given editor David English's love for tennis, a heck of a responsibility.

My debut was at the *Kentish Times* tournament played at Beckenham Cricket Club on Foxgrove Road in the first week of June. Its spot in the calendar coincided with the second week of the French Open, so that those eliminated in the first few days in Paris or who simply sidestepped clay could sharpen their grass game on prime English courts.

The paper booked me into the Bromley Court Hotel, which looked utterly majestic. I came down to breakfast on the first day and found John Fitzgerald, the Australian who had lost in the first round of Roland Garros, sitting there. He was the first Aussie player I introduced myself to and we were mates to the day I was prevented from covering the sport and didn't see him again.

To a differing extent, I'd come to know the four finalists as the years went by. American Pam Shriver, all curls and cuteness, defeated the lovely Aussie Elizabeth Sayers (later Smylie) in the women's final and South Africa's huge-serving Kevin Curren overcame local favourite Buster Mottram to lift the men's title.

There was something definitively English about writing tennis reports while sitting in a cricket pavilion.

The Birmingham tournament at Edgbaston Priory was a women-only event and then we moved to Bristol for the West of England Championships at Redlands, exclusively for men. In Birmingham the national reporters were mostly football people like me, notably John Wragg for the *Express* and Jack Steggles for the *Mirror* who would both cover Wimbledon as part of their paper's teams.

There were bloody fine champions at both locations; the remarkable American Billie Jean King in the Midlands and John Alexander of Australia in the west country. We writers were spoiled rotten by the quality on show, even if as non-tennis specialists, we didn't know much better.

Now it was time for Wimbledon.

* * *

Whether it was your first or last experience in SW19 – a span of 32 years in my case – Wimbledon possessed an alchemy that raised it above many sporting celebrations.

It was hard to put your finger on what made it different but somehow people stepped out of themselves when they walked through the gates. To me it was like that first string being cut on freshly minted newspapers at 5.30am. Something special was being released.

Yes, the place was stiff with decorum. Jackets and ties were the order of the day, especially if you worked for the *Mail*. David English's maxim was that you never knew where you might end up on any given day and if you represented the *Mail*, it was imperative to look the part.

The press was housed at the top of the first flight of stairs in the south-east hall. Two relatively plain doors guarded by a couple of old soldiers turned commissionaires opened to a Pandora's box of tight corridors, unfettered high spirits and enduring adventure.

My Wembley debut. Dad took me to the 1964 FA Cup Final where West Ham United defeated Preston North End 3-2. Celebrating are [l to r] Jack Burkett, John Bond, John Sissons, Bobby Moore and Peter Brabrook. Burkett, Bond and Moore would play influential parts in my writing career.

Arthur Rowley, manager of Southend United, in 1975. My first dealing with a professional football manager. Arthur was tough but fair.

Have boots will wander – Laurie Cunningham, who became a firm friend, poses outside The Hawthorns, home of West Bromwich Albion.

Laurie was perhaps the most naturally gifted footballer I saw. His career was cruelly disrupted by injury and his life cut short in a car crash in Madrid.

Jack Nicklaus savours his success at the 1978 Open Championship at St Andrews. I had been sent there as a rookie reporter for the Birmingham Evening Mail. *What a baptism.*

The somewhat odd couple – Graham Taylor and his assistant manager Lawrie McMenemy discuss tactics at an England training session.

'You know the ruling' – Graham Taylor and fourth official Marcus Merk of Germany clash during England's fateful World Cup qualifier against Holland in Rotterdam. October 1993.

Talking England – Terry Venables [left] and Taylor were unable to win a trophy as England managers in the 1990s. They left indelible memories.

An infamous night as Eric Cantona of Manchester United is hauled away after leaping kung-fu style into the crowd at Selhurst Park. Gary Pallister, far left, can't believe what he's just seen. Nor could we in the press box. January 1995

Fergie and referees – another poor soul in black faces the wrath of Alex Ferguson when the Manchester United manager felt aggrieved at decisions against his side.

The full force of Fergie. Clearly, Alex Ferguson didn't like the idea of struggling against Stoke City managed by Tony Pulis [left]. A linesman gets it in the neck.

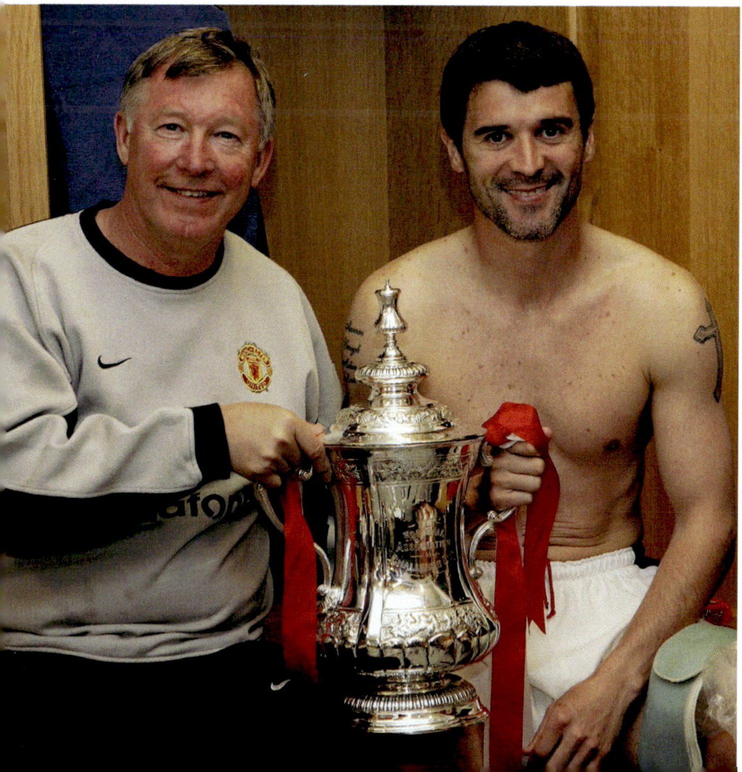

Fergie and Keano – You didn't cross these guys without good reason. Alex Ferguson and Roy Keane celebrate another FA Cup success for Manchester United.

Pointing the way – Kenny Dalglish led Blackburn Rovers to their extraordinary Premier League triumph in 1995. Kenny and I clicked for some reason.

The British writers bar the agency boys were housed in one room overlooking the Wimbledon Park golf course, with often 30 typewriters clattering away at the same time, especially as the first edition's 6pm deadline approached.

The international scribes had to make do with composing their prose at random tables in a corner of the press restaurant that was sectioned off by six-foot-tall barriers. The contempt shown by anyone not from the shires in those days would not possibly be tolerated now.

In 1982 the man in charge of keeping order was Roy McKelvie, an indomitable former correspondent for the *Sunday Express* known to all and sundry as the 'Brigadier'. He was silver-haired, bespectacled, purple-veined, loud and ran the press room as a brigadier would his brigade. Zero bloody tolerance.

The chairman was Air Chief Marshal Sir Brian Burnett, GCB, DFC, AFC, ADC. He had an incredible war record, serving his nation with gallantry and honour, the picture-perfect boss for Wimbledon. The Brigadier was the unswervingly loyal officer just right for knocking the rag-tag press into shape.

McKelvie and Pignon got on famously as a pair of eccentric Second World War veterans would. They loved Wooldridge, who was allowed to use the back of Roy's office to work his lyrical masterpieces rather than mix it with us in the confines of the official writing room. Once McKelvie knew Pignon liked me, he liked me as well.

My remit in the team was simple – to make sure no story fell through the cracks. There were a multitude of matches all over the place, especially in the first week, and the last match might be as important as the first in terms of a tale. You had to keep your wits at all times, especially in the press bar later as matches would often continue into semi-darkness.

To send your work to the office meant carrying a couple of typed sheets – or simply your notebook if you ad libbed every word like the remarkable David Irvine of *The Guardian* – to a six-yard-square anteroom on whose walls were screwed half a dozen soundproofed booths, each housing a phone.

Most of the writers buried their heads in the booths but I found concentration easier standing up straight rather than being bent double to dictate, which led to a lot of shushing from those who didn't really want to hear my rubbish while trying to concentrate on their own.

Pignon often demanded I dictate his copy for him, which I didn't mind except that his spelling was terrible and I often had to work out for myself what he was saying or I'd have spent all evening dashing back and forth to the bar. That would have really pissed him off.

This first year covering Wimbledon would coincide with the first Sunday final in the tournament's history and, because the Brigadier pulled some strings, I was able to watch it from the concrete steps next to the press seats. My arse was solid at the end of four hours and 14 minutes, then the longest final in the history of the event. Jimmy Connors won it, beating fellow American John McEnroe, and I wondered if I'd ever get to know them.

The women's final would also be an all-American affair, though Martina Navratilova only became a US citizen the previous year and the bitterness of her defection from the old Czechoslovakia still lingered. In winning her third title at Wimbledon, she defeated Chris Evert in three sets.

My Wimbledon responsibilities weren't restricted to writing about the odd match and running errands. I was the regular chauffeur for a special passenger. Geoffrey Green was a noted former football correspondent of *The Times*, a Shakespeare of the press box. The poor chap had lost the bottom half of his right leg to gangrene and a wooden stump was attached to what was left so he was able to limp around.

He was a quite wonderful old gentleman who stationed himself permanently in the higher press seats on No. 1 Court, rested his stump on the writing bench and remained there most of the day. As evening fell and the exertions of work – and the odd drink – began to take a toll, Pignon exclaimed, 'Doings [he struggled to recall my first name], time for Green to go home.'

I would help the great man into the passenger seat of my Triumph and drop him as close as possible to his front gate in Richmond, making sure he got to the door, which often meant careful manoeuvring. Geoffrey never took down the Christmas tree in his front room. 'Every day is Christmas Day if you want it to be, dear boy,' he often reminded me.

We all drank rather copiously in those days. Many an evening was illuminated – or darkened in the case of the international writers trying to finish their pieces – by a singsong at the press bar, generally led by the irrepressible Cockney/Scots duo of Peter Batt of *The Sun* and the *Sunday Mirror*'s Ken 'Big 'Un' Montgomery.

The weaker-willed among us would weave into the night to the strains of 'Daisy, Daisy give me your answer do' bouncing off the walls of Centre Court's south-east hall.

* * *

The *Daily Mail* called time on the 65-year-old Laurie Pignon in 1983, paying for him to fly Concorde to cover his final US Open that summer. No more would I be called to the imperative task at the end of the day's play of topping Laurie's brandy glass with cold water into which he would place his buttonhole so it would be in decent flower the following morning.

There was an embarrassing scene at Simpson's in the Strand at his farewell lunch, attended by the great and good of the *Mail* hierarchy. During his speech, Pignon made it clear he thought I should have been his replacement, which didn't go down well with Tom Clarke who had chosen Malcolm Folley of the *Daily Express* as Laurie's successor. I kept looking down at my plate replete with pink roast beef.

I guessed this endorsement meant I'd done an OK job, though Pignon was miffed on the last day of his last Wimbledon when

I gained front-page projection for the mixed doubles title being won by my pal John Lloyd and Wendy Turnbull of Australia who defeated America's Steve Denton and Billie Jean King. It was his fault for demanding I never leave my post.

Perhaps down deep I thought I might be in the frame to replace Laurie but I was only 26 and there was a lot more I needed to experience as a football writer to feel I really belonged. I had also fallen in love with Manchester and didn't want to leave.

The 1982/83 season in the north-west had been tumultuous for the two major Manchester clubs – United winning the FA Cup and City dropping out of the First Division. Lower down the scale, the relegations of Burnley and Bolton to the Third Division were major shocks to the townsfolk of two of the area's stalwart names.

There was an array of huge clubs in the Second Division, including Wolves, Chelsea, Leeds, Newcastle, Sheffield Wednesday and the eventual runaway champions, Queens Park Rangers. This was a tough league to escape but falling the other way had defining consequences.

Bolton were managed by a disciple of Brian Clough and Peter Taylor in their former captain at Derby and Nottingham Forest, John McGovern, with whom I enjoyed a good rapport. John was honest and circumspect and if he didn't give an awful lot away, the defenders he selected were otherwise inclined.

For Burnley these were really unsettling times. John Jackson, a barrister, had assumed the chairmanship Bob Lord used to hold with a miserly authority. It had taken some time for the club's finances to be brought under control and results were reasonably stable until a five-match losing streak in December 1982 was followed by a three-goal loss at a rain-swept Burnden Park – a match I reported on in which Bolton's goalkeeper Jim McDonagh scored direct from a punt downfield.

Brian Miller's position was coming under increasing threat but it shocked everyone when, the day before Burnley were due to play a League Cup fifth-round tie at Tottenham, he was told he wouldn't be required at White Hart Lane and first-team coach Frank Casper was placed in charge.

It was Jackson's intention to take time to choose Miller's permanent successor, so Casper was left in appalling limbo. He refused to use the manager's office until officially appointed. Burnley's form collapsed (they lost every game in March) and by the time their last two matches at Leicester and Crystal Palace arrived they needed three points to stay up.

At a packed Filbert Street, looking limp and lame, they drew 0-0. It wasn't a great deal better at Selhurst Park where a 1-0 loss confirmed the club's relegation and the end of Casper's never-quite-was managerial career.

* * *

Manchester City had been enjoying a fits-and-starts season and though they looked to be in a relatively secure league position at the turn of 1983, an ignominious 4-0 defeat at Brighton in the fourth round of the FA Cup brought long-standing managerial mistrust to a head.

John Bond and his board had lived a precarious existence and several directors were just waiting for a chance to stencil a new name on the manager's door. Bond did their job for them and resigned after the Brighton loss. It was the first week of February.

His good mate John Benson, the assistant manager, took over in partnership with club stalwart Tony Book, but the departure of Bond sucked the life out of the team's confidence levels. City lost eight of their next ten games and were hovering dangerously close to the relegation places.

I had all the time in the world for decent people like Benno and Book who seemed at a loss to turn the tide until an unexpected victory in the penultimate game of the season, ironically at Brighton's Goldstone Ground, meant City had only to avoid defeat in the final fixture at home to Luton Town to survive and send the Bedfordshire club down.

Maine Road, packed to the rafters, was in a state of suspended anxiety. I loved the ground. The press pass was a simple folded piece of white card that, when placed on your desk in the office to signify you were covering City, you treated as if it was the entry to King Tut's tomb. It allowed you to park your car on the ground's forecourt and enter up the main stairs into a ten-yard-square anteroom where directors, principal guests and fellow press men mingled.

There were three exit doors to the seats; those to the left or right took you to the press box, while the central opening was for the directors. The chairman, Peter Swales, would usually be the last to enter, walking through the throng of press on each side and straight into the jaws of the fans. Peter, to his credit, never once hid from his critics, be they written or verbal.

He was there as usual on this most tumultuous of afternoons. My old pal from West Bromwich Albion, Tony Godden, was in goal for Luton, who possessed further strong, gifted players in captain Brian Horton (later to become City's manager), Mal Donaghy, Brian Stein and Paul Walsh. They would not be easily rolled over.

City plugged their team with experience. Asa Hartford, Graham Baker, Kevin Bond, Tommy Caton, Dennis Tueart and Bobby McDonald formed a formidable backbone. Alex Williams, one of the first black goalkeepers to play First Division football, had made the number one jersey his own with performances of marvellous athleticism and astonishing reflexes.

Midway through the second half with the game heading for a goalless stalemate (and City's survival), Luton manager David Pleat decided to toss Radomir 'Raddy' Antić into the fray as a last roll of the dice. The match had become a skirmish rather than a game of football when, four minutes from time and with Luton chucking the kitchen sink at City's back line, Williams threw himself full-length to punch away a Stein cross.

The goalkeeper was scrambling back to his feet as Antić – 20 yards out – swung a right foot at the ball. Williams instinctively stuck out a right hand that deflected it beyond a couple of City defenders who may have blocked it before the ball nestled in the bottom corner.

I had never heard a ground so full descend into such mournful silence, save for a few delirious Luton fans. Moments later at the final whistle, the cream-suited Pleat came dashing from the dugout and raced across the pitch, jacket and arms flailing in wild celebration of his side's great escape.

In the home manager's office, staff were quickly collecting the champagne bottles that had been placed there in anticipation of a life-saving victory, replacing them with a sickly white wine, probably Liebfraumilch. Benno and Book sat there, ashen.

Swales, cigar half-bitten, walked in as the pair were trying to make sense to the press. He turned on his famously platformed heels and left. Benson was on his way the following week.

Help was just up the M66. John Bond and Burnley had seemed an improbable fit but the era of the irascible Bob Lord had ended and John Jackson replaced the old buzzard in the chair. I liked Jackson straight away. He clearly wanted to do things differently and Bond's appointment affirmed that.

The denizens of Burnley didn't take to Bond, especially when they learned that one of their favourite players, Martin Dobson, was locking horns with the new manager from the first training session. Dobson wasn't the only aggrieved player on the books and there was no one on the staff for them to turn to as Bond had filled those jobs with his old City pals, Benson, John Docherty and John Sainty.

Burnley possessed a formidable collection of players for a Third Division side. Billy Hamilton had starred for Northern Ireland in the 1982 World Cup finals, Brian Flynn was a Welsh stalwart and Dobson gained England caps. Bond signed his old City players Gerry Gow and Tommy Hutchison, though Gow was clearly on his last legs.

It didn't help matters that another Bond ex, Kevin Reeves, endured a hip injury mid-season that effectively ended his career.

Burnley would finish 12th in Bond's first and – as it turned out – only campaign.

There was a pre-season competition played by Lancashire clubs called the Manx Cup, with Isle of Man backers, which was a series of not-quite-so-friendly friendlies. On 18 August 1984 Burnley gave a dissonant performance and lost 2-1 at Turf Moor to Wigan Athletic.

Bond held court in the boardroom with a small press assembly. The mutterings about behind-the-scenes discontent were on the rise and I asked John if he'd speak to me more expansively. He did. The gist of the article was that he thought his job was being harmed by boardroom disagreements and that they should sort themselves out or he would be off.

A board meeting had been scheduled two days after the Manx tie. The local Burnley press on Monday evening quoted my original *Mail* article in which Bond said, 'I am still as prepared as ever to make Burnley a First Division club again but that is an impossibility when there is friction between myself and the chairman. The game has gone and the only thing that would entice me to a match if I leave Burnley would be to watch my son Kevin playing for Manchester City.'

In his book *A Director's Tale*, covering Bond's period at Turf Moor, author Dave Thomas noted the minutes of that historic board meeting, 'The manager entered and was asked by the chairman to give an explanation regarding articles that had appeared in recent national newspapers. Mr Bond said he had not spoken with the press. The manager said he would not be held responsible for that which had been written.

'The chairman then asked the manager if he had asked the press for an apology or asked them to retract the comments he was reputed to have made. Mr Bond said he had not made such a request because he had never made the statements in the first place. The manager was then asked to leave the meeting. When Mr Bond was recalled, the chairman asked him to resign his position.'

Further into Thomas's book and given an opportunity to reflect on his term at Burnley, Bond said, 'He [Jackson] didn't feel the club was doing as well as it ought to be. There were a lot of snide remarks about a "them and us" situation. And then I did an article about him in the *Daily Mail* [yet Bond told the August 1984 board meeting he hadn't spoken to the press].

'I went to a board meeting on Monday and all of a sudden he [Jackson] slammed the paper down in front of me and said, "I'm sorry, you're going to have to go." It was a relief to be honest. He put me out of my misery.'

At the height of the furore, I was invited to John Bond's home, which sat 30 yards back off the A556 in a row of majestic houses bordering Mere Golf Club. Kevin Bond lived a few doors down.

It was a pleasant experience until John asked if I was mistaken in my recollection of what he'd said about the situation at Burnley that caused the breakdown to become final. I said I wasn't. He pressed me. I said I had a very good shorthand note. There was the hinted suggestion of an inducement to change my mind, one that I didn't really take seriously.

I reported the contents of the meeting to northern editor John Womersley, who stood by me 100 per cent. I still visualise Bond in a pale raincoat coming down the staircase at Turf Moor after the board meeting and brusquely dismissing the assembled press before bustling out of the main entrance.

* * *

Manchester City's choice of manager to steady their ship raised quite a few eyebrows. Billy McNeill was a legend in Scottish football, the captain of Celtic's Lisbon Lions who had become Britain's first European Cup winners in 1967. He was Caesar; his word brooked no dispute.

I watched the final that day in the TV lounge of the seaview hotel at which Mum, Dad and I were resident in Newquay. It was our first family holiday, which was ruined by the Torrey Canyon disaster in March and subsequent oil spillage affecting Cornwall's resorts, meaning we were on a beach holiday and couldn't go to the beach.

It was not simply as the blond-haired totem of the Celtic defence that McNeill was well known. He had managed the club to three championships, the Scottish Cup and League Cup. And yet he felt under-appreciated by chairman Desmond White and leapt at the chance to become City's manager a month after their relegation, thus taking his first job in England.

Sometimes you're not sure why you bond with someone you had not previously met but – like Dave Smith at Southend – the minute I first shook hands with McNeill, it felt right. He carried an immense presence, tall, straight-backed, straight-talking. I sensed a good rapport in the making. I was right.

After 17 consecutive seasons in the First Division mostly living beyond their means, the task of rebuilding City would have to be undertaken by McNeill with one hand tied behind his back. He hoped an injection of Scottish blood would help and signed strikers Derek Parlane from Leeds United and Jim Tolmie from the obscurity of Lokeren in Belgium for a total of £30,000.

The first season in the Second Division was steady if a little unspectacular, though Parlane and Tolmie top-scored with 19 and 15 goals respectively. City won one of their final six games and finished in fourth place, eight points behind Chelsea, Sheffield Wednesday and Newcastle, which evidenced the strength of the league.

McNeill would make several significant additions in David Phillips, Jim Melrose, Neil McNab and Mick McCarthy, the latter of whom arrived in December 1983. All became firm friends with the exception of McCarthy, a rough-hewn centre-back from Barnsley.

I should have known better than to question the talents of a centre-half signed by McNeill, who happened to be one of the very best in the position the British game had produced. Yet for reasons best known to myself, I wrote that McCarthy was one of the poorest centre-halves I'd seen in City blue.

With two months to play in the 84/85 season, City were right in the mix for promotion, leading the table by six points before a relapse and nervous tension became the prevailing emotion once again.

In late April they were due at Portsmouth – a fellow promotion contender. I asked the manager if I could travel on the coach and write a piece from the inside to measure the strength of City's character at a critical juncture in the season. He said I could.

By this time McNeill and I had grown close. He proposed me for membership of Northenden Golf Club – assistant manager Jimmy Frizzell seconded the motion – noted as one of the finest courses in Greater Manchester around which the River Mersey flowed and where a stray slice, my forte, cost multiple shots.

Frizz was a steady 11 handicap, Billy and I slightly less consistent off 14 and 15. The chance to play this tremendous stretch, where Ken Lawrence of the *Daily Star* was one of the best golfers and became a regular partner, was enough to thank Billy for. Ken and I would become the first pair to defeat the partnership of Kenny Dalglish and Alan Hansen in a four-ball on their home course, Hillside, near Southport, a few years later.

On his 45th birthday – a month before the Portsmouth match – McNeill invited me to a drinks party at his home on High Elm Road in Hale. I knocked on the door and his gracious wife Liz showed me through to the kitchen.

Billy handed me a glass of wine, said I was second to arrive and would I mind keeping the first guest company until more people turned up. I was walked into the lounge and found myself being introduced to Sir Matt Busby.

The great man was settled into a cushioned corner of a sofa and we sat no more than a foot apart where I made enough sense to sustain the conversation for a quarter of an hour, interrupted a couple of times by Billy poking his head in to ask if we were getting on OK.

Sir Matt was, as you would have expected him to be, absolutely charming. We talked a little family, a little journalism, a little Duncan Edwards, he said he was a *Mail* reader, I told him he was one of my all-time hero figures and thanked him more than once for his company. For the life of me I cannot remember anyone else at the party that night.

* * *

The double-decker City team coach left Maine Road for the journey to the south coast and when Mick McCarthy found out I was travelling downstairs, he made sure he was seated as far away as possible on the upper deck. Billy had a trick up his sleeve though.

A room at the team's hotel had been set aside for the pre-match meal to which the players bar McCarthy were summoned at 11.45am. The City manager deliberately sat me by the one empty chair and when McCarthy arrived at noon – the time he'd been told the meal was to be served – there was nowhere else to sit but next to me.

Billy and the rest of his team thought it was the hugest laugh; miserable Mick didn't see the funny side at all. We just about managed to say 'hello' to each other and ate in silence.

City won 2-1 against a major contender and with three matches to play – at home to Oldham, away to Notts County and home to Charlton – could smell promotion. Typically, Oldham held them to a goalless draw, City lost 3-2 at Meadow Lane and now needed to beat Charlton in front of 47,000 fans for their dream to come true.

BBC commentator Barry Davies introduced the match as 'another of the extraordinary brushes of fate that regularly afflict Manchester City'. How right he was. McCarthy was suspended from the match because of a surfeit of bookings.

This was to be a day very unlike the Luton reckoning two years earlier. City were a goal up inside five minutes thanks to the first of several stunning contributions down the left from a young Paul Simpson. He crossed for the first three goals, a side-footed finish by David Phillips and headers by Andy May and Jim Melrose. Simpson scored the fourth himself and set up Phillips for the sweetest of right-footed finishes to complete City's five-goal haul.

There was a boisterous pitch invasion, during which a shirtless May was hoisted to all corners of the ground and finally made it back to the safety of the dressing room with just a few scratches to his torso. It was as if 1983 had never happened.

Peter Swales puffed proudly on one of his monstrous cigars. Billy McNeill had done what he had been asked to do.

* * *

By now I was well ensconced at Old Trafford as well. Big Ron was in firm control and home match nights invariably ended with his room as open house to the opposition's management, his own backroom staff, various hangers-on and assorted friendly press men. I was an unashamed regular.

These were opportunities to debate football and life with Ron's assistant Mick Brown, reserve-team manager Brian Whitehouse, youth coaches Eric Harrison and Jimmy Curran, chief scout Tony Collins and physio Jim McGregor, all football men of the highest calibre. Gordon Clayton, a former United player who became Frank Casper's assistant in his short-lived reign at Burnley, was often there. Time spent in this company was time really well spent.

Les Olive, the long-serving United club secretary, usually popped his head around the door, took a look at the numbers and at the fast-emptying drinks cabinet, rolled his eyes and said his goodnights.

As thanks for my endeavours in the department, Bryan Webster ultimately determined that I should work at both FA Cup finals under Ron's management in 1983 and 1985, two extravagant occasions that ended in success for the club.

It ought to have been a different outcome in 1983 when a minute from the end of extra time against Brighton, the seaside club's striker Gordon Smith (to become a great mate at Manchester

City) was clean through for the last kick of the match but Gary Bailey pulled off an astonishing save. A reprieved United won the replay 4-0.

Two years later against Everton, no one could have conceived the storyline. Kevin Moran and Norman Whiteside were good buddies, the pair often popping into The Park in Altrincham town centre, a pub owned by Pat Crerand, a stalwart of the 1968 European Cup-winning side. There was fabulous craic and a story or two to be gained from standing at the bar.

The sensational element of the 1985 final was Moran becoming the first player sent off in a final, for preventing a goalscoring opportunity, and though I wanted to see things from his view because he was such a lovely fellow, I felt it was a correct, if notorious, decision by referee Peter Willis.

Whiteside – who had just turned 20 – would win the final for the ten men with the most exquisite left-footed goal, a curler that beat Neville Southall into the far corner. That evening, back in Altrincham, I found Moran in a corner, supping a pint of Guinness, not the only one he had before chucking-out time. It was one of those moments you dreamed of as a journalist.

Kevin talked about his shame, his joy, his disbelief, his delight; he laughed, he came close to tears. It was a perfect Monday-morning scoop.

* * *

As a prelude to the following season, Ron Atkinson called me one morning and insisted I get to The Cliff, United's training ground, and bring my referee's kit. My presumption was that there was a youth-team match that needed firm handling.

Instead I was greeted by the entire first-team squad. Ron wanted to play a full-scale practice match before deciding on his selection for the first game against Aston Villa. When they saw me the players didn't know whether to laugh or cry. Ron admonished me to referee as I would a real match.

There was no holding back. I had to physically part a couple of rather rash tacklers – you try persuading Bryan Robson and Paul McGrath to calm down a bit when they're both telling you to fuck off – Jesper Olsen and Gordon Strachan were buzzing, Mark Hughes and Frank Stapleton fired up to be the manager's first-choice striker. I was physically shattered at the end.

* * *

The deputy picture editor in the *Mail*'s northern office was a dapper gentleman named Peter Howard. Peter was in his 60s, unflappable and kindly though sometimes inclined to be brusque if you didn't explain to his satisfaction why you needed one of his snappers for a particular assignment.

He liked his sport and I thought him tremendously engaging. I had no idea for the longest time that he was a survivor of the 1958 Munich air crash that shattered so many lives, young and old. Indeed, he had been a heroic survivor, helping stricken Manchester United players out of the inferno.

Peter, the *Mail*'s photographer on the European Cup trip, came back to some of his senses, grabbed a phone at the airport and dictated copy for the paper's final edition with as much detail as he could summon from an appalling and unfolding tragedy. In his article he wrote, 'I feel a bit wobbly but please tell my wife I'm OK.'

I found Peter sitting alone at the bar of the Abercromby one February evening in 1983 after I'd been despatched to cover a United story and popped by the pub for a quenching pint. We chatted for a bit, I said I'd been to Old Trafford and, taking me completely by surprise, he began to well up.

I asked what the matter was but he said he'd rather not talk about it. I left it at that. When I mentioned it to Webby the next day, he told me all about Peter's heroism. It was also the 25th anniversary of Munich. Bryan must have told Peter he'd told me because I could tell he then knew that I knew. I never raised the subject with dear Peter again.

* * *

The vagaries of the *Mail*'s northern edition circulation meant North Wales landed in the Manchester catchment area. As such, our office covered events that didn't particularly drive national interest – priority in Welsh road signage, repairs to the Menai Suspension Bridge, the progress of local football teams.

When the first-round draw for the 1984/85 European Cup Winners' Cup competition pitted Wrexham with Porto, runners-up the previous year to Juventus, there was no dissent when Webby said it was my match. No sane judge expected it to deliver more than a single night's interest and if Wrexham got a drubbing, he could easily pull me off the second leg to save a few quid.

Bobby Roberts, the Wrexham manager, had once managed Colchester United, Southend's great Essex enemy. I refused to hold it against him. He was a quiet-spoken Scot who didn't say silly things like Wrexham had a ghostly of winning the tie over two legs, even if he might have believed it. He was low-key and sensible in his approach. The Portuguese side were heavy, undeniable favourites.

The first leg at the Racecourse Ground in October would be remembered for how many times Wrexham's woodwork was shaken. Porto should have won by half a dozen, yet the only goal of the game from home centre-forward Jim Steel was a simplistic masterpiece as he headed in a John Muldoon cross from eight yards with no defender in sight. I'd have to cover the second leg now.

Wrexham's chairman Pryce Griffiths was a newsagent so we had a striking affinity. He was one of those local heroes who kept football alive, a total enthusiast who was not particularly worldly wise but adored the publicity Wrexham's success was delivering, much of which was being sold across his own counter.

From the reporting group, the main characters were John Hall, the *Wrexham Leader* reporter, Nick Hilton from the *Liverpool Post*, as well as John Bean of the *Express* and Alec Johnson from the *Mirror*. On the eve of the tie, Bean and I were walking the dark streets of Porto back to our hotel when a curled finger beckoned us towards a dimly lit entrance.

When we walked in, a lady behind the desk said in fractured English that she had a girl for me and one for my father. We legged it, though Bean did initially stop and engage her in conversation longer than was really necessary.

The match at the Estádio das Antas would prove to be one of the most remarkable experiences of my career. Wrexham's first-leg lead was erased within minutes and Porto's contemptuous football suggested a mauling. They led 3-1 on aggregate and were tearing the Fourth Division side's defence apart at will.

The Porto press seating was unique, a succession of glass-fronted upright boxes housing two reporters, each seated at an angle across from each other and miles away from the pitch. My cohabitant was Johnson, as lovably eccentric a character as you could find. The rain was lashing down with Noah's Ark-like intensity which made the identification of players we'd only seen play a couple of times before random at best.

Jake King assuredly scored one for Wrexham, then another that required much shouting between the British boxes so that at least we'd all send over the same name even if it was wrong. At half-time, it was 3-2 on the night to Porto, 3-3 on aggregate with an away goal in the Welshmen's favour.

Paolo Futre fired Porto further ahead in the second half and the Wrexham goalkeeper Stuart Parker performed heroics to keep his side in the game. The running copy we had been filing since half-time was laced with such words as courageous, heroic and submerged. We couldn't see a way back for Wrexham. We couldn't see much at all.

Then, with the copy already subbed and headlines written, substitute Muldoon prodded the ball on, Barry Horne launched himself at it, and his volley struck a post and landed in the net. It was the 90th minute. The score was 4-3, 4-4 on aggregate, and Wrexham had won on away goals.

Alec and I were struck dumb but couldn't remain so for more than a few seconds. A new story required writing with 15 minutes to recover our senses and file. The rain continued to pound against the glass but by now we were oblivious to it. Horne was the hero of an unforgettable, wonderful victory.

The post-midnight flight back to Ringway was one I ought to have defined but everyone was so pissed I can't tell you who I sat next to or for how long. The only memory I have is of being part of a 3am stretcher party – I exaggerate but not much – that helped manoeuvre a legless Stuart Parker through customs and to his transport home.

Pryce Griffiths was in a similar state and would not be marking the papers later in the morning. I doubted he'd see daylight for a couple of days.

Three years later with a team that contained five of the side which lost to Wrexham and still coached by Artur Jorge, Porto won the European Cup, defeating Bayern Munich in the final.

* * *

The following season saw an even more unlikely participant from the principality. Bangor City from the Multipart League had lost the two-legged final of the Welsh Cup 5-1 to Shrewsbury Town who, by virtue of being an English club, weren't eligible to compete in Europe as a representative of Wales. I hope you're following.

Bangor didn't mind a bit. They had a couple of solid Welsh stalwarts in their ranks – manager John Mahoney, once of Stoke City, had played 51 times for his country, the last of those two years previously against England in the Home Internationals. Dai Davies, the goalkeeper and an affirmed Druid, had one cap more than his manager, was 37 years old and had been persuaded to do his pal a favour as Bangor had no other fit goalkeeper.

Bangor defeated Fredrikstad of Norway in the opening round on away goals and then landed an incredible plum, drawn to face the Spanish giants Atlético Madrid. Sent to cast an eye over their unknown opponents, Atlético's scouts arrived in Bangor, Northern Ireland, to much mocking hilarity.

The first leg at Farrar Road became quite the attraction. English clubs had been banned from Europe that year after the Heysel Stadium disaster involving Liverpool and Juventus so the big names in the British press needed to cover something, even a tie to which they wouldn't normally have given a second glance.

Jeff Powell, the *Mail*'s main man, came up from London, so I was designated to write the quotes story while he supplied the match report. I shared a room in a local pub across from the railway station with Michael Calvin of the *Daily Telegraph*, another big hitter from the big city lights.

Bangor had had to spend money they didn't have to install new barriers to satisfy the rule makers of UEFA about ground safety, though when the home side went two goals down in 25 minutes, thoughts of a pitch invasion by the locals had been dashed.

Bangor – for whom the future FA chief executive Mark Palios was a dynamic midfield player – bravely offered up a couple of chances themselves and held Atlético at bay for over an hour, which meant I'd be needed for the second leg, just in case.

The travelling press helped swell the numbers on the charter flight from Manchester to Madrid and we arrived at our hotel in the Spanish capital to discover that, as a cost-cutting exercise, we were sharing rooms. I lost the toss and my bedroom buddy would be Alan Thompson of the *Daily Express*.

Tommo was Huddersfield to his core, a northern football legend whose attendance at any fixture in the region prompted the *Express* to go overboard with matchday posters on every other lamppost, declaring 'Alan Thompson is here'. At least we didn't have to put up with those in Madrid.

On the night before the match, I retired early for a football writer, around midnight, and the bed next to mine was empty. When I was awoken at 3.30am, it was to a sight to behold. All the lights were on, Tommo was sitting on the edge of his bed, glass of brandy in one hand, Capstan Full Strength in the other, dressed in the most outrageously shiny turquoise pyjamas, demanding I engage him in conversation.

I can't remember what the hell we talked about but the back and forth went on for a couple of hours.

The match itself was something of a blur after brandy at four in the morning but Bangor and Dai Davies excelled themselves in the Estadio Vicente Calderón. The only time the veteran was beaten was by a free kick by Jesús Landáburu that arrowed into the top corner from 25 yards. Bangor's effort had been truly heroic.

* * *

By late 1985 the writing was on the wall for the Manchester offices of all the national newspaper groups. Rumours were spreading that the last days of the northern powerhouses were upon us and Manchester was to become, to all intents and purposes, a branch office.

The individual case studies are too detailed to go into here but the industry as a whole was spending money it didn't have. If a directive was taken to close, there wasn't much anyone could do but sort out their own situation. This destructive diminution of the northern base was to coincide with a moment in newspaper history of eternal consequence.

Eddie Shah had newspapers in his blood and when he was fired from the *Manchester Evening News* in 1976, rather than seek another so-so job, he went that little bit further and chose to launch his own newspaper from the proceeds of the sale of his home in Sale – at the other end of the town to where I first moved in 1981.

In late 1983, emboldened by new anti-trade union laws adopted by the Thatcher government, his *Stockport Messenger* group of newspapers started to employ non-union print workers which opened a bitter conflict with the National Graphical Association (NGA) which called its workers out on strike. Shah promptly sacked half a dozen of them.

A very nasty can of worms began to spill. Union workers laid siege to Shah's print works in Warrington and despite winning several court judgements preventing strike action, there was no ending the feud until November when over 4,000 trade union members attended a mass picket to prevent lorries leaving the works with Shah's newspapers on board.

There were baton charges by the police, several protestors were injured, almost 100 were arrested and only two months later did the NGA finally call off its action. Shah had become a bastion for newspaper barons – with Rupert Murdoch and Robert Maxwell to the fore – who had wanted for years to neuter the print unions.

In his book, *The History of the Times*, author Graham Stewart wrote, 'Eddie Shah, survivor of the *Messenger* dispute, had begun to think beyond the confines of Warrington and was envisaging a far more revolutionary plan. He conceived a new mid-market tabloid national newspaper to be called *Today*, edited by Brian MacArthur [formerly of *The Times*].

'Loosely modelled on *USA Today*, it would transmit its paper via satellite to regional printing plants in London, Birmingham and Manchester. In doing so it would be free from Fleet Street's restrictive practices and could thus be produced at a cost that significantly undercut the current titles.

'Its planners budgeted that it could break even without any advertising on sales of 600,000. What was more, by using the latest technology and printing in colour it would be attractive to readers. Its journalists would have direct input.'

* * *

Len Gould was a member of the back-bench hierarchy at the *Express* in Manchester and had been plucked from that relative obscurity to be anointed the first sports editor of *Today*. I'd seen Len around a few times at functions and matches but not enough to know him that well when he called and asked if I fancied a drink one evening.

The upshot was a job offer to join the Shah revolution. On the face of it, this seemed to be too good to be true, a giant leap for technological and journalistic mankind. The *Today* staff would be guinea pigs entering a world of trial and error (mostly error as it turned out) but as a single man of 28, I didn't think I had too much to lose.

Len asked me to be *Today*'s first tennis correspondent, with plenty of opportunities to cover football. He recruited eagerly from the north, with the *Express*'s lead in Manchester, Derek Potter, signing on, as did *The Guardian*'s Patrick Barclay, a prince of football prose.

When Roy Collins, my first journalistic hero, joined the enterprise, it was both music to my ears as well as offering me a chance to doss down at his home in Highgate while searching for a place of my own. Our young thrusting football reporter in London was a chap by the name of Rob Shepherd.

Just before packing for the move, I received an unexpected phone message. Mike Dempsey, the northern sports editor of the *Express*, wanted to meet at the Britannia Hotel on Portland Street. We took a couple of high-backed chairs in the lobby area and Mike – not one to mess around – offered me a job.

Potter's move to *Today* upset him deeply and what better way to get one back than nick someone who had agreed to move but hadn't formalised anything. Although Manchester was closing down its main newspaper offices, there was still masses of work in the area. I could have first pick of the matches, Dempsey promised. It was a heck of an offer.

I told him I'd give it some thought but I not only felt accepting would be a terrible kick in the teeth for Bryan Webster and all he'd done for me but I'd given my word to Len and couldn't break it. I phoned Mike to say I was deeply grateful for the offer but couldn't accept.

To *Today* and a new tomorrow it was to be. On the day before my farewell 'do' at the Abercromby on 20 January 1986 I received this letter.

Dear Neil,

These are the sort of things I should be saying at your farewell but I am a notoriously bad public speaker and there is every chance that I may fail to pay you full credit for your time with us.

From the day you joined us four and a half years ago you have made a tremendous contribution. It is quite dispiriting to think that from tomorrow we shall be without your unfailing good humour, unflagging enthusiasm and unlimited capacity for hard work.

I have seen many people leave the Daily Mail *in my 22 years as sports editor and I know of no one whose departure was more regretted.*

Even so, I fully understand the reason why you wish to move to a job that may offer more scope. Needless to say, I wish you every success while entertaining a hope that perhaps one day you will come back to the Daily Mail, *either in Manchester or London.*

You may, of course, use this letter as a testimonial. I don't think you will ever need it.

Yours sincerely,
Bryan Webster
Northern Sports Editor

8

A Brave New World

THE HEADQUARTERS of *Today* was a corner office on Vauxhall Bridge Road halfway between the River Thames and Victoria Station. It was an obscure location for such a game-changing enterprise.

The new recruits assembled eagerly to listen to the concept of an adventure that would transform the way newspapers were produced. The reporters would file directly to the office by way of something called a Tandy 200, while the pages would be designed on computer screens and transmitted straight to the printing centres without the need for production staff.

There wasn't a great deal of time to put all this palaver into practice. The journalists began to clock in by late 1985 and the first issue was scheduled for 4 March 1986. The initial few weeks were a blur of activity, getting to know new people and how they worked, bonding sessions, learning all sorts of ropes and for us going in the field, how to work our new-fangled portable computers and what to do in case of a technical collapse other than brick it.

In essence, your copy was typed on to a screen, the computer asked you a question ('would you like to send y/n?'), you listened for a beeping sound which meant you'd connected, shoved the telephone handset into rubber couplers, pressed y, held the ends down and prayed. A cursor was meant to cross the screen and when it stopped your copy had – theoretically – reached the computers in the office.

There were all number of dummy runs before the big night was prefaced by the screening of a TV commercial where some of the main writers, Derek Jameson, Simon Jenkins, Anthony Holden, Peter O'Sullevan and Patrick Barclay, were to the fore as the remainder of us gathered round, raised our thumbs and shouted, 'We're ready Eddie!' into the camera. We hoped to hell we were.

I had two articles in the first issue, one on Jesper Olsen being dropped by Manchester United and a report on the Brighton v Peterborough United FA Cup fifth-round replay which merited a dozen paragraphs. The Tandy had worked its magic.

That night, as many *Today* reporters who were within reach gathered in the pub across the road from the office and toasted our existence, the edition arrived to the popping of champagne corks, and on the front page there was a rather blurry colour image of HM The Queen on her Australian tour.

* * *

No one could be sure how far *Today*'s largesse stretched but the owners didn't scrimp on my account. The first tennis tournament of note after the launch was the renowned Monte Carlo Open. Len sent me without a quibble considering there wasn't a single British player in the draw.

I'd been told to expect a gala occasion and it didn't disappoint. The Country Club was simply exquisite, set in rock a quarter of the way up a mountainside, to which the rich and famous of the principality, including the Grimaldi royal family, meandered their way to be wined and dined.

They weren't the only ones. The press restaurant was an elegant eight-to-ten-tabled area, tucked away from public view with waiter service and as much food and drink as you could possibly desire (and receipts!). A circular staircase – taken very carefully after lunch – led you to the press seating where the view stretched out beyond Karl Lagerfeld's palatial home, copious yachts and to the Mediterranean horizon.

The British press contingent numbered at least ten, which was incredible until you saw the food. Reg Brace of the *Yorkshire Post* attended, as did Peter Blackman of the *London Evening Standard* and the two agency reporters, John Oakley of the Press Association and Bryan Cutress of Exchange Telegraph. There was plenty for all.

Most of us were stationed at the far end of town in a *pension* by the railway station, an unpretentious antidote to the rest of the place that was stacked to the gills with millionaires. John Parsons of the *Telegraph* was resident at the Beach Plaza, the best hotel on the promenade to which we weren't invited.

As for the sport played on majestic, tan-coloured dusty courts, Joakim Nyström of Sweden won the title that year, defeating the French hero Yannick Noah in straight sets. I probably only got half a dozen paragraphs in the paper on the match but frankly cared not a jot.

There were three tennis events in my time with *Today* that, in retrospect, were history-makers concertinaed into a few weeks.

After his victory in the French Open in June, I decided it might be beneficial to try to break the glacial interface between Ivan Lendl of Czechoslovakia and the rest of humankind.

Lendl had won two grand slam titles including a remarkable success in Paris in 1984, from two sets to love down from which John McEnroe's hopes of ever winning the French Open were dashed. Now Lendl wanted Wimbledon more than any other.

I asked his agent Jerry Solomon if he might be open to an interview. The response was positive. We met at a new coffee shop in the village called Racquets. Lendl was as eloquent and open as I could have wanted. We played golf at Coombe Wood in Kingston where he didn't give a single putt that most would have accepted as a gimme. No wonder he was such an arse to play professionally.

Lendl's grass-court game was sticky to say the least. He wasn't confident moving on the surface and eked wins. In the second week of the 1986 tournament he won five-set marathons in both the quarters (against Tim Mayotte of the USA) and the semis (against Slobodan Živojinović of Yugoslavia). In the final he was chicken feed to the defending champion, Boris Becker of Germany. I determined to know Lendl better.

The same was true of McEnroe, the most fascinating of sportsmen. He had taken a nine-month sabbatical from tennis from the end of 1985, during which he became a father for the first time with wildchild actress Tatum O'Neal.

The couple were married on Long Island a few days before John's appointed return to competition in beautiful Stratton Mountain, Vermont. The British press were heading there en masse. It promised to be a tumultuous week.

We were billeted in ski chalets, for the location was renowned for its winter sports clamour rather than summer sunshine and tennis. It was a spectacular setting for the Volvo International, a tournament run with sophistication and good humour by Jim Westhall who would need to draw upon all his charm as the week progressed.

McEnroe was scheduled to give a press conference on the eve of the tournament but pulled out to widespread consternation from those who had travelled thousands of miles to hear him speak. John's father, also John, stepped in to say his son was worried the whole event was becoming a circus.

The big top duly arrived on cue the next morning. John was practising on a court at the foot of a grassy slope and, from the corner of his eye, saw British freelance photographer Tommy Hindley approaching. The pair had previous. McEnroe had once lashed out with his foot when Tommy poked his camera through the canvas backdrop of the old bullring court at Roland Garros.

'Get that asshole outta here!' McEnroe raged. Tommy was not for moving, the Stratton sheriff was summoned and with backup he attempted to frogmarch a spluttering snapper from a scene made the more comic as everyone kept losing their footing on the slippery slope. Tommy called a press briefing of his own the next day to denounce his treatment.

When we did get down to some tennis, McEnroe was in decent nick and celebrated his first-round victory over Marko Ostoja of Yugoslavia by saying how many people had told him they missed him on the court and that it was about time he was afforded such affection.

Westhall, who managed to placate Hindley with a room upgrade, was thrilled that McEnroe had one match under his belt and was still in the event. The director then told me that if I had some time to spare, I should spend it watching a 16-year-old phenomenon with crazy bleached hair and a wild forehand, name of Andre Agassi.

The first sighting of the kid was quite something. He was all bristling US bravado and colourful array, as if something from a freeway billboard. A marketeer's dream. Agassi not only struck the ball with amazing power, he also spoke with a confidence born of his Las Vegas upbringing. There was nothing you thought this boy couldn't do.

Mac had to cede a little of the spotlight to this devil-may-care teenager and when they were matched in the quarter-finals, the Stratton stands were heaving. John tamed Andre in straight sets and admitted later that he'd rarely seen a tennis ball hit with such venom.

The semi-final line-up would not have embarrassed a grand slam – Ivan Lendl v Jimmy Connors and John McEnroe v Boris Becker. Lendl and Becker would prevail in two mesmerising three-setters, though McEnroe didn't go down without choice words to the German who had won back-to-back Wimbledon titles and was still only 18. 'Just because he won Wimbledon, he still has to show me some respect,' John said.

The final was played to a backdrop of thunder clouds forming atop the mountains of Vermont and saw Lendl defeat Becker in straight sets. Then the rain pelted down.

* * *

There had been not a cloud in the sky in Prague a few days earlier where a bride in blue and a controversial homecoming took centre stage. The Federation Cup women's team event was staged across a week in late July in the capital of Czechoslovakia. Representing the United States was Martina Navratilova, a Czech by birth who had taken US citizenship five years earlier.

Navratilova had won 14 grand slam singles titles and seven WTA Tour Finals by the summer of 1986. She was without doubt the dominant player in her sport and hadn't been back to the country of her birth for 11 years. The atmosphere was thick with tension.

The Czechs had been told by the tennis authorities that if they wanted to stage such a prestigious event, they would have to grant Martina a visa, even if it stuck in their craw. Though the 1986 Wimbledon final – when Navratilova defeated the Czech heroine Hana Mandlíková in straight sets – was shown on state television, Martina's name had been scrubbed from many of her country's record books.

Prague was an entirely breathtaking city, one of the centrepieces of which was the Old Town Hall. David 'Noddy' Irvine, *The Guardian*'s correspondent, was taking in the sights one morning when he happened upon a wedding party and made a mental note of how incredible the bride looked, especially as she was dressed in blue.

David was regaling us with the scene as we awaited a press conference at the tennis stadium when suddenly Ted Tinling appeared complete with a huge cake. Ted didn't often require additional decoration. He stood 6ft 5in, was bald, gay, wore an earring, outrageous clothes, his false teeth had a mind of their own and he was a huge name in women's tennis, as a one-time controversial dress designer turned public relations man. Ted used to say that he loved walking on to an airplane and seeing the alarm on the faces of the passengers, all of whom were thinking, 'Please don't take the seat next to mine.'

Tinling laid the cake on the dais and told us he had such happy news to impart, that Hana Mandlíková had been married that day to Australian Jan Sedlak. Noddy – so named for his habit of falling asleep at the dinner table – spluttered in disbelief, realising he'd been witness to the wedding and hadn't recognised the bride as a major tennis champion.

It had to happen that after a week of elimination matches, the final would be a duel between Czechoslovakia and the United States. The first match was really close, Chris Evert defeating Helena Suková in two tight sets and leaving the stage for Mandlíková v Navratilova, three weeks on from their Wimbledon final.

The home crowd was rooting for Hana but as it became clear Martina was the stronger and was going to win, they cheered her every move. The body of Czech politicians in the front-row seats departed before the presentations but this empty gesture neither diminished the worthiness nor the glory of another chapter in one woman's incredible story.

* * *

Martina Navratilova would win the US Open a month hence. Indeed, all four singles finalists in 1986 were Czechoslovak-born: Navratilova, Helena Suková, Ivan Lendl and Miloslav Mečíř, which didn't do much for CBS television ratings, or space in the British papers.

It was my New York debut where a recurring memory of a first meal in the city was a corned beef sandwich the size of a loofah served at Stars Deli on Lexington Avenue, a block down from the Loews Summit Hotel, known to the British press boys as the Slummit (Stars is now the Paris Baguette and the Loews is now the Doubletree).

The Big Apple was as one had dreamed it with vast indiscriminate movement, vapour rising from drain covers, yellow taxis hurtling through vast potholes, coffee and bagel vendors selling their wares from little carts on every corner, great bars, sirens and screams. *Hill Street Blues* played out for real.

The tennis complex was in Corona Park in the borough of Queens, a journey that averaged out at three-quarters of an hour from midtown Manhattan through teeming traffic. The main court at Flushing Meadows was the Louis Armstrong Stadium, named for the famed jazz musician who had lived near the site.

The press box stretched across the top of the full width of the main stand and doubled as your office space in a three-decked affair from which you could gaze at the Manhattan skyline in the distant. It was easier to pick out the Chrysler Building ten miles away than who was playing tennis some 100 feet below you.

In the afternoon, seeing anything at all was almost impossible because the sun was directly in your face, and behind glass the press box took on the properties of a greenhouse. It was stifling and blinding at one and the same time and you often emerged with a face like a tomato.

The written press corps, numbering 100 or so, had two access points: a couple of elevators one at each end of the box that worked half the time and into which you could squeeze at most a dozen people. It was often a nightmare when a press conference was called because the interview room was down in the depths and you needed to give yourself at least ten minutes to make it.

Many a time you arrived breathless to face a player throwing a tantrum at having to wait so long for the room to fill and who then went obstinately schtum when you asked them a simple question.

The scores from the outside courts were scrawled in chalk on boards at either end of the box. It was all very primitive but at the same time it tested your athletic as well as cerebral talents. With a five-hour time difference to the UK, much of the day was a race against the clock. After the first edition copy had been sent, the Chesterfield's bar on the main concourse was the regular location for alcoholic replenishment.

There was a healthy British contingent who worked hard and never shirked playing hard. The need for everyone to stay for late-night matches was not as pressing then as it is in today's 24-hour world of blanket rolling news. When the newspapers' final edition shutters went down, it was permissible to draw breath. Even John Parsons didn't stay for *every* match.

Peter 'Blackers' Blackman of the *Evening Standard* had to be at the courts at night for the next morning's London first edition and would type and print off any relevant late-night quotes which he slid under the door of each of our rooms while we slept. That's if we were sleeping.

The Brit pack had their regular social haunts like Harglo's and Eamonn Doran's on Second Avenue, which were two blocks apart and where it wasn't unusual for us to be the last to leave well into the early hours. I do look back and wonder where we got our stamina from.

My favourite haunt was Bill's Gay Nineties on 54th Street, a one-time speakeasy turned saloon/restaurant to which I went more for the piano players and opportunities to sing than the amount of gin Nick the barman determined a single measure. Robert Monet was an old-time crooner whose renditions of 'If You Go Away' and 'I'm So Afraid' evoked golden days. Robert would see out his days performing on the cruise ships of Florida. Lovely man.

Bill's was full of sporting memorabilia, mostly of boxers – the greeter Aldo Leone had been a cornerman for the great Rocky Marciano – and thoroughbred horses. Behind the bar hung a huge picture taken in 1902 of George M. Cohan – the original Yankee Doodle Dandy – and his manager Sam Harris, signed 'To Bill'.

I returned to my hotel room from a singsong there one evening to find the red message light on the phone flashing. It was Peter Moss, sports news editor of the *Daily Mail*, saying he wanted me to call him at my earliest convenience. I slept on it and made contact first thing the next morning.

Mossie said that Arthur Firth, recently appointed sports editor after the departure of Tom Clarke, would like to meet me when I returned home.

* * *

Firth had been a short-lived editor of the *Daily Express* – a position that changed hands as often as guards at Buck House – had worked on the *Mail*'s back bench and was a long-standing associate of David English. The announcement of his new position came as a surprise given his lack of experience in sport.

The current *Mail* tennis correspondent, Malcolm Folley, had decided to leave for pastures new and Firth said he wanted me to replace him. I said goodbye to *Today* after nine hectic, immensely fulfilling months.

Firth definitely wanted to make the pages brighter. I liked him tremendously and he gave tennis its head. For my first Wimbledon as the *Mail*'s man, I went out on a limb and tipped Australian Pat Cash, a relative outsider at the 11th seed, to win the title.

The headline on our championship pull-out was 'Cash's tunes of glory', with a picture of Pat playing guitar. His father Patrick snr told me I was 'a bloody great judge of tennis'.

Patrick's 22-year-old son would enjoy a life-changing two weeks, winning his last three matches against Mats Wilander, Jimmy Connors and, in the final, Ivan Lendl, without dropping serve. His mastery of the volley was complete. As the props were wheeled on to Centre Court for the trophy presentation, Cash made his historic dash into the players' box where his family and coach Ian 'Barkers' Barclay were waiting to greet him.

The 1987 US Open was memorable for many things – Lendl's third title in New York, Andrew Castle giving Boris Becker a four-set run for his money on the old Grandstand court and a bourgeoning courtship between myself and Maureen Hanlon, one of the WTA media staff, who had long strawberry blonde hair and a determination to knock me into shape, especially what she said was my hideous clothes sense.

There was more love in the air. Ron Atkin of *The Observer* acquired seats at Carnegie Hall and not for any old concert. Frank Sinatra was celebrating the reopening of the landmark venue after years of restoration work and Atkin was offering half a dozen tickets, obstructed view, in the upper gallery. I snapped his hand off.

Sinatra may have been in the autumn of his vocal years but lit up the place with two hours of mainstays like 'My Way', 'I've Got the World on a String' and, of course, 'New York, New York'. His finest work was a pitch-perfect rendition of Billy's soliloquy from the musical *Carousel.* The encores were frequent and tingled the spine.

We were about to endure an emotional upheaval of our own on *Mail* sport. Arthur Firth was in the midst of trying to persuade ex-*Express* man Joe Melling, a tremendous football writer, to join the *Mail* from its sister paper the *Mail on Sunday* but dropped dead of a heart attack.

His position passed to Peter Lea, once Tom Clarke's deputy, and now the man in the hotseat. He was a safe, capable pair of hands. Everything on the sportsdesk returned to normal.

* * *

David English rubber-stamped my first visit to the Australian Open in 1988, the year the championship switched venues from the cramped grass courts in the quaint suburb of Kooyong to a multi-purpose stadium on the banks of the River Yarra named Flinders Park.

Peter Lea protected company money as if it was his own when it came to foreign expenditure but the editor said attendance at grand slam tournaments was an essential element of covering one of his favourite sports and the trip was signed off, even to the extent of flying business class.

From the minute I arrived I fell in love with Melbourne, a city that felt more like a village with its tidy, spotless trams, coffee bars, water taxis, university rowing clubs on the Yarra, bountiful flora and fauna, architecture old and new somehow meshing and all bound together by the spirit and informality of the people. The only downside was the bloody flies that attacked in battalions, constantly getting into your mouth and up your nose.

The Aussies were proud of their shiny new tennis centre directly across the railway tracks from the Melbourne Cricket Ground from which it was difficult to draw your gaze such was its majestic form. The MCG had an awful lot to commend it but it would never have a roof. Tennis had well and truly moved into a different age.

Not only a new ceiling but the Australian Open unveiled an original playing surface called Rebound Ace, a synthetic amalgam of fibres and textures which played not quite hard court, not quite indoor court, but somewhere in between. By and large the players were entirely in favour.

There were 15 Brits in the singles, ten women and five men, which meant plenty to write home about, though losing seven first-round matches on a single day was rather over-egging the pie. The two who remained standing in the men's draw, Jeremy Bates and Stephen Shaw, made more than a bit of noise.

Shaw confronted the giant Yugoslav Slobodan Živojinović after an exchange of on-court insults and if Stephen was powerfully built himself, 'Bobo' was Giant Haystacks in tennis gear. Shaw didn't back down and somehow survived.

Bates was not pleased when his first-round opponent Kelly Evernden of New Zealand suggested to his local press that he couldn't have wished for a kinder draw. Batesy got so riled he won in five high-octane sets and it made you wonder what he might have achieved if every one of his opponents pierced his skin before he played them.

At the time of these relatively minor disputes, Steffi Graf of Germany was setting out on a year that would shake the game to its core. It ended in a Golden Slam, as the 19-year-old won all four grand slams and Olympic gold in Seoul, South Korea. Never before had women's tennis revelled in such an achievement.

The German media, already invested heavily in the teenage brilliance of Boris Becker, now had another superstar on their hands and didn't know which way to turn, lucky buggers.

In the final of the ensuing French Open, Graf routed Russian Natasha Zvereva 6-0, 6-0 in 34 minutes; at Wimbledon Martina Navratilova led decisively but couldn't repel Graf's incredible fightback, and at both the US Open and in the Olympics, Gabriela Sabatini of Argentina was Steffi's last victim.

The old stagers of the women's game, Navratilova and Chris Evert, were being challenged on a sustained level of wondrous tennis by a girl who disguised her innate shyness with free-hitting abandon on court. Bud Collins, the seer of American tennis commentators, dubbed Graf 'Fraulein Forehand'.

A sense of mystery clung to Graf which meant her story engaged like few others. Peter, her father, was a domineering presence and the pair ploughed a distinct path that unnerved opponents and the Women's Tennis Association (WTA), which thought it ran the women's game. Peter was outspoken and unpredictable which was great copy for us writers but less enjoyable for those who preferred not to be told all the time how useless they were.

There was, therefore, much relief in the hierarchy when a handful of newcomers sprang forth, all younger than Steffi and exuding free spirit and promise. Sabatini was the olive-skinned Argentine beauty, Arantxa Sánchez Vicario an excitable bundle of Spanish energy, Monica Seles an uninhibited left-hander from Yugoslavia, and when Jennifer Capriati emerged from Florida at 13 without an apparent care in the world, the sport was spinning on its axis.

The *Mail* headlined them the 'Million Dollar Babies'.

* * *

In my last 18 months as the *Mail*'s correspondent, I would report on both the single finest match I witnessed live and what was arguably the most remarkable grand slam tournament the sport ever staged.

The two venues were markedly contrasting; Madison Square Garden in New York City at Christmas time and Roland Garros in the full scent of a Parisian spring. The Garden staged the climax to the men's season, the Nabisco Masters, an eight-man event based on the points accrued across a year of competition. A surprising semi-finalist was the Swiss, Jakob Hlasek; the very unsurprising final pitted Ivan Lendl, a three-time champion, against Boris Becker.

There are many distractions to tempt even the most ardent tennis buff in New York when it's all twinkly outside, there's snow in the air and warm bars beckon but few left their seats in the Garden during four hours of levitated, cut-and-thrust tennis, encapsulated by the very last point.

The match was drawn into a final-set tie-break, Becker led it 6-5, missed his first serve and slid in his second. The resultant rally was interspersed with more oohs and aahs than the final scene of an Agatha Christie mystery, slice from Becker, slice from Lendl, power from Lendl, deft reply from Becker until the German's backhand drive clipped the top of the net and faded over. Lendl stood, hands on hips, Becker arms aloft. It was truly the most magical match.

In Paris six months later, it was not one match that necessarily stood out, but the entire fortnight. Each year I stayed in the same room in a three-star hotel, the Poussin, a 15-minute walk to the site. A few press lads would often start the day with clay-court combat on local public courts, usually myself, Malcolm Folley, Hugh Jamieson, Nigel Clarke and occasionally Bryan Cooney of the *Star* who wasn't my pick of people, nor I him.

The one downside to the tournament was that its proximity to Wimbledon meant British sports writers who didn't cover tennis regularly were despatched to Paris to stoke fires and get under players' skins. Cooney was expert at taking the written piss out of British players for what he deemed was lack of bottle and backbone.

Disagreements between red-tops and the rest about how the sport should be reported would repeatedly rear their head at evening get-togethers after one Ricard liqueur too many. I got rather pickled at Le Congres, a posh restaurant on the Porte D'Auteuil, and told Cooney precisely what I thought of his (lack of) style. He said I was an arrogant shit. I said he was an arsehole.

There was one significant social ritual to which all members of the British press – arrogant and arsehole included – were invited, a dinner hosted exclusively for us by Philippe Chatrier, the president of both the French Tennis Federation and the International Tennis Federation (ITF).

Chatrier was a charming man who wielded the power of his twin positions with both velvet glove and discreet force. Once introduced, he never forgot a first name, oldest and novice alike.

Ted Tinling organised the dinners which were held in the grandest places and often degenerated into fractious division as one argument after another broke out. 'The boys will have their orgasms,' Ted said. David Irvine of *The Guardian*, when chairman of the Lawn Tennis Writers' Association, once made a coruscating speech denouncing everything the ITF stood for, sat down and promptly dropped off.

None of this bothered Chatrier, after whom the centre court at Roland Garros was named on his passing. He rather adored what he regarded was our passion for the sport which would be at its height as the 1989 version of the French Open unfolded.

The unrest in China arrived at a sinister juncture; the tanks were rolling into Beijing's Tiananmen Square to crush student uprisings demanding reforms of the political system. In a Paris hotel, 17-year-old Michael Chang, the American player of Chinese descent, was shocked as he watched the dramas unfold with the rest of his family.

Chang was to face Ivan Lendl in the fourth round and few gave him much hope. Chang was a committed Christian and Lendl a committed champion. And each year around this time in Paris the French chose to go on strike about some dispute or another, so the sounds of blaring horns and raucous demonstrators from adjacent boulevards would interrupt the relative peace reserved for tennis.

Put all these ingredients together and something weird was bound to happen. It did. Lendl led by two sets to love which, usually, progressed to three very quickly. Chang was a soft-baller who didn't possess tremendous physical power, rather an unsettling hang-in-there attitude which, astonishingly, brought him level. But all the muscles in his body were tightening.

In the seventh game of the final set and as the crowd willed him to victory, Chang suddenly tossed in an underarm serve. A nonplussed Lendl managed to scramble the ball back into play but the ruse meant he was off balance for the rest of the rally and lost it. 'I was just popping my serves in anyway and I needed to break his concentration,' Chang said later.

When the Czech was match point down and missed his first serve, Chang hustled forward to within a yard of the service box. Lendl was raging but no rules were broken. His second serve flicked the net, floated long and Chang collapsed where he stood, the victor.

Chang subsequently survived four-set matches against the Haitian Ronald Agénor and Andrei Chesnokov of Russia to set up a final against Sweden's Stefan Edberg, coached by Tony Pickard, a former British Davis Cup player who relished the limelight his role provided and rightly so.

Edberg led by two sets to one and had nine opportunities to take a double break advantage in the fourth set but Chang wouldn't buckle. All the power suddenly left Edberg's legs, his forehand began to fail and Chang it was who kept his nerve to triumph.

My report was the following day's back-page lead, 'They say faith can move mountains. And so it came to pass at Roland Garros that Michael Chang became the youngest grand slam champion the world has seen. It was an astounding success for the 17-year-old made all the more remarkable because his total time on court throughout the tournament added up to 21 hours and 28 minutes. And this on the most gruelling tennis surface God created.'

The women's event was just as exceptional. Steffi Graf was still rolling over the sport, having won the past five slams and carrying an aura of invincibility. She defeated a rare delight of a girl, the Yugoslav Monica Seles, in the semi-finals and faced another upstart 17-year-old in Arantxa Sánchez Vicario two days later. It would not end well for the German.

Though she had been dominating on the court, Steffi's life was suffering away from it. She was distracted by a loony tunes Florida millionaire who turned up uninvited to her matches, lavished her with flowers and said he would buy her any colour Porsche she wanted.

A jar of poisoned marmalade was sent to Graf's home in Bruhl which was discovered in the nick of time. In January, a bomb threat was made against the flight the family were taking home from Australia. Surreptitiously, they chose to leave by another route.

Peter Graf told me of 'horrible things that have happened to us, and you don't know the half of it'. Under the heading 'The Torment of Steffi', I wrote, 'For two years, the German media with an intrusive desire to see Graf as they want to see her, ridiculed her for not being able to attract a boyfriend. "Now that I have a boyfriend [Alex Mronz, a male player ranked in the mid-100s]," she said, "they write so much garbage I can't leave home."'

In the final throes of his daughter's defeat to Sánchez Vicario in Paris, Peter disappeared from the stadium without a backward glance and all seemed to be crumbling apart. He said he was suffering from a bronchial problem.

The upside was the Sánchez Vicario story, a lovely little kid from Barcelona who was 'getting a character' after years growing up never wanting to say a word. Her 7-6, 3-6, 7-5 victory was some elucidation. Steffi, out of her own character, hugged Arantxa at the net. She longed for someone to really hug her back.

How extraordinary that a month later, Graf responded by winning Wimbledon as if France had been a hallucination. What powers this woman had. Martina Navratilova, the grass-court supremacist, didn't play badly at all; in fact, she would have beaten any other woman on tour on the final day. But Steffi was driven to heights I'd not seen. Her backhand slice was quite the most devastating shot, consistently luring Navratilova forward where Graf would gleefully pick her off at the net.

In New York, Steffi repeated the dose, once more beating Navratilova in a grand slam final. The following day, Boris Becker would make it a German *eins-zwei*. Becker was in his hard-court element, swinging into his serve, withstanding much of Ivan Lendl's formidable baseline ball-striking and on his first match point, bounced the ball once more than usual, pointed his racket at his opponent and delivered an unreturnable serve down the T.

* * *

The cheers as I stepped off the coach when we returned to midtown Manhattan were a nice touch from my tennis-writing colleagues. I had asked Maureen's parents, Richard and Joan, for permission to marry their daughter and, five days after the US Open, we celebrated our wedding at St. John the Evangelist Church, Attleboro, Massachusetts, her hometown.

Sean Rafter, the Southend youth-team goalkeeper from those very first days as a kid reporter, was my best man.

My bachelor party was held in Bill's. I sang Harry Secombe's 'If I Ruled the World' to kick-start proceedings, 'Every head would be held up high, there'd be sunshine in everyone's sky, if the day ever dawned when I ruled the world,' before a coachload of 60-something women from Florida gatecrashed our party. David Irvine completed the night by performing a terribly pissed rendition of the Dance of the Seven Veils which the ladies thoroughly appreciated.

Irvine and John Parsons attended the following week's Wightman Cup, an annual women's tournament between the US and Britain staged that week in Williamsburg, Virginia. The US trounced our girls 7-0 and decided it was time to pull the shutters down on an event that had become so one-sided.

The chaps then flew in from Virginia to Providence, Rhode Island, where I collected them to be guests at the wedding. George Gordon, the *Mail*'s New York correspondent and a wonderful guy, drove a 400-mile round trip to be there.

Maureen and I had searched long and hard for a honeymoon venue when I noted that Dave Hall, an old *Evening Echo* news reporter, had relocated to California and was working as a public relations man for a city called Indian Wells, in the Coachella Valley. The place sounded idyllic.

Thanks to Dave, we secured a week at the Hyatt Grand Champions, the first four nights of which were free of charge on the hotel's executive floor which overlooked one of its two golf courses. My new wife and I played alternate courses each day. I hadn't realised the hotel hosted the Newsweek Champions Cup tennis event and thought how wonderful it would be to return there sometime.

* * *

In February 1989 I had flown to Milan to interview John McEnroe on his 30th birthday. 'McEnroe reaches the age of reason,' the *Mail* headlined the piece. A premature judgement as it turned out.

We sat on a wooden bench inside the Palatrussardi, the venue for the indoor tournament in the Italian city. I mentioned that his first and ultimate adversary, Björn Borg, had retired from the sport at 26.

'For any athlete the figure 30 seems to represent a gnawing despair,' he replied. 'There are days when I think about it and they're scary. Hopefully, there are still things I can improve. Back in my youth there was so much innocence.'

We were close to a year on from that sit-down when the sport gathered in Melbourne for the first grand slam tournament of a new decade. The period of McEnroe's utter domination of the men's game was a dim and distant memory. But he was still box office, you couldn't take your eyes from him.

He was seeded fourth, won his first three rounds in straight sets and faced the unseeded Mikael Pernfors of Sweden in the last 16. In the third set, dissatisfied with a few line calls, he stood directly in front of a lineswoman, bouncing the ball on his racket a foot from her nose.

Gerry Armstrong from East Sussex, one of a new intake of professional umpires, saw this as intimidation and warned the American. At two sets to one down, Pernfors was mounting a spirited challenge and when McEnroe missed a forehand drive in the sixth game, he smacked his racket into the court surface, causing the frame to split, bringing an instant second penalty that gave Pernfors a break of serve and a 4-2 lead.

McEnroe was as steaming as the day. He didn't think a small crack merited such a punishment, though that was the rule. He argued over and again with the umpire, who summoned Ken Farrar, the match supervisor, and Peter Bellenger, the referee. They explained the situation to John but he wasn't calmed.

As the two officials turned to leave, McEnroe muttered the words 'fuck' and 'mother' among others which meant an instant default if either men or the umpire heard them. Farrar spun on his heel and told Armstrong to disqualify the player there and then.

'Code violation, verbal abuse, default Mr McEnroe,' intoned the umpire. It took about ten seconds for it to sink in. McEnroe smiled, packed his bags and left. Farrar described his words as 'extremely abusive, the worst I've heard in 11 years of officiating'.

The scramble from the press seats on centre court to the interview room began in earnest. We were knocking spectators out of the way, assuming McEnroe would go straight in, say a few words then flee the site. 'Only two people heard what I said, I don't think that's enough to disqualify me,' John said. 'This is the icing on the cake. They've written the rules for me, it's not like they're for anyone else.'

The *Mail* cleared the decks to tell of the first time a player had been defaulted in a grand slam – a back-page lead and an entire page on op-ed, headlined, 'Is this the downfall of brat morality?'

I wrote, 'At Wimbledon in 1981, tennis officialdom shuddered at McEnroe but swallowed his outrage. The McEnroe morality became ingrained in tennis, in other sports and even, I suspect, had echoes in the selfish, ugly behaviour of so many young people across the world. Nine years, a thousand curses, a few exquisite brushstrokes of tennis genius and several million dollars in the bank later the sight each and every umpire would pawn their gold badge to see, actually occurred.'

The following day the McEnroe family – John, Tatum and young sons Kevin and Sean – escaped photographers camped outside their hotel by exiting through the garbage trollies by the back door. Gerry Armstrong received an anonymous death threat. He is now the Wimbledon referee and McEnroe the sport's sagest commentator.

* * *

The sport was in need of some fun and games. Behind the scenes in the men's game, there was talk of breakaways and player power, vested interests and crude tactics. A players' tour was touted; the performers wanted a bigger cut of the cash swilling around in the game and threatened revolt.

The Men's Tennis Council, which oversaw the rules and regulations, didn't want any erosion of its power base. Mark McCormack, famed head of International Management Group (IMG), which was responsible for marketing Wimbledon and also represented leading players, said that tennis required 'a breath of fresh air'. It arrived in March on McCormack's doorstep.

The Virginia Slims of Florida was staged at the Polo Club, Boca Raton, where Chris Evert owned a home. There was one entry to which all eyes were drawn, the 13-year-old Jennifer Capriati who was about to take the sport by storm. She had come to my notice in the week before my wedding, defeating Clare Wood of Britain 6-0, 6-0 in that final Wightman Cup humiliation.

Capriati held a conference call the week before the tournament with 15 journalists from around the world, enthralling us with her bubbling naivety. I had wanted to be there from the start but Peter Lea prevaricated. At the editor's conference on the Monday morning, David English asked why I wasn't at the event and before I knew it, I was packing for Florida.

Jennifer had Italian ancestry and country's foremost sports clothing company Diadora had dangled a deal worth $6m over six years in front of her parents. Diadora already had Boris Becker, the Dutch footballer Marco van Basten and the Italian football team on its books but was desperate for Capriati. Prince rackets were talking even grander figures. I asked her about Wimbledon, 'Yeah, all that grass, it's really neat.'

She said she didn't know how good she was going to be. 'No one can answer that but I'm going to have fun,' she told us. Her father Stefano, a former stuntman, said, without blinking, 'She's a killer, there's no doubt about that.'

Jen-Jen, as her family knew her, reached the final that first disbelieving week, eventually losing to Gabriela Sabatini. Five years earlier, at the age of 14, Gabriela had been the youngest player on the women's tour to reach a final. The torch of teenage abandon had been passed.

Capriati reached the fourth round of her first Wimbledon before succumbing to Steffi Graf, who in turn lost to American Zina Garrison who became only the second black woman after Althea Gibson to play a final on Centre Court. There, Zina would lose to Martina Navratilova who took her ninth, and last, singles title.

I tipped Ivan Lendl to win Wimbledon that year (I was perfectly sober). For more than two months in the spring, Lendl had been honing his grass-court game in Australia, staying at the home of Tony Roche, his coach. Roche said Lendl needed match practice but they were located in Salamander Bay, north of Newcastle, New South Wales, quite a way from regular tennis civilisation.

Roche went quietly about organising a small tournament for Lendl's benefit and asked some friends to play. When your friends are John Newcombe and Ken Rosewall, it is quite a party.

In front of an invited audience, Lendl played a set apiece against all three, regarding it as one of the highlights of his life, even when

Rosewall struck two backhand beauties beyond his reach and beat him with a backhand lob. Ivan made sure they were the only times Rosewall – 25 years his senior – won a rally.

He took the lessons learned on a hideaway location in furthest Australia into Queen's Club, where he won the pre-Wimbledon event, dropping a mere six games to John McEnroe in the semi-final and five to Boris Becker in the final.

Lendl might have won the championship he cherished above all else had not Stefan Edberg played the finest grass-court tennis of his life, defeating Ivan in the semis and extending Becker to five sets, over two days because of rain before the Swede edged a classic final.

I did have my own classic encounter with Ken Rosewall some years later. Neale Fraser, the 1960 Wimbledon champion and hugely successful Australian Davis Cup captain, became a firm friend and during one Australian Open invited me to Kingston Heath, a golf course on the Melbourne sand-belt regarded by many as the finest in all Christendom.

As we walked to the first tee, 'Frase' said he hoped I didn't mind but he had invited someone else to play. He introduced me to 'Muscles' Rosewall. Did I mind? This was heaven, playing golf with two tennis legends.

All was blessed until Ken, a left-handed golfer, struck his tee shot on the 18th into a steep-faced fairway bunker. Frase and I saw a club twice swishing into the air, bits of sand flying out but no ball. There was a pause and suddenly a crescendo of 'bugger, bugger, bugger' and the thumping sound of sand iron on sand.

* * *

No one, least of all me and my wife of less than a year, expected that I would become chief football writer of the *Daily Mail* in the late summer of 1990. The three years as tennis correspondent had been blissful, the world was pretty much my oyster, I was reporting on the exploits of some extraordinary icons of sport and life was good.

Every four years the football World Cup would coincide with Wimbledon and, though concentration was squarely on the tennis, England's exploits in 1990 were close to any patriot's heart and so, as the boys neared the final, anticipation grew and the Wimbledon press room became more agitated as the matches mounted in significance.

We wanted to feel part of the sea change in the English game, inspired by a team moulded by Bobby Robson who, with such notables as Gary Lineker, Bryan Robson, Peter Shilton and an emerging maverick called Paul Gascoigne in their ranks, was increasingly daring.

The semi-final against the West Germans was – as something in the pit of the stomach forewarned – a savage let-down. The images of Chris Waddle and Stuart Pearce as they missed the decisive penalties were seared on our hearts.

For that summer – our first as a married couple – I was preparing to take Maureen to her parents before some 'we' time on Cape Cod at our regular home from home, the Beach House at Bass River. I would then pack my bags for New York and another two weeks of mayhem at the US Open. But something had come up.

Len Gould was the new *Mail* sports editor after the departure of Peter Lea. He asked me after Wimbledon why I hadn't applied for the football job. To be honest, I hadn't realised that Jeff Powell, the best football writer in the country for 20 years, had been promoted to a more wide-ranging brief. Even if I had, my reaction would have been the same – lovely job but what chance have I got to succeed him?

The football writing talent across the board in England was immense. I could count at least a dozen candidates who had more experience, know-how, contacts and writing ability than me. To my mind, Len's question answered itself.

The boss asked me to join him for a drink in Scribes, the watering hole of a generation of journalists that had – since the *Mail* transferred its headquarters from antiquated Tudor Street to the bright and busy Kensington High Street – relocated in our wake and transfigured into Scribes West.

I walked down to the bar and found Len with Powell being pampered, as was his wont, by Geoffrey Van-Hay, a legend of the Fleet Street drinking world who had managed the famed El Vino before transferring to Scribes. I wasn't important enough to be one of those journalists around whom 'Van' fluttered condescendingly but perhaps that was about to change.

The gist of the conversation was that if I put my hand up, they would back my application and I stood a fair chance of success. Then again, editor David English was a fervent tennis fan and might not want me to abandon a sport I thought I'd covered with a decent degree of success.

My unexpected support team didn't believe that would be a problem. Stiffened by their egging on and wondering what I had to lose apart from soul-destroying rejection, I said I'd be interested. I sent no formal written application. Len and Jeff said they'd make the appropriate people know I was keen.

Thinking back on it, Jeff couldn't lose in promoting me in his stead. He knew he was the far better football writer and that future questions about my suitability for the role would inevitably begin with, 'He's not a patch on Powell.'

* * *

A couple of weeks later, Ina Miller, David English's PA, approached me on the editorial floor. I wouldn't say that such an occasion made one nervous but Ina – the wife of the *Mail on Sunday* and former *Daily Mirror* chief football writer Harry Miller – cut a forbidding figure.

Her hair was styled in a tan-coloured 1960s beehive and her eyes lined with the darkest mascara I'd ever seen. She reminded me of a middle-aged Dusty Springfield. Any curl and beckoning gesture of Ina's index finger struck fear into the heart of the sturdiest journalist. It meant the editor was demanding an audience.

David was Sir David by this time, knighted for his services to journalism (and the Conservative Party) as a stalwart supporter of Margaret Thatcher, who gained unswerving loyalty from the *Mail* under his stewardship.

Mrs Thatcher's daughter Carol appeared regularly on the pages of the paper, writing across the features spectrum, often promoting all manner of winter sports, a particular favourite of the boss. Carol and I once covered the British bobsleigh team's preparation for the 1988 Winter Olympics in the Italian resort of Cervinia. These were very brave people.

Needless to say, when a chance presented itself to have a go in the bob down a fearsome ride, Carol stepped up and I played my (genuine) hangover for all it was worth and chickened out. If the *Mail* sports pages were filled only with skiing, bob and tennis, English would have loved it.

The only time I had personal dealings with the editor during my time as the tennis correspondent came in 1988, when Steffi Graf won the Wimbledon singles for the first time at the age of 19.

For some reason Peter Graf took a shine both to myself and Malcolm Folley, my predecessor at the *Mail* who had moved back to the *Daily Express* via a short-lived spell with a project called *Sportsweek* – a glossy magazine that never caught the imagination or readership it had rightly aspired to.

Peter ushered Malcolm and I to a small bar in the corner of the members' restaurant, where journalists were not really welcome, and gave chapter and verse on his daughter's success and why she would be a dominant champion for the next ten years. This was manna for the Monday edition.

We chose to ignore the fact that Mr Graf was taking slugs from a brandy glass and had tomato ketchup stains down his white shirt, which made for a not entirely pleasing scene. Then again, if the brandy fortified his convictions and enhanced his quotability, what the heck.

The daily paper news reporters – an unfortunate by-product of the power of Wimbledon – were unshakeable and invasive on these occasions and found out we had cornered Mr Graf. The *Mail*'s newsdesk asked me for his number, which I wouldn't give them. They persisted.

English became involved and I told him I'd worked hard to gain the Grafs' trust which could suffer irreparable damage if a news reporter started to poke his nose into a sports story.

Talking this firmly to an editor was a bit of a risk but if Steffi was to be the player her father championed – and she was – I needed to stay as close as possible to them and that ultimately the paper would benefit. English told me to keep the number to myself and I'm sure the fact that I managed to get a couple of Centre Court tickets for friends of Lady English that year helped my cause.

* * *

As Ina and I made our way across the editorial floor towards the editor's office, I could sense necks were craned and eyes raised. What's Harman been up to?

Ina told me that if David showed me to the settee in the corner it generally meant positive news and if he drew back the chair across from his at his desk, I should steel myself for something less appealing. The armpits began to moisten.

She tapped on the door, announced me, David rose from his chair and said, 'Neil, come and sit over here,' gesturing to the sofa. I had a bit of a knee tremble. The next five minutes or so were a blur but I do recall he said something about tennis being a prized job, how well I'd done, but that football was the most important position in the sports department and I'd earned the chance to take over. I asked if I could talk it through with Maureen. He said I had 24 hours.

There was only one decision a journalist could make in these circumstances. It was the job to which I'd secretly hankered, never believing I was equipped for it and worried I didn't have the requisite talent to do it properly. But here it was jangling in front of me. A fool would say no.

I asked Ina for an appointment to see David the next day and once he was free from scheduled meetings, I was invited back to his office and told him I'd be proud to accept the challenge. We shook hands and it was done.

It was a giddy sensation. I crossed the floor to where the sports guys were full of congratulatory handshakes and good wishes. We poured into Scribes where Geoffrey Van-Hay and I became best buddies. I was 33 years old and about to set forth on an incredible journey.

* * *

On 24 August, this letter landed on my doorstep:

> *Dear Neil,*
> *I am delighted to appoint you as from 1 September chief football writer of the* Daily Mail.
>
> *This is one of the most important jobs on the paper and it is a tremendous step forward in your career to succeed to this title.*
>
> *You have got it because you have earned it. I wish everybody had the same dedicated and enthusiastic approach to their work as you have. I very much respect it and am pleased to reward it.*
>
> *Your salary will be increased by £5,000 a year from 1 September and, with this new position, you will be given a company car. Please see Brian Vine or Garth Burden* [the managing editor and his deputy] *about this.*
>
> *I look forward to reading your reports with interest and, even more, to discussing specials and features with you on the very intriguing wide world of football.*
>
> *Yours sincerely,*
> *David English*

There was now the *Mail*'s tennis position to consider. Len didn't really know of anyone in that particular world and so asked me if I would suggest any candidates who might be talented enough to join the paper.

I told the boss that there was a lad who had recently partnered Chris Martin in his freelance radio business and wrote with a very nice touch for *The Independent*. I thought he had the right stuff for the role. I recommended Mike Dickson.

9

The Football Job

MY FATHER had passed away from prostate cancer in 1983 and so the elation in my heart at this major transformation in my life was tempered by wishing I could have seen his face when I told him.

Mum wasn't sure what to think when I invited her to dinner at the lovely Padrino Pizzeria on the seafront in Westcliff-on-Sea seven years later, on the premise of having something special to announce. I felt she was slightly disappointed when I didn't say she was going to be a granny.

I remained torn between gratitude for the job, insecure about performing it well enough for a paper I loved and an eagerness to get started. I had a new set of writers with whom to engage, the *crème de la crème* of football reportage, those at the very top of their game whose verdicts framed the public's perceptions and could make – and often ruin – a career.

How would they take to me? Would I be perceived as worthy of the accolade I'd been given or someone they could push around? How many of them had applied for the *Mail* job for goodness sake? For a tennis correspondent to become chief football writer in one spectacular bound was unheard of.

There was one important ace in the hand I'd been dealt. Graham Taylor had succeeded Bobby Robson at the helm of the English game. He was a *Mail* reader, despised my predecessor and was eager to covet any journalist he could, given such a pressurised position. I wondered if he had remembered an occasion when we had crossed swords.

Taylor was appointed England's youth-team coach under Robson, a move that was not without its controversies. Back in my northern beat days, I wrote a piece about young players being withheld from youth-team gatherings because of what certain club managers felt was Taylor's primitive tactical approach at Watford.

Graham was beside himself and said that 'these people' – the managers I quoted – were confusing the boys, 'The players read about things that are said to have happened at Lilleshall [the FA training HQ in Shropshire] that simply did not happen. My remit from Bobby was to get them [the youth players] to play in a more positive and progressive manner and has nothing whatsoever to do with being manager of Watford.'

Now Taylor had won English football's first prize after proving his worth at Aston Villa where he oversaw promotion to the First Division in 1988, and inspired those he coached to give Liverpool the only run for their title money in 1989/90. Howard Kendall and Joe Royle had their supporters but it was to Taylor, seen as a coach on the up and an FA 'type', that the governing body turned.

* * *

The number ones were an eclectic mix and like all sports writing cabals they worked to diverse moods and rhythms. It was a reassurance that two of their number had been colleagues at the *Mail*. Colin Gibson at the *Daily Telegraph* and Harry Harris at the *Daily Mirror* had worked in the *Mail*'s London office and I considered them acquaintances even if our paths crossed only occasionally.

My direct opposition in the middle-market domain was Steve Curry of the *Daily Express*, a Lancastrian who reminded me much of Phil Brown from the newsagent in Leigh-on-Sea. Steve was 15 years my senior, given to wearing flamboyant shirts but more importantly he possessed a well-thumbed contacts book and an impressive track record for breaking stories. Steve led with his chin, which possessed the sharpest cleft I'd seen.

Curry had been around the top of the game a long time and everyone seemed to get on with him, Jeff Powell for one. They were regarded as professional running mates despite working for rival papers when every copy sold really mattered.

I could sense that Curry discerned in me a far more appealing opponent and felt he now had our particular field to himself. If I had been in his shoes I'd have wondered what possible threat a tennis writer, albeit one with some football experience, could really pose.

The *Mirror* and *Sun* were too engaged going for each other's throats to worry much about me. There was no personal love lost between Harris and *The Sun*'s number one, Alex Montgomery, a Scot of stature both in size and journalistic reputation. Harry could be excessively irritating yet there was something oddly personable about him. He used up an awful lot of newsprint, some stories more fanciful than others.

Tony Quested, not long since a local reporter in Blackpool, had risen without trace to become the *Daily Star*'s number one, though Bob Driscoll, the paper's chief sports writer and Montgomery's good friend, never strayed far from the scene.

Then there was Rob Shepherd who had been at *Today* with me on day one in 1986 and had lost none of the enthusiasm and tenacity that unnerved some of the elder press-box dwellers. Shep had made a significant mark on Italia '90 when he was parachuted in at the last minute to cover England after his predecessor Bob Harris suddenly left the paper.

Shep was in a small advance party of writers who arrived at the Forte Village headquarters in Sardinia a couple of days before the official FA bandwagon landed. The group had decided to dine together that evening.

He checked in with his office as soon as he reached his room to be informed that decent intelligence had reached *Today* that manager Bobby Robson had told the FA he was leaving after the tournament to take over as head coach of the Dutch club PSV Eindhoven.

Rob called a couple of FA bigwigs, neither of whom would deny the story, so he wrote it.

As those he was due to dine with started without him, Shep waited until *Today*'s first edition was off the presses and then he broke gently to them what he had done. To seek verification from the horse's mouth, Curry rang Robson who said it was true and gave the lads a couple of quotes to use. The England team landed the next day into a fusillade of camera flashes, microphones and hostile questions.

Shep would have been delirious at getting a scoop on his first day in the role, except that the front page of his paper carried the headline 'Lock Him In The Tower' over a comment piece essentially calling Robson a traitor.

It was a prime example of how news reporters and comment writers could completely fuck up the relations between sports writers and their contacts on which papers thrived and not really give a damn.

* * *

The broadsheet correspondents were a splendid mix. Colin Gibson was a shrewd operator who knew which way football's political wind blew and wrote and spoke with an impressive command of his brief. When Jacques Georges, president of UEFA, the European governing body, couldn't see Colin at one press conference and asked, 'Ou est Monsieur le Grand?' his nickname just had to become Mr Big.

The Times's Stuart Jones was the son of Peter Jones, the bedrock of radio sports coverage on the BBC, who perfected the art of commentating so that the listener was held captive by a voice that would have felt soothing when describing the greatest sporting events in the world or reciting *A Book at Bedtime*.

There was something in Peter's manner that oozed calm authority. In concert with Bryon Butler, the BBC's football correspondent, they could not be bettered. Bryon's 15-minute preview of the day's football at 1.15pm on Saturday was lyrical poetry and delivered with absolute authority. And there were no ex-footballers around to call them Jonesy or Butters or any of the folksy shit that fills today's airwaves.

Peter, who had commentated on numerous World Cups, Olympic Games, Wimbledon championships and occasions of state, would tragically collapse with microphone in hand at the 1990 University Boat Race and pass away a couple of days later at the tender age of 60.

His son was a character in his own right. Stuart, too, possessed a syrupy voice – though smoking too much added to its bass texture – as well as a very pleasing turn of phrase but, as I would discover over the ensuing months, he had a disregard for timekeeping and a quirky manner that could have been construed as indifference to his role.

Stuart didn't drive and was thus held captive by British Rail's untrustworthy services, often arriving flustered in his seat ten minutes after kick-off to ask for the 'salient points' from his neighbour in the press box who'd then have to describe the action to the point of Jones's appearance.

He would sit throughout a match with huge earphones clamped to the sides of his head. Whether he was listening to the BBC radio commentary or Genesis, cutting yourself off from the atmosphere inside a ground limited your ability to properly gauge the occasion on which you were reporting.

David Lacey was *The Guardian*'s correspondent, a quite lovely man whose work was never anything other than beautifully crafted. He had a sense of the mischievous, a questioning mind, piercing insight and when you read his pieces, either match reports, features and especially his Monday column, it was with a degree of awe unmatched by many before or since. David never had to strain for effect.

You could hardly have found two more polar opposites than David and *The Independent*'s number one, Joe Lovejoy. Joe was peppery in character and language. I liked both him and his talents enormously. The man could write a brilliant piece.

There were other regulars, notably Michael Hart of the *London Evening Standard*, known as 'Coach' because of his shrewd tactical appreciation. Coach was a West Ham nut like quite a few of the lads. Bob 'Bomber' Harris, with his outlandish collection of colourfully framed glasses, had worked for United Newspapers, a conglomerate of regional titles, when he wasn't writing books, one of which seemed to be published every other week. He was now sports editor of the *Sunday Mirror.*

Without me having much say in the matter, Steve Curry and Colin Gibson chose to anoint me a Morris Man. It had become a rolling saga in the football-writing fraternity that Steve and Gibbo in concert with Jones and Harris formed an alliance designed to cover their arses by sharing information at appropriate moments. They were christened the Morris Dancers.

There were no restrictions on doing your own thing. That could never have been tolerated. In my circumstances I was happy to aid self-preservation and was accepted into the group as Morris Minor. The guys were great company, Colin and Steve loved to hold court and what they didn't know about football hardly seemed worth knowing.

Nights abroad around a restaurant table often ended with Steve's particular party piece. He would rise, clear his throat, clasp the front of his shirt and – as incredulous diners around us replaced their cutlery – launched into the St Crispin's Day soliloquy from Shakespeare's *Henry V*, Act IV.

'We few, we happy few, we band of brothers;
For he today that sheds his blood with me
Shall be my brother; be he ne'er so vile,
This day shall gentle his condition:

And gentlemen in England now a-bed
Shall think themselves accursed they were not here,
And hold their manhoods cheap whiles any speaks
That fought with us upon Saint Crispin's day.'

We'd leave many foreign premises to roars of approval, even if most of the customers hadn't got a clue what he'd been going on about.

* * *

Becoming the number one writer on any sport on a national newspaper brought accolades and envy in equal measure. I already knew that. Brian Scovell, who took on the lion's share of the England coverage for the *Mail* at Italia '90, had been leapfrogged. Nick Townsend, a new talent recently signed by the paper, probably thought he had a chance of the main job.

Brian, a former *Daily Sketch* man, had been the eternal number two in cricket to *Mail* correspondents Alex Bannister, Peter Smith and Peter Johnson, and probably didn't want to give up his favourite sport entirely. If you were a chief football writer, those lazy, hazy summer days at The Oval would become a thing of the past.

How would Brian and I get on? He was a total gentleman though I sensed his ego had been deflated by David English's decision not to promote him. This could be a bloody cut-throat business. I simply had to try to make sure I did the job I had been asked to do and not worry what others thought of me.

The day after the editor's letter confirmed me in the job, the headline on my introductory piece was 'Dawn of the Crusader', not about me but Paul Gascoigne. I was granted an interview by virtue of my new position and chose to pinpoint the perils of the English game asking too much of a single character, however frighteningly talented.

'It is a long time – probably since Manchester United wondered whether George Best would turn up for the kick-off at all – that the ideals of a new season are harnessed to the precociousness of one man. How remarkable that he remains so outwardly unaffected by it,' I wrote.

'I'm worried I'm built up so high,' Gazza said. 'Sometimes I feel like doing a runner for a few days and just hide. I'm safer on the field with my boots and strip on. When I'm in the centre of the pitch no one can get to me.'

The last line of the piece was delivered with as much optimism as I could muster, 'Reach for the sky, lads. Lead them there, Gazza.'

The article called on Graham Taylor to have the courage of his convictions, whatever they may be. I asked that Matthew Le Tissier of Southampton be given the chance to shine internationally. Gascoigne and Le Tissier together could open the most stubborn of defences. I also tipped David Rocastle of Arsenal and Manchester City's Paul Lake for places in Taylor's first squad.

The initial post-Italia '90 England trip didn't involve players at all. It was a reconnaissance mission for the lead writers with the manager to Budapest, as Hungary were coming to Wembley for a friendly a week later and their opponents, Turkey, were drawn in the same qualifying group as England for the 1992 European Championship.

That first night in a plush restaurant overlooking the Danube was cordial and positive. Taylor had an open manner and an ease and self-confidence in the company of journalists. He was certainly loquacious, there was something of the Humphrey Appleby in his tactical explanations. We'd start to learn some of his favoured comments, such as 'not wishing to appear boastful', or 'without putting a halo over my head', which were generally followed either by a boast or a sense that he was absolutely sure of his ground.

Graham hadn't long settled into his position when he invited Maureen and I to join he and his wife Rita for an evening meal and a performance of *Bubbling Brown Sugar* at a theatre in Birmingham. It was a very pleasant evening.

Steve Curry found out about it and his reaction shook me. 'You should have said no,' he said. 'It looks like you're accepting a bribe.' I think he was pissed off that I might become closer to the new manager than he would. After all, Steve had a long-standing friendship with Bobby Robson which probably extended to a personal invitation or two.

It didn't take long to realise this job offered not a minute's respite from scrutiny from your office, fellow writers and the entire company of football and that if reporting on England was the golden burden, the First Division contained a cast of characters jostling for attention and not shy in complaining if they felt you were favouring another. There was a daily clattering and clashing of inflated egos.

Starting out, I was happy to be on first-name terms with a few managers in post – Brian Clough (Nottingham Forest), Howard Kendall (Manchester City) and Steve Coppell (Crystal Palace). In Kendall's case I was still 'lad' and to Clough I remained 'young Neil Harman'.

It was time to acquaint myself with those I knew about only from what I'd read and seen on television and who were going to be central to my writing. I needed to meet George Graham at Arsenal and Terry Venables at Tottenham (both great mates of Jeff Powell), Bobby Campbell at Chelsea, Howard Wilkinson at Leeds United and two Scottish variations on an enigma, Kenny Dalglish at Liverpool and a chap by the name of Alex Ferguson at Manchester United.

* * *

It was going to take time for these men to get used to me and giving a new kid a break wasn't something I should expect. I knew Graham and Venables would be tough to break down because they had known and respected Powell from their playing days and confided in him for years.

They were hardly likely to offer unswerving allegiance to someone who just happened to be the *Mail*'s new football 'voice'. What was Jeff telling them about me? In all likelihood he would say what was in *his* best interests rather than mine. I'd have to fight this battle on my own. I soon had a battle to write about.

Graham was standoffish and arrogant and chances of building a mutually agreeable relationship were dashed when Arsenal went to Old Trafford in October and became embroiled in a free-for-all against Manchester United. The unholy spectacle of 21 players and coaching staff going hammer and tongs at each other demanded a comment from the correspondent. It was the first occasion to make a stand – eight weeks into the job and about two of the biggest clubs in the land.

I knew the story had to be handled sensitively. Arsenal reacted almost before I could. Chairman Peter Hill-Wood and his board chose to fine Graham and five of his players – Nigel Winterburn, Paul Davis, Anders Limpar, David Rocastle and Michael Thomas – each two weeks' wages.

The FA summoned the clubs along with the referee Keith Hackett – who had booked two players when he could have sent off five – and imposed £50,000 fines on both clubs and controversially deducted two points from Arsenal and one from United.

My take was, 'Arsenal have attracted unwelcome headlines in recent months followed by a litany of fines and poisonous invective. All this does little to enhance anyone's reputation indeed it reflects more than anyone on the man at the top. That man is the manager. For the chairman to have given him such a public dressing-down is little short of extraordinary.'

This was hardly going to endear me to Graham but it needed to be said. What nobody could have known was that these would be the first shots in a rivalry destined to get a lot uglier as time passed. As would my relations with both managers.

* * *

On the face of it, Terry Venables ought to have been a more straightforward personality to deal with. He had an outward charm, a remarkable record as a coach, and Tottenham – though long since a recognisable title pretender – played football with a daring dash that attracted acclaim if not enough points.

I say 'on the face of it' because I wasn't aware at the time just how enmeshed Venables was in the throes of entrepreneurship.

It wasn't as if you had to go far to find him, for he had taken a large slice of equity in the Scribes West club directly beneath the *Mail*'s offices on Kensington High Street. To what extent wasn't initially clear, though Geoffrey Van-Hay was around one day and the next he seemed to have disappeared.

Jeff Powell would be back and forth to Scribes, which had become a secondary *Mail* HQ. I needed to show my face there regularly in case some deal or other was being done which I – and the readers – should know about. Bloody hell, it was like a revolving door of lawyers, business partners, journalists, agents and hangers-on. A sort of Tramp for scamps.

Terry loved playing the *bon viveur* but I found the place classless and superficial. This was emphasised when Eric Hall, the agent known for his 'Monster, Monster' catchphrase and who clung to Venables like a limpet, picked up the microphone on karaoke nights. It was time to head for home. Give me the Abercromby any day of the week.

Though the fault of neither of us, this was an awful time to try to get close to Dalglish. Less than 18 months had passed since the horrors of Hillsborough, Kenny had taken it upon himself to be the city's conscience and the responsibility was bearing down on his ability to manage with a clear sight of his priorities.

The Liverpool 'mafia' of local writers still proved fiercely protective of the manager, the team and their patch. Our own man Colin Wood, though I admired him immensely, was never overly welcoming when I used my chief football writer's prerogative to cover either Liverpool or Everton.

Reading Kenny's autobiography *Dalglish,* I gained a genuine sense of the man's anguish, as he wrote, 'I would not admit to myself that I was under pressure. Why should I feel pressure? The people under pressure were those who had lost loved ones [at Hillsborough]. All I had lost were tears.

'But I *was* under pressure and realised as much before I left Liverpool. I had become unpleasant company at home. I was shouting at the kids. I didn't want to become this tetchy father who kept bawling his children out. It became pretty obvious I had to get out. I had wanted to leave in 1990, the year before I eventually resigned.'

Alex Ferguson was exceedingly wary and needed to establish if I was to be friend or foe. Steve Curry, Colin Gibson and Stuart Jones never disguised their bias where United were concerned. They may as well have worn red rosettes in the press box.

Was it a condition of Morris membership that I should become a red as well? I hadn't been a United apologist when Ron Atkinson was manager so why would I start now?

On the contrary; I became deliberately nuanced when writing about the club, preferring to counter my colleagues' red-misted positivity with a more sceptical approach. I might have gone a tad too far the other way and my reporting on United didn't take long to get right up Ferguson's nose.

Any negative review was greeted with an intimidating scowl. When he gave you that look, it wasn't easy to retain calm. He told Curry he mistrusted me because of the paper I worked for (he loathed the *Mail* which meant it was the first he read each morning), I was from the south of England and worst of all was a 'fucking referee' who knew the laws of the game almost certainly better than he did.

If referees were the United manager's weekly target practice, a journalist who refereed and regularly took their side in debates and match reports was akin to a boil he couldn't lance.

On 26 September 1992 I reported on a goalless draw at Old Trafford between United and Queens Park Rangers. It was an untidy game, interrupted by several questionable decisions. Ferguson was asked – not by me – to comment on the referee's performance. He fixed me with a withering stare, pointed and said, 'Why don't you ask Mr fucking Harman, he knows all the rules.' I thought it quite the tribute.

Ferguson hadn't objected to my face about anything I'd written until the League Cup Final at Wembley in March 1991 between United and Sheffield Wednesday, of the Second Division and where my old chum Ron Atkinson was the manager, and I considered it more likely I'd get a decent preview line from him rather than Alex.

We met at Hillsborough and Ron was persuasively confident about Wednesday's chances, enough so that I tipped the lower-league side to win, an opinion at variance with every paper bar the *Sheffield Morning Telegraph*. Curry told me I was bonkers. Wednesday won 1-0.

Ferguson didn't make anything of it in the official press conference but turned a couple of days later, raging that I bore a grudge against United because I preferred Atkinson to him – I'd known Ron for 14 years and Alex less than eight months – and that my article was a disgrace to fair reporting.

If United's manager would be so touchy over a preview, what if I wrote something *really* contentious, like the end of the road was nigh for him if United didn't win a title soon? The club's board had demonstrated remarkable patience where he was concerned.

What improved Ferguson's position dramatically was his team's performance in Rotterdam three weeks after the League Cup loss when United lifted the European Cup Winners' Cup against the mighty Barcelona, coached by Johan Cruyff and tormented for much of the night by an old player of theirs, Mark Hughes.

In full, physical flow, there were few players to touch 'Sparky' with his thighs like tree trunks that offered explosive power in both right foot and left. He was bloody brave with it. He really did let his feet do the talking for it rarely proved rewarding to ask him for a quote. How did a person so outwardly shy play with such devastating self-confidence?

The second of his two goals was quite brilliant, running on to a threaded pass from Bryan Robson, forced out to a crazy angle by goalkeeper Carles Busquets and smacking the ball as hard as he could with the outside of his right foot into the bottom-left corner of the net. Ferguson described his team as heroes and legends.

They were still a long way from a title-winning side, though. United completed the domestic season in sixth place, a distant 24 points behind champions Arsenal.

Then came the summer break and the sprouting buds of an upheaval in English football whose effect on Ferguson and the rest of us would last for years to come.

* * *

The Football Association Council's summer meeting was generally an occasion for a gathering of worthies to indulge in social chit-chat and supplement their tans. The venue for the 1991 gathering was Torquay, on the Devon riviera, so an application or two of factor 30 was on the cards.

I had never attended one of these jollies before but in the company of Steve Curry, Colin Gibson, Joe Melling of the *Mail on Sunday* and our ladies it seemed like a good excuse for a few days away. We stayed in a lovely village named North Huish, half an hour from the coast.

FA chief executive Graham Kelly – a more genial fellow than his public persona suggested – greeted us one morning by introducing us to Rick Parry as 'someone you lads need to get to know'. Rick, with his wavy hair and eccentric shirts, was a financial consultant at Ernst & Young who had been employed to see an extraordinary mission through.

Parry's plan – not entirely revolutionary – was to break up the age-old 92-club Football League and establish at the helm of the game a standalone, self-governing 18-club Premier League which would have the effect of enhancing the England national team's hopes of success. The FA endorsed this enthusiastically.

Manchester United, Liverpool, Tottenham, Arsenal and Everton – none of whom gave a tuppenny toss about England – had been foremost in negotiating a deal serving their interests and, to be frank, let the rest fall as they may. The majority of professional football clubs shuddered.

As far back as 1982 I'd written a piece for the *Mail* with United chairman Martin Edwards who responded to the Liverpool chairman John Smith's revelation that an English Super League was being considered, something that caused shudders all the way down the professional ladder. Smith said, 'Wealthy clubs are helping others who don't want to help themselves.'

The headline on my Edwards interview was 'Poor relations pull United down'. He said, 'Sooner or later people at my level are going to have to be brave. It is unrealistic in today's world for the poorer clubs to expect the big clubs to bail them out. I believe a Football League continuing with 92 clubs is ridiculous.

'Hard-earned money is being syphoned off and going out of the game which sorely needs it. The time has come for people to vote against what may be in their best interests and in favour of what is proper for the future of football.'

Fast forward nine years, the scene hadn't shifted and now defining decisions were to be made. If United remained the most glamorous club in England, it was upon Tottenham that much of the financial spotlight would be trained. Nothing at White Hart Lane was ever quite what it seemed.

* * *

In his autobiographical tome *What You See Is What You Get*, the entrepreneur Alan Sugar reflected on the spring of 1991 when he was reading about 'a lot of aggravation going on with Spurs' finances and how the club was on the verge of bankruptcy'.

It was a year that would be profound in the history of a club that registered powerfully in my memory because John Hall – my sister's then husband – had taken me to White Hart Lane in 1970 to watch a friendly against Glasgow Rangers where I was lifted on to a seat on the dirt track in front of the terracing.

I had seen Jimmy Greaves, Alan Gilzean, Mike England and Pat Jennings at close quarters and so I felt some affinity with Tottenham. For the next seven years of my writing life, the events at the club would not stray far from the back page and several others.

Sugar was at home watching the 1991 FA Cup Final between Spurs and Nottingham Forest where much of the pre-match interaction surrounded Paul Gascoigne and his upcoming move to Lazio of Rome. The £5.5m being discussed as the transfer fee would radically reduce the club's restrictive debt. Gazza refused to sign until he had played at Wembley.

Sugar recalled, 'The fans weren't happy but saw this as part and parcel of the survival of this famous club. We [Sugar had been taken to Spurs by his father and uncle in the 1950s] beat Forest but Gascoigne suffered a serious knee injury which meant the transfer to Lazio was off and the £5.5m wouldn't be coming.

'To this day I don't know what possessed me but the following Monday I put in a call to Spurs manager Terry Venables. The newspapers had been reporting on various consortiums buying the club from existing owner Irving Scholar but all failed because none of them had the funding.

'There was talk that Venables was trying to put his own consortium together but was at loggerheads with Scholar who as chairman had been cast as the guy responsible for the club's demise. Scholar was the devil and Venables the white knight – only without any money.'

As a result of his call to Venables, a meeting was called at the Hilton Hotel in Park Lane where Sugar met Terry's business associate Eddie Ashby. Sugar was invited to match Venables' £3m and provide a fighting fund to buy Scholar's shares and those of another shareholder, Paul Bobroff, to take control of the company.

'It never dawned on me to challenge whether Venables actually *had* £3m of his own money,' Sugar said.

Alan had been a rising star in the financial firmament when at 21 he formed a company called Amstrad, from Alan Michael Sugar Trading, that began with him selling car radio aerials from the back of a van and became a behemoth in the home computer market. He didn't splash the cash willy-nilly.

The moment Sugar thought his part in the purchase of Tottenham was settled, a fly landed in the ointment in the formidable shape of Robert Maxwell, the owner of Mirror Group Newspapers, who was fixated with becoming a big mover and shaker in the football world. *He* was going to be Spurs' saviour. The story, dictated by Maxwell to Harry Harris, was all over his own newspaper and quite a few others besides once word got out. Sugar said Maxwell 'was full of shit' and called his bluff.

Maxwell went off in a huff and Sugar put £3m on the table to secure his side of the deal. Ashby then said there was a 'technical issue' with Venables' money. It would take a couple of days for it to be sorted. Sugar thought, 'What the bloody hell have I let myself in for with this pair?'

The Venables money still hadn't arrived when Tottenham convened a press conference to announce the takeover. A few days later the cash was banked, though Sugar said, 'I never thought of asking whether it was from Venables' own pocket or whether it had come by way of some form of funding or loan. I was just grateful to receive it.' That sense of gratitude wouldn't last long.

The memories of Spurs' 1991 FA Cup campaign lingered for many moons longer than Venables and Sugar worked together. Gazza more or less won every tie with extraordinary goals and unfettered brilliance. Oxford, Notts County and Portsmouth were all torn asunder by him.

In the first FA Cup semi-final played at Wembley rather than a neutral club venue – a precedent of which I was hugely critical – he struck a 30-yard free kick past Arsenal's goalkeeper David Seaman that reverberates over 30 years later. That was north London taken care of.

I had heard that Gascoigne was in Scribes West the evening before the final against Nottingham Forest, consuming brandy. His team-mates knew him to need mind and body settled on the eve of massive matches and so much was riding on this one. In the hours leading up to the final itself, he was metaphorically climbing the dressing-room walls.

He was all over the place in the opening exchanges, raising his right foot kung-fu style into the chest of Forest's Garry Parker. It was a clear red-card offence. Instead of sending Gazza off, referee Roger Milford gestured for him to calm down. This was crazily indulgent officiating.

Not long after, as Gary Charles burst into a dangerous forward position, Gascoigne took a massive right-legged swipe which caught the Forest full-back flush on the shin. Charles hopped to his feet but the tackler had injured himself seriously, tearing the cruciate ligaments around his knee. As he was being stretchered off, Gazza asked Spurs physiotherapist John Sheridan if he would play again.

The loss of Gascoigne for a year dashed myriad plans and promises. Lazio refused – with justification – to contemplate paying the amount they had agreed with Spurs; the player was damaged mentally as well as physically and Graham Taylor's preparation for the rest of England's European Championship qualifying campaign was right up in the air.

* * *

Before a few not-so tranquil days in Torquay, we undertook a more demanding journey. England embarked on a trip no one really wanted except the press and Gary Lineker. Taylor was bequeathed a tour of Australia, New Zealand and Malaysia that encompassed seven flights and four matches in 13 days.

I was settling in for the first leg from London to Bangkok and found myself next to Rob Shepherd, which promised to make it a lively trip. Shep never could keep still until the slightest touch of turbulence when he would go rigid in his seat. This meant 19 hours or so of constant anxiety between alcoholic refills. We arrived in Sydney very much the worse for wear.

Taylor was pissed – in the metaphorical sense – that the FA had rubber-stamped the trip so soon after the 1990 World Cup in the midst of the qualification process for the 1992 Euros and it was designated a 'full' tour. He appreciated England had to fly the flag but why have to go to the other side of the world to brandish it?

His squad was not the mightiest England had sent on a diplomatic mission. Goalkeeper Peter Shilton and central defender Terry Butcher had retired after Italia '90 and neither Peter Beardsley nor Bryan Robson were to figure prominently in Taylor's time. I think back now and realise that Graham was never sure of himself in the company of those players with far more significant profiles than his own.

The injury to Paul Gascoigne had rendered him *hors de combat* and so there were several surprise names in the party.

John Salako, Brian Deane, Earl Barrett, David Batty, Geoff Thomas, David Hirst and Nigel Clough wouldn't turn a head in an airport departure lounge. Taylor had to put out scratch teams and it was no wonder the results were scratchy too. One unforgettable moment was the first touch by Salako of Crystal Palace as a second-half substitute in Sydney, an impudent drag-back which left an Aussie defender floundering. He was a confident young pup.

As the tour unfolded, so Gary Lineker's career route was taking him in his autumn years to pastures new. Japan were preparing to launch the professional J.League and a player like Lineker with his profile, personality and goals would deliver rich commercial dividends.

A team named Grampus Eight, with close links to the Toyota motor company, was to be located in Nagoya. Japan wanted a superstar to help sell its league, Tottenham needed the money, Lineker had played abroad before and as his playing days were winding down, why not enjoy one last adventure?

What upset Taylor was that he felt his captain should be concentrating on international responsibilities, rather than using the trip to feather his individual nest. Even the fact that Gary would return to score all four goals in the final tour match against Malaysia in Kuala Lumpur on a horribly humid night would not quell the manager's innate sense of betrayal.

He was exasperated by the whole affair, 'If we had lost any of the games, no consideration would have been given to the players having to make their debuts. All hell would have been let loose at home.' Taylor only had a few months to wait for that prophesy to come back and bite him on the arse.

Talking of which, Steve Harrison's promotion to England coach had alarmed the FA. Harrison, an old friend of Taylor's, was on that arduous trip and at Wellington airport he emerged on to the baggage carousel in the foetal position. Those crusty stalwarts with three lions on their blazers looked on incredulously.

Millwall, the club to which Harrison was attached at the time, was preparing to sack him for 'conduct unbecoming'. I wrote that if this was true, his position with England was untenable. His party piece was – it was said – to defecate into a paper cup while balanced on the top of a wardrobe.

My article on his status with the national team ended with the line, 'There is a danger of English football falling between two stools.' Harrison soon departed.

* * *

Of the seven qualifying groups for the 1992 European Championship, England were drawn in one of the two that contained four teams. The rest had five. Taylor's men would face the Republic of Ireland under Jack Charlton, Poland and Turkey. Each of the six matches proved an absolute slog.

A few highlights stood out if the matches themselves didn't particularly. A late headed equaliser from Tony Cascarino – an old favourite of Taylor's – gave the Republic a 1-1 draw against

England in Dublin, in which the manager preferred another former Villa stalwart, Gordon Cowans, in a prosaic midfield with Steve McMahon and left out Paul Gascoigne. Our headline was 'England hijacked on Route One'.

The nations drew 1-1 again at Wembley the following March – England let another lead fall through the cracks – and had the Irish not squandered a 3-1 second-half advantage in Poland before having to settle for a 3-3 draw, who knows how the group would have played out.

England – jeered from Wembley after a single-goal victory over Turkey in October – would sneak qualification by a point after yet another unconvincing performance in Poland, a 1-1 draw secured by Gary Lineker's stunning swivelled volley 13 minutes from complete embarrassment.

Graham Taylor was heading to his first major championship as England's manager by the skin of his teeth.

* * *

In his highly recommended memoir *After Extra Time and Penalties*, the former BBC football correspondent Mike Ingham wrote of head Morris Man Colin Gibson, 'If he hadn't become an accomplished writer, he would have made it as a top travel agent or supplier of sponsored kit.'

It was the perfect summing-up by Mike, who had replaced the retiring Bryon Butler in one of the Beeb's top sporting roles and was filling it with real aplomb. Mike – aka 'The Boy Ingham' – became semi-attached to our group, which was a benefit in kind to all as he was a real gent and smashing company. He knew his football.

Gibson, Mr Big, was team leader when it came to touring requirements. He organised flights, booked accommodation, hired cars, scouted surrounding countryside for the best golf courses and probably taste-tested the hotel food on the quiet to make sure it was fit for our consumption. We just sat back in our newly acquired Nike get-up and enjoyed the views.

As a precursor to the Euros, the FA had – at Taylor's behest – decamped in Lahti, Finland. The scenery was spectacular, if the place itself was a bit like Chelmsford. Taylor held his daily briefings at five in the evening, so when Gibbo discovered the scenic Messila Golf Club and arranged regular early tee times for the team (us, not England) it was a blessing. We'd have gladly played 36 holes a day and often wished we had.

Taylor constantly agitated that some of his players weren't taking the process seriously. He organised orienteering events through the Finnish pine forests for team-bonding purposes – though running around with a compass and a map was not exactly an international footballer's cup of tea.

Had the players found their way to our hotel, they'd have had much more fun. There was a shooting incident one evening when some tanked-up Russian got involved in an argument with dear old Rob King of the Press Association and fired into the hotel's ceiling, sending everyone scrambling for cover. There was never a dull moment when Kingy was in the company.

We thought the same might be true when Lawrie McMenemy was named Taylor's assistant, even if it was a partnership that never sat well. The two were so different, the earnest coach and patrician manager appointed, we assumed, to act as a friendly bulwark between Graham and us.

At the end of one session Taylor asked McMenemy if he had anything to add, expecting the ex-Southampton manager to throw in a tactical insight or two. Lawrie paused and said, 'Lads, when you check out today make sure you leave your hotel rooms nice and tidy.'

* * *

The England squad hunkered down in preparation for the Euros in Lund, Sweden's second-oldest town, whose medieval buildings and streets were largely unsullied by the passing of the centuries. It would have been a nice place to stay but Colin Gibson had discovered a Morris Men alternative.

Snogeholm Castle was 40 minutes east, an imposing building that stood next to a lake whose waters were accessed by way of a rowing boat attached to a short wooden jetty. The castle had a small number of guest rooms and we took a vote whether to stay or return to Lund. It was 4-1 for the castle. Harry voted against.

We couldn't have wanted for lovelier quarters or food, especially the succulent daily catch from the lake. On hazy Swedish summer evenings, having filed our reports and dined expansively, we took it in turns to row to an island on the lake we christened 'Contemplation Point'. Our one accompaniment was a glass of wine precariously balanced on the bottom of the boat.

It was permissible to swim in the lake though weed-like plants attached to your legs the minute your body hit the water. One evening Gibbo plunged in from the jetty and hadn't surfaced after at least 20 seconds. I screamed 'Colin, Colin' but the other guys didn't react so I dived in for what would have been an astonishing rescue given he weighed two stones heavier.

I could neither move nor see through the thick pondlife and came up spluttering 'I can't find him' to discover Gibbo lying on the grass verge. The bastard had clung to the bottom of the jetty waiting to see if any idiot would jump in to try to save him.

Graham Taylor too was waving, not quite drowning. England's lukewarm victory at the Helsinki Olympic Stadium was tarnished when Liverpool's John Barnes ruptured the Achilles tendon in his right leg and was out of the Euros. A Finn stamped on the foot of Gary Stevens, the Everton right-back, and he was done for as well. Then there was the silly Mark Wright saga.

The Liverpool centre-back was troubled by an Achilles injury and communications between club and country on his fitness satisfied neither side. Wright was in the 20-man squad notified to UEFA, the governing body of European football, and it was too late to call anyone in if he didn't show up.

Taylor kept apologising to the Finnish media for our obsession with the story but the manager wasn't on top of his brief about his squad players as a major tournament loomed. Did he really expect us to overlook a rather significant instance to spare him embarrassing headlines?

The whole group needed a fillip and it arrived with the news that Yugoslavia, a powerful football nation drawn in England's group, were to be banished from the tournament. The Yugoslav Wars were still raging and UN sanctions had been imposed on Yugoslavia which left UEFA with little choice but to expel them.

The replacements were Denmark who had taken the precaution of recalling their players from summer holiday and putting a preparatory plan in place. They would now be England's first opponents, exactly what Taylor and the FA would have wanted. France and hosts Sweden formed the rest of the group.

After much unnecessary shilly-shallying, Wright refused the trip – a story broken in the *News of the World* by the legendary Reg Drury – and so for the opener in Malmö, Arsenal's Martin Keown partnered Des Walker of Nottingham Forest in central defence and the novice Keith Curle of Manchester City took Stevens's spot at right-back.

The outcome was a turgid goalless draw, though the Danes – not long off the beach – were by far the better side. That said, their goalkeeper Peter Schmeichel of Manchester United did make one crucial save to deny David Platt who didn't often snatch at chances from six yards out.

Bobby Moore, attending the tournament as a summariser for radio station Capital Gold, was in Morris Men company later that evening. 'We should be grateful for small mercies,' he said, 'perhaps this is as good as it gets.'

The next day, Gibbo, Steve, Bobby and I enjoyed an early tee time at the magnificent Falsterbo Golf Club on the waterfront. Bobby sliced his opening tee shot too close to the clubhouse for the members' comfort. Even the finest of men was fallible. And Bobby was looking tired and careworn. We'd soon discover why.

* * *

France were up next, which offered the heady prospect of England versus Eric Cantona. The striker joined Leeds United on loan from Nîmes midway through the previous season and had been so instrumental in their unexpected First Division title success that manager Howard Wilkinson chose to make the transfer permanent just before the Euros.

Cantona had a volatile reputation, falling out with team-mates and opposition players alike. He had once thrown the ball at a referee and when a disciplinary panel banned him for a month, he walked up to each member in turn and shouted 'idiot' in their face. The ban was extended by a further month.

The meeting with England could have done with a bit of Gallic livening up for it became a classic stalemate, an England team that didn't want to lose against a France without much inclination to win. Taylor said his selection was determined by a lot of 'ifs and buts', which was hardly rousing in the Agincourt manner.

Nottingham Forest's Stuart Pearce, dabbing blood from a cut beneath his right eye, awakened the game from its inertia when he rattled the French crossbar with a free kick near the end but that was as close as it got. After two matches, England hadn't conceded but neither had they scored.

The team had one chance remaining and they flew to Stockholm to pit what remained of their wits against the hosts, who were atop the group with three points. France and England had two points apiece and Denmark a single point from one draw and a loss.

Tony Daley of Aston Villa and Andy Sinton of Queens Park Rangers were picked to provide attacking width with Platt – who had signed a £6m deal to join Juventus from Bari during the week – playing off Gary Lineker.

Platt celebrated his monster move with England's first goal of the tournament after four minutes, a crappy half-hit shot whose awkward bounce deceived Thomas Ravelli, the Swedish goalkeeper. There was a little light in the distance.

It was a pity that two viable chances to double the lead both fell to Daley, who was lightning fast but not a cool-headed finisher. He scuffed a right-foot opening across goal – where Lineker was the length of a boot from turning it in – then missed with a header he should have directed down rather than up.

The second half became a tale of two substitutions. Sweden withdrew Arsenal winger Anders Limpar for the experienced Johnny Ekström and were transformed. They equalised with a header from a corner and began to descend upon England like a yellow-shirted swarm. After 61 minutes, the England bench stirred. Alan Smith of Arsenal was coming on but when the number ten board was raised, we couldn't believe our eyes.

Taylor had chosen to take his captain off with half an hour to go and his country in need of a goal to stay in the tournament. Did the decision have anything to do with the manager seeking retribution for his perceived slight on the previous year's tour to the Antipodes? Surely, he wasn't that thin-skinned. What other explanation was there?

Lineker – one short of the England scoring record held by Bobby Charlton – tossed his armband into the air, Carlton Palmer caught it, looked at it and was at a loss to know what to do with it. The disarray in the England setup was captured in that one moment of farce.

Sweden would score the game's winner, a beautifully crafted exchange of passes through the middle of England's half between Martin Dahlin and Tomas Brolin from which Brolin – who like Platt was honing his talents in Italian football – finished with daring.

England were eliminated and their captain humiliated. My report concluded, 'Lineker, his face a picture of sadness, was walking down the tunnel when both sets of players exchanged shirts in the centre circle. The England manager, in a moment of terrible folly, had already torn his from him.'

Next morning we assembled in the lobby of Grand Hotel in Stockholm for Taylor's post-tournament conference just as the

British papers were placed in the racks. The *Mail* headline was 'Lineker's last act'. Trevor Brooking, the former international now a radio summariser for the BBC, was standing next to me and let out a gasp. 'Take a look at this, Neil,' he said, handing me *The Sun*. Its back page said in massive type, 'Swedes 2 Turnips 1'.

Initially the headline drew a degree of admiration and even a snigger or two. I marvelled at the headline writer's balls. There was a sports subeditor on the *Mirror* who famously came up with such off-the-wall novelties all the time. When he heard there was a rumpus in the University Boat Race, the crews had clashed oars and a scholarly argument ensued, he walked behind the back bench and whispered, 'Blazing Paddles.'

It took a certain talent to capture a moment with such explosive definition. The turnip bit was emphasised with a mock-up of Taylor's head shaped as one. OK, England had played some pretty average football during the finals, but there was a scornful cruelty to this that disturbed me.

We could have no idea that this lampooning of Taylor would continue throughout the rest of his international employment. Once a turnip, always a turnip as it turned out. *The Sun* played its hand mercilessly and we began two years in which England would attempt to qualify for the 1994 World Cup with the manager ranked on a par with a root vegetable.

* * *

The England footballers departed Sweden thoroughly mocked but a handful of us remained to see the tournament through. The semi-finals pitted the hosts against Germany while Holland faced off against Denmark. Our group moved to Gothenburg where, once more, Colin Gibson came up tour guide trumps.

He booked the Morris Men into the Stenungsbaden Yacht Club on Hakefjord beach – 30 minutes from the city – and a stunning location. As we arrived at reception, a posse of tracksuited Danish players walked by. They were staying there as well. This was a massive coup.

The Danish press boys couldn't believe it. They would turn up breathless for conferences to find the five of us luxuriating in the spa or lying by the pool. What made things more special was Denmark's semi-final penalty shoot-out victory over the Dutch meant the team would be in our company for the next four nights.

Manager Richard Møller Nielsen, initially alarmed to find a group of British press ever present in his slipstream, became very chilled with us, much like the Lindeman's white wine in the Kookaburra bar. He walked the jetty each evening, often alone and lost in thought. This was his Contemplation Point. He regularly paused to greet us and say a few words that enhanced our pre-final build-up.

It helped having Peter Schmeichel in the squad given we all knew him from his first season at Manchester United. He was erudite and positive. Brian Laudrup would regularly stop to have a word and the Danish skipper Lars Olsen happily shared his confidences.

Alex Ferguson arrived at the hotel one morning to wish his goalkeeper the best of luck in the final. We found him on the wooden deck deep in conversation with the BBC radio lads Mike Ingham and Alan Green, the latter of whom Ferguson would come to loathe more than me.

Greenie was a fan of Liverpool which was never helpful when trying to extract a soundbite from Manchester United's boss. Once, in the tunnel at Anfield, when Green was live on air with Ferguson, Kenny Dalglish was walking by carrying one of his children – presumably Kelly who is now a Sky presenter – when he stopped and said, 'You'll get more sense from her.' Cue muffled raised voices and a cut back to the studio.

Away from madding Manchester United matters, Ferguson could be terrific social company and there were many reasons to want to raise a glass in convivial company – even ours – at the end of the week when Denmark went and won the cup.

Reigning world champions Germany were deemed by most students of the game to be hot favourites, a team studded with experience and excellence in the likes of Matthias Sammer, Jürgen Klinsmann, Karl-Heinz Riedle and Stefan Effenberg. They would take some stopping.

To widespread objective joy, Denmark took the lead through John Jensen's ferocious strike, and after Schmeichel and his defensive crew repelled all reprisal efforts, the outcome was decided 12 minutes from time when Kim Vilfort spun two German defenders and shot home off the inside of a post.

Denmark, the Beach Boys, had won their first football trophy. The sun was rising in Stenungsbaden on Monday morning when the Morris Men – now ordained as Danes by a jubilant and pissed squad – clambered, temples throbbing, into our beds.

* * *

Len Gould had departed the *Mail* to join the *Sunday People* as deputy editor. He had brought in as his number two Cammie Stewart, a sidekick at the *Express* in Manchester who I knew well from those days. We may have expected Cammie to be promoted but David English was looking elsewhere.

The Independent was a paper the editor much admired, particularly its use of a sports pull-out with an emphasis on dramatic use of pictures. He wanted to add something similar to the *Mail* and so Vic Robbie, high up in *The Independent*'s sports team, was lured to Kensington.

One of the upshots was an unveiling of a *Mail* 'Sports Pictorial' with big pictures and long reads. That suited the correspondents just fine.

Vic was a steady hand on the tiller. He didn't force it one way, then another; in fact there were times you barely knew he was in charge at all. On a Monday he'd lock himself in his room all day to write a column for Tuesday morning. He let me get on with my job without a great deal of vocal interference.

It was important to place England's position in the football order in a proper perspective after the Euro '92 debacle. As an entrée to the new season, Graham Taylor decided to assess the fitness of his players and summoned them to Lilleshall in Shropshire for a series of beep tests; in essence, 20-yard shuttle runs against the clock to test aerobic capacity.

David Platt was a player with whom I had formed a close bond. I travelled with him when he signed for the Italian club Bari from Aston Villa in late 1991 and had found him articulate, sensible and through his father Frank's long association with *The Guardian* in Manchester, eager to engage with journalists to pick whatever brains they had and learn how they operated.

On his arrival at the squad's lodgings, Taylor asked Platt if he should bet on him to finish top in the fitness tests and David hesitated, suspecting players like Tony Daley and Carlton Palmer, who he considered more natural athletes, would outlast him.

As it turned out, while his comrades were falling like flies, Platt was still running and realised he could have run a lot longer had the exercise continued. Paul Gascoigne, who had spent the previous year in Italy building up fitness after his cruciate ligament injury, finished second.

'In England the fitness focus is strengthening the heart through tough physical running, as if we think we will always win the race,' Platt said. 'In Italy we train the muscles which gives us the ability to change direction and push off quickly. It is the quality of exercise that matters, rather than the quantity.'

The harsh truth was that England were way behind when it came to educating the body for football rather than imposing football on the body.

All eyes were on the draw for the World Cup qualifying groups, staged in New York where I became a Morris Man big shot by pointing the boys to the nightspots I'd favoured from my tennis days. The evenings were noisy and convivial and so would be a number to come as the draw placed England in a pot with familiar foes Turkey and Poland along with Norway, Holland and San Marino. Six wins from ten should suffice, seven definitely.

We assuredly had the quality of players to succeed and if the fissure between the manager and the press could be repaired, a real togetherness might develop. The initial signs weren't encouraging. Taylor was deeply wounded by the 'turnip' taunts and many of us felt tarred by *The Sun*'s brush. The manager was falling deeply out of love with a group of people he felt certain would keep his faith.

I was sent to report on the friendly between Norway, England's first group opponents, and our Euro '92 nemesis, Sweden. Taylor blanked me at Heathrow Airport so I offered my hand as we awaited our luggage in Oslo. There was a pause and he declined it.

When I tried to make conversation, he said, 'You've got your job, I've got mine,' and climbed into a taxi before winding down the window. 'Why are you turning up to this match? I've attended matches in the past and never had this sort of attention. Why now?' Because it was our job, Graham.

By the time England kicked off their qualification programme in October 1992, Norway were on a high with three wins – San Marino home and away for an aggregate of 12-0 and against Holland at home. 'The Norwegians have such a rich vein of confidence that even Wembley, with all of its intimidating qualities, may not afford the protection England assume,' I suggested from Oslo after the Holland victory.

Taylor picked a team replete with strong personalities that very few could argue with: Woods; Dixon, Adams, Walker, Pearce; Batty, Gascoigne, Ince; Platt; Shearer, Wright. When Platty reacted quickest to a low-slung Pearce free kick to sweep England into a 55th-minute lead, all was set fair.

But nothing about this process was going to be as simple as we hoped. Slack marking at a throw-in left Norway's Kjetil Rekdal free 25 yards from goal. Nine times out of ten his shot would have gone looping into the crowd. This one flew high into the top-right corner of the net. Not a positive portent.

10
The FA Premier League

ALAN SHEARER was a tremendous striker, the best in my period in the job and a man who few have come close to emulating since. It was Shearer's instinct, bravery and calmness among a posse of defenders and an incredible confidence that his right foot would never let him down that stood out.

His lofted right arm was to become a symbol of English might. Manchester United wanted to sign him as the man who could inspire them to the elusive title in the first season of a new era in English football.

Alex Ferguson thought nothing would dissuade Shearer from moving from Southampton to Old Trafford until Blackburn Rovers came along. Something remarkable had been stirring for a while at Ewood Park. Jack Walker, the local boy turned steel magnate, was throwing the weight of his fortune around and making the grandiose big-city clubs very twitchy.

That Shearer would join a club that had been ramshackle five years earlier signalled Blackburn meant real business. Kenny Dalglish had become the manager only eight months after his resignation stunned Liverpool and far beyond. For homespun Rovers most especially, English football's 'Whole New Ball Game' was exactly that.

Blackburn's chairman for many years was a delightful soul named Bill Fox who was president of the Football League and one of the most vehement protagonists against the formation of a Premier League. He felt the wreckers would have their comeuppance but sadly Bill passed away not long before the 1992 play-off final at Wembley from which his Blackburn would be promoted to the league he so hated.

I had to confess a sense of unease when the BSkyB/BBC deal was announced, fearing the saturation coverage they promised could kill what made football so special. There was enough of the national game on television to satisfy most palates and now we were being prepared for wall-to-wall exposure, the usual Saturday afternoons extended through *Super Sunday* to *Monday Night Football.* Toss in midweek matches, replays, European competition and we'd never escape the game.

Maureen was concerned I was behind the wheel all hours in all weathers almost every night of the week and insistent that it was my duty to cover as many matches as I could to stay at the sharp end of everything happening in the game. It was the way I felt it had to be.

I wrote a comment piece asking what had happened to the shining principles of the FA's blueprint for the game, with its promise of a future based on quality, at whose essence was a successful England team? That idea was dropped like a hot coal to satisfy media tycoon Rupert Murdoch whose satellite company now owned football – though it was paying more than £300m over five years for the privilege. Would England's success matter a shit to an Australian tycoon who wouldn't know Wembley from Wollongong?

The first frontmen for Sky's presentation of the Premier League were old mates Richard Keys and Andy Gray. I'd known Andy from his playing career at Aston Villa and was invited on to the pitch with fellow press men to witness his record £1.5m move to Wolves in September 1979. Many were the times I'd pop into the Holy City Zoo, the nightclub Andy owned in Birmingham.

Richard – born the same month and year as me – had been a popular radio presenter in the north-west, both at Radio City in Liverpool and Radio Piccadilly in Manchester, before branching into television, first at TV-am. The three of us got on famously, even if they regularly railed against what they regarded as my insistently negative reporting where Sky was concerned.

The boys wondered if the *Mail* put me up to an anti-Murdoch stance, which I told them was bollocks. I made my own judgements without interference. One evening in the car park at Elland Road they beckoned me across to where they were sat in the front of Richard's car, a bit of a debate ensued, Andy trapped my tie in the passenger window and I was dragged 20 yards before being released from an uncomfortable choke hold. I'm (pretty) sure it was done in jest.

If I could breathe, I'd have mentioned they were lucky to be in their jobs. The leading clubs, including Liverpool, Manchester United, Arsenal and Leeds, preferred the counter-deal on the table from ITV of £262m across five years. ITV bosses Greg Dyke and Trevor East, the latter an old pal from my Birmingham days when he was the big sports cheese at ATV, were confident of getting a majority of hands raised.

Alan Sugar of Tottenham was desperately keen for BSkyB to succeed, not least as his company was the prime manufacturer and supplier of the satellite dishes everyone who purchased the Sky package would need to attach to the outside of their homes to watch the never-ending stream of live matches and magazine programmes.

Sugar broke off from the defining chairmen's meeting, dashing to a public pay phone (remember those?) to call Sam Chisholm, managing director of BSkyB and lead man for their bid. It was during this conversation Alan famously told Chisholm he had to come up with something to 'blow ITV out of the water'.

Chisholm contacted Premier League chief executive Rick Parry, who was chairing the meeting, and proposed a vastly improved offer at the moment Sugar was trying to recuse himself from the vote because he felt it could be construed as a conflict of interest given his business operation.

After two hours of intense debate, Tottenham were allowed to have a say and BSkyB's groundbreaking, gigantic bid triumphed by a single vote.

* * *

By the end of the first season of the FA Premier League, the millions spent to purchase the rights was an open and shut case of Murdoch daylight robbery. Alex Ferguson and Ron Atkinson would be further testing my neutrality and there was a refreshing club on which to spend quality time reporting.

For three-quarters of the season, the Canaries of Norwich City sang a charming tune. Mike Walker, a former goalkeeper with little managerial experience, was unabashed in his pride that a team without notable stars maintained a level of resilience no one expected. Even a 7-1 defeat at promoted Blackburn in October did not dull their positivity.

There were good people everywhere at Carrow Road. Walker had an old friend of mine from our Midland days, the former Aston Villa and West Brom striker John 'Dixie' Deehan, on his coaching staff so it wasn't a surprise Norwich played enterprising football.

They possessed a defence-untangling right-winger in Ruel Fox, tireless midfield enterprise from Tim Sherwood, Ian Crook and David Phillips – who I knew from his Manchester City days – a pair of potent young forwards in Efan Ekoku and Chris Sutton and a poacher supreme, Mark Robins.

Some colleagues thought Walker too fond of his own voice – Steve Curry especially – which I put down to Norwich refusing to bend to Manchester United's determination to land the title for the first time in a quarter of a century, rather than their manager's undoubted relish for self-promotion.

Most eyes and ears were trained on Ferguson and Atkinson, whose Aston Villa side refused for months to throw in the title towel. If United were to win this elusive crown, it became increasingly clear Eric Cantona would have to be their renaissance man.

The Frenchman's move from Elland Road for £1.3m – a real steal – was confirmed in November 1992 and about which I wrote, 'When Cantona is not painting, writing poetry, studying the architecture of Leeds city centre or shooting on the moors, he is making sweet music on the football field and denouncing officialdom off it.

'The Leeds anthem "Marching On Together" became "Marchons Ensembles" so Eric would feel at home. He was summed up in one Yorkshire paper as "a bit like Vinnie Jones but with class". On selling him, Leeds manager Howard Wilkinson said, "The big question is whether Eric has the intelligence and character to adapt his ability. The next season or so will be make or break for him. If you scrutinise the evidence you have to admit his chances are less than even."'

United's need for anyone with an eye for goal was terribly urgent once Dion Dublin, a £1m signing from Cambridge United, broke his leg in the initial skirmishes of the season and Ferguson was down to the bare bones. Even he didn't really know if Cantona would work out but when Eric scored in four successive matches over Christmas, United and their fanbase were beginning to sense a new hero rising in their midst.

I initiated an A to Z compendium in the paper at the turn of each new year, an alphabetical reflection on football's fortunes. In the 'what will happen in 1993 version?', I wrote, 'A is for Aston Villa – the most entertaining side this season whose title success, if confirmed, would be a great stimulant for the English game.' Ferguson was livid when he read it.

With ten matches to go, United faced Villa at Old Trafford when only goal difference separated the two teams. Ferguson refused all requests for interviews that week and didn't take too kindly to an article in which I asked Tommy Docherty, the former Scottish manager of United, how he saw the season unfolding.

Ferguson was refusing to communicate with the local radio station that employed The Doc as a co-commentator after he had criticised Gary Pallister's defending earlier in the season. Docherty wasn't for turning on that and told me, 'A lot will come down to how he [Ferguson] handles it. Atkinson might be worked up inside but he doesn't look as if he has a care in the world.'

Manchester United against Aston Villa finished 1-1. Both sides had still to visit Carrow Road where it was United's three-goal blitz in the first opening 20 minutes that inspired them to search for some long-lost red and white bunting. Ferguson said after a 3-0 thrashing of Chelsea on 17 April, 'If we do our job properly it doesn't matter about anyone else. I think fate is on our side.'

United would win their last seven matches of the season, a truly champion finish. Ferguson was playing golf at Mottram Hall near Macclesfield on 2 May when Oldham Athletic won 1-0 at Villa Park to settle matters. A United fan marched on to the course as Ferguson was preparing to play his approach to the 18th. 'Excuse me, Mr Ferguson,' he said, 'but we're the champions.'

The following day I became a father for the first time when Maureen delivered Elizabeth at the Royal Berkshire Hospital in Reading, presaging hours of unprecedented joy for both the manager of Manchester United and the Harman family.

* * *

Steve Curry decided to arrange a special celebratory lunch for the number one writers of all the daily and Sunday papers and Mike Ingham of the BBC, to which he'd invite Alex Ferguson and a couple of his coaching staff. A truly red-letter occasion.

Ferguson replied to Curry's fulsome overture that he would love to join us so long as 'that fucking Harman' wasn't there. I told Steve to leave me out because Maureen would appreciate some help with a ton of shit-filled nappies but he wrote back saying it was either all of us or none at all. Ferguson said he would come on the proviso I didn't speak to him.

Steve booked a table in an ornate dining room at the Royal Lancaster Hotel for 30 and mischievously sat me directly opposite the United boss, who was accompanied by assistant manager Brian Kidd and reserve-team coach Brian Whitehouse. We nodded at each other like a collection of dummies.

At the end of a sumptuous meal and Curry's OTT speech, we toasted the champions. Everyone was getting up to leave when Ferguson told me to stay where I was. The order was for me alone – even Kidd and Whitehouse left the room. Steve dragged his feet for the longest time, desperate to hear what was about to happen.

Ferguson ordered a further bottle of the rather splendid red we'd been drinking for the previous two hours to be decanted. The wine waiter placed it on the table between us before he, too, was dismissed.

Ferguson opened by saying he didn't like me and surmised that I didn't like him. I said it wasn't personal and to suggest I favoured others (i.e. Ron Atkinson) over him was wrong. I just knew them better. He insisted I had it in for United and continuously accentuated the negative.

As I tried to absorb the weight of his words, I saw flashbacks of John McEnroe's father, John, who sought out British tennis writers critical of his son, produced a sheaf of cuttings from his inside jacket pocket and waved them in the offenders' faces, often accompanied by frequent use of the word 'asshole'.

Ferguson didn't need exhibits; he recalled examples of my 'negativity' with alarming clarity. I insisted that I wrote what I believed was right at the time and had no hidden agendas. I respected and admired Manchester United, I loved Manchester like a second home but I wasn't beholden to any person or club. He said I was far too fucking clever for my own good and expected better.

As the decanter emptied far too swiftly, we agreed to put our differences to one side and start the relationship afresh the following season. A new leaf was being turned, or so we imagined.

We emerged from the lobby where Harry Harris had loitered – hoping for a quote on a day we'd all agreed was strictly off the record – whereupon the manager of Manchester United and I threw our arms across each other's shoulders for a semblance of balance before making our way, in an unsteady meander, towards Lancaster Gate tube station.

* * *

One man's championship was another's retirement. On the penultimate weekend of the season I was at the City Ground to witness Nottingham Forest's final home game and Brian Clough's farewell to the club for whom he had delivered unfathomable success.

Clough would always be a giant among Nottingham people and though he was beginning to struggle physically and had broken out in red blotches, his saviour status and masterful past would never be dimmed in their eyes. The ground was heaving and quite a few people parked their cars nearby and stayed with them, just wanting to be close to the occasion.

The route to Clough's seat on the bench before the match was blocked by photographers, TV cameramen and their handlers, pushing and shoving. Cloughie stopped, waved his hands and they magically parted. Charlton Heston couldn't have done it any better though I don't recall him kissing any policemen in *The Ten Commandments*. A 2-0 loss to Dave Bassett's Sheffield United was a cruel last act.

We were in the tunnel afterwards and a couple of us managed to sneak into Brian's room for a farewell tipple. 'I said hello to the team afterwards and thanked them for all they'd done and told them I'd see them at Ipswich next week. I'll see you there as well, boys,' he told us. That would, sadly, not be possible.

Alan Hill, Brian's long-serving chief scout, knocked on the door. 'Come on, gaffer, the grandchildren want to go home,' he said. With that and a quick kiss on our cheek, Brian Clough vanished into the world of *Mr Men*. By God we'd miss him.

* * *

Four months prior to Brian Clough's departure from football, we lost a man forever who it would be impossible to replace.

On a bitter February night at Wembley, the place where he achieved something no Englishman had before or has since, World Cup-winning captain Bobby Moore was commentating for Capital Gold on the qualifier between his country and San Marino. How far we as a footballing nation had stumbled from the glorious summer day 27 years earlier.

Bobby, huddled in a greatcoat and wearing an extravagant cap pulled down to just above his eyes, was a very sick man. I had suddenly appreciated how yellow his skin had turned. Only Bobby and those closest to him, including his great chum and fellow commentator Jonathan Pearce, had recently learned how ill, and even they did not expect him to succumb so quickly.

Within a week of the match, Bobby had passed away from the bowel cancer he had kept secret from all bar his wife Stephanie for the best part of two years. A nation really did mourn, most especially in the East End of London where he had a God-like status.

From first seeing Bobby in real life at the age of seven to befriending him in the latter years of his earthly journey was a pleasure beyond description. We played golf in Sweden and Spain, the latter on the Pedreña course where the Ballesteros brothers learned their skills and had grown into such fine players.

The press group was in nearby Santander for a friendly between England and Spain in September 1992. Colin Gibson booked the course and Manuel Ballesteros, Seve's older brother, came out to meet us and almost prostrated himself at Bobby's feet. Five months later Mooro had gone.

The day before the match in Santander, Bobby and I sat on a sofa in the hotel lobby watching the current squad walk by for a group meal. I found it hard to believe how few of them came across to speak to our captain emeritus. Paul Gascoigne, for one, made the effort.

I said to Bobby I thought he deserved so much better. He told me not to make such a fuss. That was the man.

11

A Little Light Turbulence

MORE OFTEN than not in the 1990s, the press flew with football teams on their foreign jaunts. It helped the FA and individual clubs enormously when newspaper groups softened their travel expenses.

We went with Arsenal from Stansted to Lisbon in late 1991 for their European Cup tie against Benfica. The only thing I recall about that trip was that it didn't feel like being with a team of champions, for we flew in a BAe 146, unable to get any blood to our feet for three and a half hours there and back. And they lost.

Rather more upbeat was the Gunners' return from winning the European Cup Winners' Cup against Parma in the 1994 final in Copenhagen. Not only was the result memorable, so was the moment the team captain Tony Adams came over the plane's intercom to harangue the press and implore his team-mates to 'get lamped'.

Graham Taylor took a rather different approach. It was at his insistence that on England flights the press sat at the front of the plane and he, the coaching staff, players and FA officials went to the rear. The seating was all economy class but I could sense that members of the FA international committee were not used to seeing the back of other people's heads when they took to the air.

The seating plan among the press group stayed exactly the same for as long as we flew together. Steve Curry and I were in row one (him window, me aisle) with Colin Gibson and Stuart Jones across from us and Harry Harris in the row behind, usually with the BBC's Alan Green and Mike Ingham for company.

One of my first excursions was in December 1990 to Algeria for an England B international. God, what a forsaken place. The night of the match a huge lightning storm blew out all the stadium lights for 15 minutes, the linesmen wore anoraks, Bryan Robson was booked for a tackle made by Liverpool's David Burrows and Neil Webb was sent off for retaliation. Our motorcycle escort back to Algiers airport consisted of a solitary policeman who refused to go more than 20mph on a night when only a masochist would be out driving.

It had not only been an exhausting night working with an archaic phone system but after the laborious journey to the airport the customs officials seemed determined to keep us forever. I was in my usual seat when Taylor came to the front of the plane, stood outside the door to the pilot's cabin and started his press conference there.

We had taken off into pelting rain and thick cloud so a bit of shut-eye couldn't be avoided and I nodded off with Graham in mid-flow. He kicked me on the foot to bring me around and didn't look the least bit happy when I jolted awake.

After the 1992 Euros went all ends up, Taylor unilaterally banned alcohol from England flights from the start of the 1994 World Cup qualifying campaign. Curry was incandescent. We usually departed Luton Airport before nine in the morning and he and I would have a 'heart-starter' (a strong Bloody Mary with plenty of Worcestershire sauce) as soon as the plane levelled off. What now?

Steve came up with a ruse. Which of our number was least likely to be suspected if Taylor thought we were trying to sneak some strong stuff aboard with our duty-free confectionary? Ingham was the appointed stooge.

The boys had a whip-round and the BBC correspondent was deputed (strong-armed) into putting a couple of bottles of blue

Smirnoff into his plastic bag. 'Don't bloody clink them going up the steps,' Curry admonished Mike. When the first ten rows of the plane had all ordered tomato juices, the vodka was quietly opened and passed around.

We thought we were undone when Lawrie McMenemy loomed in our rear-view mirror and asked what was going on. Poor Mike turned ashen. When Steve topped up Lawrie's tonic water with a soupçon of Smirnoff, he went back and told Graham we were all behaving ourselves nicely.

A couple of trips later the ban was lifted.

* * *

Most of the time players didn't particularly engage with us on foreign trips; the odd nod and handshake but very little else. We were the bastard press. There were the exceptions.

Gary Lineker would make a point of coming over to ask after us, often staying for a coffee. Only if you had a heart of granite – or presupposed that he was doing it for a decent report a couple of days later – would you not appreciate such concern from the England captain and star striker.

David Platt was happy to mingle, mostly to chat with Midlands pals John Wragg and Dave Harrison, the number two reporters for the *Express* and *Today*, though I often sneaked a few words with him on my own. Geoff Thomas was always good value for a quote or two.

Rob Shepherd moved with industrious intent amid his long-time London pals Paul Ince, Ian Wright and Paul Merson and was often rewarded with a strong storyline. No one talked to Des Walker. He was the only England player with whom I didn't pass a single word when covering the national team. Stuart Pearce would snarl, as did Tony Adams. They didn't scare me, much.

The Morris Men were seen more as 'FA people'. We were the establishment group and would often mix with the chattier elements of the international committee who included three long-term contacts of mine in chairman Peter Swales of Manchester City, Liverpool's Noel White and the loveable 'Swinging' Jack Wiseman from Birmingham City. The best time to catch them for a quote was usually at the airport carousel, hoping our baggage had landed on the same flight we were on.

Nobody wanted to be on a losing flight home – they were unbearably morose journeys, often taken into the early hours of the morning, where defeat was exacerbated by tiredness and irascibility.

Any flight delays were normally down to the photographers who carried their offices with them. It wasn't one man and one camera but all the paraphernalia required to transmit the pictures back to London. Once we filed our reports, that was it – straight on to the coach. The last snapper always got a sarcastic jeer as he staggered aboard loaded down with equipment.

On one dramatic occasion I caused a late-night flight to be held on the tarmac and it couldn't have happened at a worse time and involve a worse club from my perspective.

Manchester United's trip to Istanbul in the 1993 Champions League to face Galatasaray was a cursed enterprise. The Turks had promised 'Welcome To Hell' and 'You'll Die Here' before United flew in for the second leg and when we arrived it felt as if they were going to be true to their threats.

The first match at Old Trafford had finished 3-3, United tossing away a 2-0 lead by proceeding to play with an arrogant sense of entitlement that inflamed and inspired the Turks. Galatasaray responded by slicing time and again through a soft United centre and scored three fine goals. A late Eric Cantona strike brought the Reds level. Nothing could be taken for granted on the return.

The reception at the Atatürk Airport was worryingly provocative. Even Ned Kelly, the United security chief who would throw you into an arm lock if you said 'good morning' to him, was alarmed how close the several hundred fans who had congregated were able to get to United's party. The police were dressed and armed as if expecting a full-blown riot. It came pretty close. A few players smiled but most were crapping themselves.

From the middle of the following afternoon, the stands at the Ali Sami Yen Stadium were full to choking point. When we arrived at the ground in two coachloads it required the police – most of whom were clearly on overtime and not happy about it – to form a human shelter before we could disembark.

I expressed surprise in print that Alex Ferguson chose to leave Mark Hughes on the bench as United needed one goal at least to advance. How they would miss their spark.

It was to be a frustrating as well as frightful night. The din from the terracing never subsided as the Turks defended for all they were worth and stalled the match at every turn. Cantona decided to take the matter into his own hands.

Late in the proceedings he ran to collect a ball that the Turkish bench had refused to throw back and kicked it straight at them, knocking over an official with his follow-through. The Turkish players went mad, the fans madder and at the end of a goalless draw, a red card was flourished at Eric for an insult directed at the referee, a Swiss who taught primary school French.

The dressing rooms were reached via a steep flight of concrete steps behind one of the goals. As he left the field with Bryan Robson for protective company, a riot shield was thumped into Cantona's back. Robson was also hit, requiring two stitches in an arm gash. Cantona described the incident as a 'giant scandal'.

The office wanted the 800-plus-word match report and a short, sharp news story for the back page. Those of us flying solo needed a helping hand and it was provided by Rob Shepherd and Ken Lawrence of the *Star* who fought their way down into the tunnel area to gather post-match reaction and gladly handed the quotes around. This was the kind of selfless teamwork often required on foreign trips.

The wide-eyed Turks surrounding the press box were baying for British blood and it took an age to dictate two pieces in a febrile atmosphere where so much had happened out of your sight. We were all relieved to make it back to our transport in one piece.

In the frenzy of the airport boarding process, I didn't hear the announcement for the flight and was mooching around in duty free when United's assistant secretary Ken Ramsden came racing into view, 'Neil, Neil, you're holding up the flight, the manager has told them to close the door and leave you here.'

Picture the greeting when I reached the end of the jetty, red-faced and panting, to see every passenger and crew member giving me the evil eye. Ferguson and Brian Kidd were in row one, the rest of the coaching staff next, the board of directors behind them, Ned Kelly polishing his knuckle-duster, then the players, Bruce, Schmeichel, Ince, Cantona and the rest, all pissed at being knocked out of Europe and wanting to get home.

'Get tae fuck,' the manager hissed. I tried to look everyone else in the eye until I reached Roy Keane's row and something on the floor demanded my undivided attention.

12

Did We Not Like That?

A FEW weeks before Manchester United's first campaign in the European Cup – by now the Champions League – for almost three decades fell apart, Graham Taylor's career as England manager had gone the same way. It was a sad and often unedifying spectacle.

Taylor's decision to allow a film crew to record the second half of the misadventure was an act of hubris that badly backfired, as did the FA's failure to pull the plug on the whole thing.

To be fair to the Chrysalis production team, they blended so well into the background that the media had no clue they were there, or at least no one mentioned them. That took some doing. Taylor's avid participation meant that he was trying to be a football manager and an actor all in one and got lost halfway up his own ham-fisted hamming.

The rest of us, players, staff and writers, were his extras. The most toe-curling part was a meeting at the FA, chaired by Peter Swales, at which Taylor presented a report that made no sense to me at all. 'Very good that, Graham,' said Swales. Graham Kelly, the chief executive, had clearly been briefed that the meeting was being filmed because he eschewed his normal owl-like glasses and wore contact lenses, which I'd never seen before.

Taylor became a victim of his belief that he was always one step ahead of the press and would prove to be a master of tactical discernment. He really did feel he could talk his way out of anything, as if he was smarter and slicker and that everyone would buy into his management.

He had brought in a chap named David Teasdale as a personal media guru, a former Whitehall civil servant who from what we could tell had next to no knowledge of football. We ran rings around him.

On the field, England recovered from the shock of Norway's late equaliser in the first qualifier to defeat Turkey 4-0 at Wembley where Paul Gascoigne was in his pomp and Alan Shearer scored with a flying header. It was a defining blow to both Blackburn and his country that Shearer would soon pick up a knee injury that kept him out for the rest of the season.

Still, England knocked six past San Marino, won 2-0 in Turkey (our plane was rocked every which way by a lightning strike on its descent into İzmir) and approached the meeting with Holland at Wembley in April in a mood of buoyant defiance. It became a pivotal night for countless reasons.

The previous week I had been granted an interview with Dutch winger Marc Overmars, who played for Amsterdam club Ajax. 'I am a bit of a showman,' the 20-year-old said as we took a coffee at the training centre. 'I want to show the English people how good I am.'

He should never have had the chance. England were a goal up in a minute from a free kick from 20 yards by John Barnes that rose over the wall and dipped beneath the crossbar. In the Sky commentary box, Martin Tyler screamed, 'That puts the critics in their place – they have no place really,' which was biting the hand that fed him all his storylines.

Not long later, Les Ferdinand shot against the foot of a post and when the ball rebounded into play, David Platt was the sharpest of all to react to make it 2-0 England. Dennis Bergkamp pulled a delightful goal back but Paul Gascoigne had been caught flush on the cheekbone by a jutting elbow from Jan Wouters and England began to play in a similarly disjointed manner.

Six minutes from time Overmars knocked the ball past Des Walker on Holland's right-hand side. Platty screamed at Des to 'fucking take him out'. The Italian philosophy on dealing with counter-attacks – both men played in Serie A at the time – was to kill them at source, not give them time to breathe.

Walker should have taken one for the country but was undone for speed – supposedly his forte – and yanked at Overmars's shirt. The first tug didn't stop him but the second did, inside the area. Peter van Vossen, a stone-cold substitute, rolled the equalising penalty into the bottom corner. This was even more of a kick in the teeth than Norway's late fluke of a goal.

Teasdale had a humdinger of an idea the next morning. He persuaded Taylor to come into his press conference, pluck an alarm clock from Teasdale's briefcase and place it on the desk in front of him.

Graham told his bewildered audience that because we complained about the length of his answers he'd set a time limit of two minutes for each one. He then burst into song, 'Oh misery, misery, what's going to become of me,' from Buddy Holly's 'Rainin' in my Heart'. I really thought he'd lost a few marbles.

England had played five matches, four of them at Wembley where they had twice been held to a draw. The next two qualifiers, in Poland and Norway, were five days apart in June. Gascoigne's club Lazio demanded that he wear a protective mask to limit the potential for further damage to his face. Taylor was more worried about weaknesses in other parts of his body.

A 1-1 draw in Katowice courtesy of substitute Ian Wright's late strike took us back to Oslo and the occasion Taylor threw his most outrageous tactical curveball – choosing to play with three centre-backs. Was he a genius, or had he lost the plot? David Miller, a doyen of football writers, climbed on to the press coach behind me going on and on about Taylor's tinkering.

The negative atmosphere was already stoked when the manager chose the day before the match to raise what he described as

Gascoigne's 're-fuelling' habits, a comment that was like throwing a lit match on to a fuel spillage. The red-top tabloids had a field day.

The way England performed the next evening, a few more than Gazza must have been indulging in the hard stuff. By far the most listless performance of the campaign gifted what was in truth a limited Norwegian side a 2-0 victory. We were pretty well fucked.

* * *

What better location than New England – my wife's birthplace, where we had wed and holidayed joyously every summer – for replenishing the spirit? Venture a few miles south of Boston and I was immediately reminded of the lyrics to Patti Page's wonderful song, 'Old Cape Cod' with its evocative images of winding roads that beckon you to sea views and lobster stews.

The portents for a happy tour were immediate. Colin Gibson had come good with the travel arrangements again, the Morris Men plus Mike Ingham and Alan Green from the BBC travelled first class on American Airlines and really couldn't believe our fortune. It was to be one of only two luxuries on the trip.

England had three matches scheduled, against the USA at Foxboro Stadium, home of the NFL's New England Patriots, on to Washington's RFK Stadium to face Brazil and finally taking on the Germans in the Detroit Silverdome with its closed roof. To come home unbeaten would be something to celebrate.

England lost 2-0 to the US, performing horribly. I wrote, 'The Americans outplayed, out-passed and out-schemed England and none of us here considered we would be writing words like that.'

I was woken in my room at 6am the next day. Vic Robbie, the sports editor, had emerged from editorial conference with a demand from David English. 'You have to say one way or the other if the *Mail* supports Graham Taylor,' Vic said. 'There's plenty of space in the paper. It's your choice.'

I had never truly appreciated the weight of the responsibility of being the chief football writer. I sat on the edge of my bed for half an hour gathering my thoughts. I rang Steve Curry to tell him, which was a little unprofessional. 'Fucking hell, Hawkeye [my nickname because I was brilliant at finding supposedly lost golf balls],' he said. 'Just do what you think is right.'

I took a deep breath and wrote the first paragraph, 'The haunted Graham Taylor must be stood down as England manager for his own sake as much as anything to do with the rotten-to-the-core state of English football. The nation's favourite fall guy has fallen too far this time.'

From there the piece flowed. I said Graham had performed proudly and nobly and it would be compassionate for the FA to relieve him of his duties if he wouldn't step down of his own accord. I telephoned FA chairman Sir Bert Millichip, my old friend from West Bromwich Albion, to ask for a quote but he said he'd prefer to consult with his colleagues, not members of the media.

We flew to Washington the next day. Lawrie McMenemy, who had been in France at an under-21 tournament and missed the US debacle, walked into the press conference room with the British papers and tossed the *Mail* in my general direction.

The back-page headline was 'Time to put fall guy Taylor out to grass'. Next to it was a cartoon depicting the manager standing on a wooden floor with a saw emerging from the boards beneath. 'Thanks, Neil, you've killed us,' Lawrie said.

The next two matches, a draw against Brazil and a loss to the Germans, barely registered. What cleared the head was a 500-mile round roadtrip from Detroit to Traverse City in Michigan with Curry to play golf at The Bear, a course designed and named for Jack Nicklaus.

As for the England manager, he was done with me. That night watching *Bubbling Brown Sugar* and sipping a rather splendid Pinot Grigio seemed an awful long time ago.

* * *

There were three World Cup qualifying games remaining and only three wins would guarantee a place in the 1994 jamboree. Poland at home were despatched with ease and even England couldn't lose to San Marino in their final match. That left the Dutch in Rotterdam on 13 October 1993.

When we touched down in Rotterdam, Rob Shepherd was in bouncy form. I asked why and he was coy. An invitation to join the Morris Men for drinks that evening was declined. Shep had a scoop and didn't want to risk alcohol loosening his tongue before the first editions dropped.

Paul Merson had tipped Rob the wink at Luton airport that he was in the starting line-up so while most of us plumped for his Arsenal team-mate Ian Wright to start, we'd grabbed the wrong end of the stick.

As we waited for Taylor's 10am conference the day before the match, Shep appeared in the hotel lobby the worse for a late night. David Teasdale had confirmed the team to a few of us and I mentioned to Rob about it looking like the kind of selection that dumbfounded us in Norway.

Taylor was in a strange mood and when Shep blurted out that the team selection felt much like Norway and how worried it made him, the manager went full rant about the whole country being concerned about Rob Shepherd being worried. 'You worry,' Taylor said, 'but don't make the fucking rest of us worry. Go and worry on your own.'

One Dutch journalist was convulsing so hard he stumbled over his tripod and almost brought the whole row of TV cameras around him crashing down.

My misgivings about Taylor to one side, I still felt that player for player England had a decent chance to win. The Dutch had been outclassed then reprieved at Wembley. This night was to be very different, thanks to a German referee who cheated the very laws he was meant to apply.

When in the middle of the second half Andy Sinton helped a ball beyond the high Dutch line, a race ensued between David

Platt and their defender Ronald Koeman. 'I knew I was quicker than him, or perhaps should I say that he was definitely slower than me,' Platt said.

'I sensed what Andy would do and already had an image of the goal in my mind. When I was away from Koeman, I'd flick it up and over the keeper. I knew I'd score.

'When Koeman grabbed me by the arm, he pulled me right around so I couldn't keep my balance whether I wanted to or not. I was unhappy that Jimmy Greaves said on TV that night that I could have stayed on my feet. That was rubbish. I heard the referee's whistle and went to collect the ball because I was the designated penalty taker.'

It dawned on Platt a few seconds later that referee Karl-Josef Assenmacher had not only given a free kick outside the area but ignored a recently toughened FIFA ruling about fouls on the last man requiring an obligatory dismissal. He showed a yellow card to Koeman. As the free kick was being lined up, Koeman whispered in Platt's ear, 'Sorry, David, I should have been sent off.'

Koeman would score Holland's first goal from a twice-taken free kick (again the referee was abject in his interpretation of the laws) and Dennis Bergkamp struck a second that squirmed under David Seaman and meant that, to all intents and purposes, Holland were through and England out. Assenmacher never refereed again.

A month after that loss and the added humiliation of a postman from San Marino, Davide Gualtieri, scoring after eight seconds of the final qualifier in Bologna (England did win 7-1 but it mattered not), Graham Taylor resigned.

A letter arrived a few weeks later asking if I'd like to attend a private viewing at a Soho club of a documentary called *An Impossible Job*, to which 30 football writers had been invited.

It was astonishing viewing notwithstanding my three brief, non-speaking cameos. Our silence at the end spoke eloquently. What was this? Why had Graham agreed to it being aired after an abject failure? Why had the FA acquiesced? Would it have made a difference had England qualified? Instead, Graham looked like a fool. He wasn't the only one. Poor Phil Neal, the coach, was derided for coming across as little more than Long John Silver's parrot.

As time has passed with 21st-century Amazon and Netflix dressing-room exposés emerging every other season, we are inured to the genre. In 1993, the Taylor documentary was a total groundbreaker and barely a soul in the country didn't watch it. For that, Graham has our undying admiration.

Taylor also extended the lexicon of English football sayings with such pearls as, 'What have they been instructed?'; 'It's got to go big!'; 'Can we not knock it?'; 'Whether Gascoigne is ten stone or 15 stone the Norwegians are in awe of him'; 'You play the game with your heads'; 'Now this is a real, real test'; 'Linesman! Linesman! the referee's got me the sack, thank him very much for that won't you?'

And most famously, 'Do I not like that!' I didn't speak to Graham again.

13

Musical Chairs

MANCHESTER UNITED signed Roy Keane from Nottingham Forest for £3.75m in August 1993, the most expensive transfer in the English game. The lad really was some talent, a player with a ten-stroke engine now playing for a five-star club.

Steve Curry and I were staying at the Four Seasons Hotel in Hale – a regular stopover of ours – to cover the story and when we walked into the bar, young Roy was sitting there on a stool. This was a stroke of fortune. We engaged him in small talk but he was really shy and didn't offer much. After a couple more pints of Guinness, we helped him down and he was sick over my rather nice loafers.

United's 1993/94 season – their European exploits in Turkey apart – would be more restful than previous campaigns; indeed, they retained their title by eight points, losing only four league matches over nine months and completed the double, defeating Chelsea 4-0 in the FA Cup Final on a rain-swept day at Wembley.

From where would the challenge to them come moving ahead? There were considerable stirrings at Blackburn Rovers where Jack Walker, guarded in media terms, led off the pitch and Kenny Dalglish on it; similarly at Newcastle United on the back of the charismatic partnership of Sir John Hall and Kevin Keegan.

The clubs were second and third behind United in the final analysis of 1993/94 whereas Liverpool ended eighth, an astonishing

32 points adrift of Ferguson's team. Graeme Souness had resigned as manager in January to be replaced by the last surviving member of the famous coaching Boot Room, Roy Evans.

There were powerful Mersey links with both Blackburn and Newcastle given their manager's legendary playing status at Anfield but their minds were now elsewhere. Two close-season transfers stood out. Blackburn broke the British record by spending £5m on the 21-year-old Norwich striker Chris Sutton and, at the other end of the age scale, Jürgen Klinsmann, the stalwart German, moved from Monaco in France to Tottenham for £2m.

Klinsmann's opening game at Hillsborough was an epic of seven goals and his first for the club, a lovely far-post header, was celebrated by throwing himself full-length as a piece of humour – yes, Germans did possess a sense of fun – against those who had smeared him as a diver.

I didn't have long to hang around in Sheffield as I was appearing that night on a new Sky Sports football show, *Hold the Back Page*. Before each season, the network's head of sport Vic Wakeling took the number one writers for lunch at Shepherd's on Marsham Street and during our usually sparky repartee, we had the idea of cloning it in a studio in Osterley on a Saturday night.

The first airing featured Brian Woolnough of *The Sun* and Pat Butcher of *The Times* as joint hosts. The guests were me and Chris 'Crash' Lander of the *Mirror*, a cricket and rugby man, which opened the debate to a multitude of sports. There was one large circular table, four chairs and the whole studio was enclosed by long black curtains. It was difficult to pick out the movement of the huge cameras and we were told not to look straight into them anyway if we did spot them.

The programme soon became solely a four-way football conversation with 'Wooly' Woolnough as the chairman. He was terrific in the role, bringing the best out of so many of us, though if there was something football journos loved, it was the sound of their own voices.

Joe Melling, Bob Cass, Harry Harris, Nigel Clarke, Rob Shepherd, Alex Montgomery, Colin Gibson and, of course, Steve Curry were at their lucid finest in front of the camera, the punters loved it given the viewership figures and, ego aside, such prime-time exposure meant an increasing chance of recognition at Premier League grounds, even if it led to the odd verbal altercation.

Steve would puff out his chest if he was spotted. If not at Old Trafford where he was minor deity, he'd often be greeted by cries of recognition like, 'There's that fucking United fan, Curry.' I generally had to make do with, 'Who's the twat with him?'

It didn't take long for certain managers to clock into every Sky debate. Alex Ferguson – wouldn't you know it? – would call to tell you what he thought of your performance, which was never much. Kenny Dalglish did the same.

Wakeling had chosen the perfect time to unleash us scribes on to the small screen. This inaugural season of *Hold the Back Page* would become one of those periods when we did precisely that. Time and again.

* * *

Manchester United, so long starved of domestic bragging rights, were now chasing a third consecutive championship. If it was to mean anything, the Premier League had to be a decent contest and so the surges of Blackburn and Newcastle were welcomed everywhere bar the district of Salford.

Whether you wanted to or not, it was difficult to take your eyes from United, who had won the Double in 1994 with Ryan Giggs and Andrei Kanchelskis, the Ukraine winger, providing so much thrust and explosive power that they blew the opposition away. The need to watch them endlessly meant the M6 seeing serious rubber.

Blackburn provided an obstinate challenge. Their 4-2 loss to United at Ewood Park in late October, rather than knocking the stuffing out of them, galvanised Kenny Dalglish's men to a

12-match unbeaten run until they lost 1-0 to United on 22 January 1995 to a goal scored by Eric Cantona.

Back at our Hale base camp, Steve Curry and I found Cantona in a quiet corner and asked if he might spare a few minutes. He had been reluctant to give the press any time but goaded by Bryan Robson, he chatted for a few minutes. The upshot was he'd never been more contented at United and believed the best of the side was yet to come.

It was the perfect intro to a preview for the following Tuesday night when United were to play Crystal Palace at Selhurst Park, always a feisty venue and especially under the lights.

Palace were managed by the exceedingly likeable Alan Smith and had a decent sharp edge about them. They may not be a side equipped for a top-five spot but possessed the talents to upset any apple cart and the idea of chipping at United's perceived arrogance was right up their street.

Richard Shaw in central defence was the epitome of Palace's rugged determination and gave Cantona a truly uncomfortable night, close-marking and tapping at his ankles. Then there was one tap too far, Cantona retaliated and referee Alan Wilkie – a prima donna himself – flourished the red card.

The press box at Palace was at the back of the stand inside the half closest to the tunnel at one end of the ground. Cantona was being shepherded along the touchline directly beneath us by United's kit manager Norman Davies – a lovely bloke – when the next thing I saw was Eric freeing himself from Norman's clutches and flying feet first into the crowd. Fucking hell. Did I see that right? Yes, it had definitely happened.

Merry hell broke loose. The sportsdesk was calling. Had I seen it? Yes I had. The front page wanted something. A match report of 800 words had suddenly become a comment piece, front-page decoration and two-page spread. The brain was absolutely racing. The back-page headline was 'Crazed Cantona'. I called for him to be expelled from football for a long time.

To think that 72 hours earlier, Eric had had Curry and I eating out of his hands and now this.

* * *

The nation was discussing nothing else. The amount of newsprint usually devoted to the royal family was being devoured by a commoner – two commoners if you included Matthew Simmons, the arse of a supporter whose as-yet unverified comments towards Cantona drew such an extraordinary reaction.

Alex Ferguson had been so busy reorganising his side in the aftermath of Cantona's dismissal that he didn't see the incident 'live' and only picked up on it when his alarm went off at four the following morning. The manager's first reaction was that his talisman would have to go.

Maurice Watkins was both a considerate director of the club and its legal eagle. He told fellow board members that justice had to take its course and United shouldn't pre-empt anything. The club banned Eric until the end of the season and fined him two weeks' wages. The FA would incur Ferguson's extended wrath – not for the first time – when they increased Cantona's suspension to the first two months of the following season.

The crime scene switched to Croydon Magistrates' Court where Cantona – shadowed by Ned Kelly, who was absolutely in his security chief's element – was standing trial for assault. There was not a spare seat to be had in the public or press galleries and audible gasps went up when Cantona was sentenced to two weeks in prison.

The magistrates wanted him sent down straight away and refused to consider an appeal. Watkins dashed to the nearby 'superior' crown court where the judges granted Cantona bail. On appeal, his sentence was reduced to 150 hours of community service.

United wanted to get the show back on the road and called a press conference where Ferguson and Watkins sat at a top table with Cantona, whose agent Jean-Jacques Bertrand had asked the United party beforehand what fishing boats were called in England.

Kelly confirmed 'trawlers'. What was the name of the small fish in the sea? 'Sardines,' replied the security man. Bertrand passed the message on to his client.

'C'mon, Eric, say something,' whispered the man from *The Sun* in the second row who so far had only dry quotes from a lawyer to excite his readers. Cantona, milking the moment, looked up, paused for enigmatic effect, and said, 'When the seagulls [then took a sip of water] follow the trawler, it's because they think sardines will be thrown into the sea. Thank you.'

We'd need a bigger supply of newsprint.

* * *

In the first week of March, United thumped Ipswich 9-0 at Old Trafford (who needed Eric Cantona?) but Blackburn were not going to be so easily swept aside. United had spent £7m signing Andy Cole from Newcastle United, with Irish winger Keith Gillespie as the £1m makeweight. Cole scored four against Ipswich and United hadn't been fatally derailed.

Kenny Dalglish's team still led the Premier League by three points and one goal separated the two clubs on goal difference. A month later Blackburn had extended the lead to five points and now had a game in hand. It was Rovers' title surely with six weeks of the season left.

United had gone out of the Champions League in the group stages once more, a 4-0 mauling at the Nou Camp in Barcelona when they wore their second change strip of grey shirts – never again avowed Alex Ferguson – a particularly grievous blow to their prestige.

They were still in the FA Cup and had reached the semi-finals to play Crystal Palace on my 38th birthday. Blackburn lost in the third round to Newcastle so there were no impediments to their assault on the title Jack Walker yearned above all. Four days before United's attention turned elsewhere, Blackburn had won 1-0 at QPR with a goal by Chris Sutton.

I wrote that a year on from being criticised as a striker who was nowhere near worth the £5m Rovers paid for him, he had scored a goal worth ten times that figure. 'We're going to keep fighting for everything,' Dalglish said. So, in a critically different sense, were United.

Palace had seduced Ferguson's men into the frenetic league game three months earlier that pre-empted Cantona's dismissal and lunge. I interviewed United's 1968 European Cup stalwart Pat Crerand in the semi-final build-up and both photographer Ted Blackbrow – God bless him – and I were amazed when Paddy agreed to a request to sit on a fence for a picture.

I asked Crerand if what happened at Selhurst Park might have cost United their hope of retaining the title. 'I suppose it would make a lot of people very happy if United didn't win anything,' he said. 'Tell me how many people in Britain want Blackburn to win the championship? Is ITV going to offer *them* a contract to show all their matches in Europe?

'There's a great deal of jealousy because of who United are and what they stand for. What's wrong with getting support from all corners of the country? We might not get into Europe next season and people say we'll miss the prestige. Does Manchester United need any more prestige?'

The semi-final against Palace at Villa Park required extra time and finished 2-2, United twice recovering from a goal down and Gary Pallister bringing them level again in the 97th minute. A replay was required at the same venue.

It was not going to be a quiet night. There had been an appeal from Ferguson and Alan Smith, the Palace manager, for calm, after a fan was stabbed and died outside a public house before the initial tie. This time, it was the players who showed a lack of restraint.

United were cruising two goals to the good when Keane lunged at Palace captain Gareth Southgate, who didn't take to the challenge kindly. Gareth tried to scythe through Keane, fell on to his back and the Irishman stamped on his chest. In the ensuing furore, Keane and Darren Patterson of Palace were both sent off. The *Mail*'s back-page headline was 'What a disgrace'.

The next day I felt obliged to pen a piece about these constant displays of United ill-discipline. I knew it would enrage the manager but didn't expect it to wound so deeply.

As I was putting the piece together the Manchester-based press boys were waiting to be summoned into Ferguson's office at The Cliff. The lads made a pact that they would delay as long as possible mentioning Keane, otherwise the conference would come to a grinding halt amid fruity language. All agreed to hold off.

Before anyone could say, 'Any injuries, Alex?', John Bean of the *Express* piped up, 'Now, about Roy Keane, matey [as John addressed everyone].' Fergie lost it. The other lads were fuming. Bean's explanation was, 'I prefer the hand grenade down the trousers approach, matey.'

I pulled a pin from one the following day. Under the heading 'Time for United to read the riot act' my comment appeared, 'The words and pictures are no strangers to Manchester United. A foot is raised, an opponent is trapped under the studs and as a consequence, shame is heaped upon a club which once embodied dignity in adversity.

'Last season the culprit was Eric Cantona who had Swindon's John Moncur pinned beneath him. On Wednesday, when two clubs were asked to give peace a chance, it was Roy Keane bringing a boot down into the chest of Gareth Southgate. Are United planning that this image should represent them on a new coat of arms to go with their monthly changes of kit?

'The behaviour of certain individuals is eating away at the club's soul. What is just as alarming is that the directors may be too busy congratulating themselves on the profits from their merchandising and marketing prowess to have the wit to see it.'

* * *

The next day United were playing Leicester City at Filbert Street with six games left of the season and their title chances beginning to fade. Given the widespread commotion after the semi-final, I needed to keep close to the side dominating the news.

At half-time United led 2-0 and were in absolute control of everything, including themselves. I was in the press room with a cup of tea in one hand and helping myself to a mini pork pie when there was a commotion by the door.

The press steward was attempting to block United's chairman Martin Edwards and Professor Sir Roland Smith, the chairman of the PLC, from barging in as they didn't have a pass. Edwards caught my eye and beckoned for me to leave the room.

We were in a corridor where the public had been stilled by a raising of voices that had nothing to do with anyone shouting a drinks order. United fans couldn't believe their eyes. I was pinned against a wall where Edwards and Sir Roland were in my face saying I had damaged United's share price and they would sue both me and the *Mail* if it fell exponentially.

I remember my teacup shaking in the saucer and a half-eaten pie falling to the floor, so vehement was their protest. The only thing I could think of to say at the time was that I was entitled to my opinion and the *Mail* was entitled to print it. The 6ft 4in John Wragg of the *Express* emerged from the press room to see if I was OK, at which moment my detractors withdrew.

United won 4-0 and at the post-match press conference Alex Ferguson gave me the worst daggers of all time and when I started to ask a question, he kicked back his chair and left without a response. There was no lawsuit.

* * *

The last month of the season was a wondrous blur. Blackburn had the title in their grasp, then tried to toss it away, even to the point of losing at home to Manchester City the Monday after United's win at Leicester. Nerves were jangling everywhere.

Blackburn were beaten 2-0 at West Ham and the following night it was Atkinson v Ferguson revisited, as United won 3-2 at Coventry, Ron's latest club, with the vibrant Cole scoring twice. Going into the last weekend, Blackburn were on 89 points and United 87. Kenny Dalglish was returning to Anfield where he remained an absolute icon; United had to visit Upton Park to play West Ham.

The last-day story would assuredly be told at Liverpool whatever the results. The announcement of each member of the Blackburn team was greeted as if they were local heroes. A few early confident Liverpool touches of the ball drew jeers from the Kop.

A creeping self-doubt had consumed Rovers for weeks, illustrated by a return of seven points from a possible 18 before the last match. After an initial 15 minutes of misplaced passes and wasted possession, Blackburn took the lead, Stuart Ripley weaving down the right to provide Alan Shearer with an opening he buried with his famed right foot. West Ham had scored through Michael Hughes against United, so it seemed settled.

Then United equalised through Brian McClair, as did Liverpool via John Barnes. Siege was being laid to West Ham's goal in London; Blackburn were staggering like zombies around Merseyside. Then, almost simultaneously, Jamie Redknapp gave Liverpool a last-minute lead from a stunning long-range free kick and the wires buzzed that the Hammers had held firm. Blackburn 89 points; United 88.

Blackburn's players, almost en masse, were looking to the press box for confirmation. A couple of us held up one finger on each hand to signify the result from Upton Park. Henning Berg, Blackburn's Norwegian defender, almost fainted.

As the game continued around them, players in blue-and-white-halved shirts were leaping into each other's arms and shaking opponents' hands. Kenny Dalglish disappeared into a bear hug from Liverpool's staff and stewards.

I completed my report with, 'What an afternoon it had been for the smallest town in the Premier League who, ten years ago, had to win at Grimsby to avoid relegation to what is now the Third Division. It's quite amazing what the odd £55m [the level of Jack Walker's investment in his hometown club] can do.'

14

Coming Home and Playing Away

THE FOOTBALL world was gearing for the USA's first dip into the pleasures and perils of hosting a major 'soccer' event and more parochially, we in England had the small matter of replacing Graham Taylor to get our heads around.

My information was that the FA was keen to split the role of England manager by appointing a head coach and apprentice, who would be schooled in the role and then succeed to the top job. I suggested Don Howe, who had been Bobby Robson's number two, and a coach of great respect and virtue, working with Ray Wilkins, a distinguished international player and a manager in the making, and went so far as to describe it as a dream ticket (getting in the American mood).

The FA had to get this one right. What better man to entrust with seeking the best way forward than my old press-box buddy Jimmy Armfield, now a member of the BBC's radio commentary team and who didn't have an enemy in the world?

Jimmy canvassed opinion far and wide – he even spoke to a couple of us football writers – and discovered a groundswell of support for Terry Venables (he wasn't my choice). This was a disconcerting verdict for the powers that be. Terry may have been a free agent as he had been sacked as Tottenham chief executive by Alan Sugar, his one-time partner, but he was spending more time with his lawyers in meeting rooms in Scribes than watching football.

Every time you turned on the TV there was one investigative programme or another focusing on the same man. Our Tel.

During his formal interview, the FA panel were somewhat disengaged as through the window they could see a woman being talked down by police from leaping to certain death from the building across the street. Ultimately, she was saved and so was Venables. He was given the title head coach rather than manager and his contract would be extended until the conclusion of the European Championship of 1996, hosted by the FA.

That left two years for experimentation on the field and the same to settle the mounting swathe of court cases off it. I was very uneasy about the whole thing.

* * *

There was time to relish a bit of a busman's holiday to the USA. It was my first – and as it turned out only – World Cup finals to report on and without the 24/7 need to dissect England's every move and moment, we could concentrate on enjoying some decent football.

The *Mail* decided to split its writers into geographical areas for ease of travel costs across such a massive land. David Walker was our resident Republic of Ireland writer, so he would cover all the group matches of Jack Charlton and his boys, while Jeff Powell had the west coast gig.

I was based at the New York Helmsley on 42nd Street, which was within decent reach of Giants Stadium, north to Foxboro in Massachusetts (half an hour from my in-laws who put me up a couple of times), south to Washington, DC, and firstly to Soldier Field in Chicago for the opening match between Germany and Bolivia on 17 June.

On a stifling afternoon Germany won 1-0 with a present of a goal for Jürgen Klinsmann, but that day soccer was a long way from anyone's mind in the US and just about everywhere else. O.J. Simpson, the famed NFL running back turned film actor, was the prime suspect in the grisly murders of his former wife Nicole

Brown and waiter friend Ron Goldman in the Los Angeles suburb of Brentwood five days earlier.

Simpson was now a fugitive, being driven along various interstates near LA in a white bronco, apparently with a gun to his own head. Every television station in the country had a helicopter in the air pursuing this incredible scene. The US was transfixed. What World Cup?

Then we did have a football story to get our teeth into. Few of us in the crowd at Foxboro could have believed that when the great Diego Maradona scored the second of Argentina's four goals against Greece it was to be his last in international football, though his eye-bulging, maniacal celebration was rather extraordinary.

The next match, against Nigeria, would be Diego's final hurrah. A couple of days later in Dallas, he failed a routine drugs test for ephedrine, a performance enhancer. Maradona claimed he had been coerced by a personal trainer, by Argentine officials, and that he was fed a cocktail of treatments to treat growing weight concerns and sinus problems. FIFA heard his pleas and threw him out of the tournament. It was his Willie Johnston moment.

I flew to Orlando to cover the last-16 match between Holland and the Republic of Ireland, which was to no avail for Jack Charlton, whose side, on a blisteringly hot afternoon, were beaten 2-0 by the Dutch who included Marc Overmars, Dennis Bergkamp and Peter van Vossen, like three ghouls dancing on the grave of Graham Taylor. We landed back in Boston that evening of 4 July through hundreds of firework displays.

The quarter-final victories for Italy and Bulgaria pitted them at Giants Stadium on another 95-degree day, one ripe for Roberto Baggio to pick his way through the eastern Europeans' defence, scoring two such splendid goals that the Italians sincerely believed they had a World Cup winner on their hands.

A pity then that the final in the Rose Bowl in Pasadena would be such a damp squib, even with Brazil as the opposition. The press seating was out in the open, we had to smother our skin in suncream, wetted headgear was provided, and it was hot and hazy. The opportunities were largely restricted to shots from 20 yards or more and so we went to penalties.

The first for each team was missed, Daniele Massaro's weak effort was later saved by Brazil's Taffarel, so when Baggio stepped forward he had to score, but swept his effort over the bar. A few Englishmen knew how that felt.

* * *

Terry Venables flew to meet David Platt in Genoa in the spring of 1994. They went to Platt's favourite restaurant, Il Tipico, with its wondrous views across the Mediterranean. The former BBC sports reporter David Davies, recently appointed FA director of public relations, had joined them, not wanting to miss out on anything as was his wont.

Platt was now with Sampdoria and remembered that Venables – who had just visited Paul Gascoigne in Rome – was keen to talk tactical preferences and the conversation had barely started when the England head coach paused and relaxed. 'I'm sure he made his mind up there and then I was going to be his captain,' Platty recalled. 'It was as though I knew what he was thinking at the same time he was.'

These two aligned minds promised much for the new England era. If there were many misgivings about Venables's ability to deal with the myriad complications in his business life, the man's coaching qualities could not be questioned.

This put me in an invidious position. Terry thrived on his capacity to persuade his 'pals' in the media to see things his way, to downplay precarious off-field proclivities and steer the coverage towards unswerving loyalty, that all would be well on the night and if you doubted it, a glass of champagne was waiting on the bar at Scribes.

I was thrilled when Rob Shepherd joined the *Mail* in 1995 from *Today* because he was the best-informed, most energetic young reporter in London and also had Terry's ear, which meant he was an invaluable addition to our England coverage and beyond. *Today* had sadly been closed.

Shep and Jeff Powell defiantly promoted Terry's footballing propriety and that was perfectly fine. My relationship with him was more distant and nuanced. This worked perfectly for the paper as we had all bases covered. I'm sure Terry thought I was against him, as Alex Ferguson had.

There was so much murk in the background, it was difficult to discern right from wrong. One morning one newspaper would contend one thing about Venables's business dealings, the next there would be a twist and something else emerged. I was able to recite the names of High Court judges (one was Mr Justice Harman) before I knew Terry's England formations.

The companies involved in these stories blurred – Edennnote, Silver Rose, Scribes, First Wave, Landhurst Leasing. Sides were taken, set positions hardened. I couldn't keep up, nor could the most forensic of financial journalists which I definitely was not. No wonder the FA were nervous.

On the pitch Venables was trying and testing new players and subtle variations. Rob Jones, Barry Venison, Graeme Le Saux, Matthew Le Tissier, Stan Collymore, Neil Ruddock and Steve Howey all won caps against an assortment of opposition. We then played a nation we knew only too well, the Republic of Ireland, in Dublin in February 1995.

David Kelly gave the Republic a 22nd-minute lead and five minutes later, a block of English fans in the upper tier started to tear Lansdowne Road apart, ripping up seating and throwing it indiscriminately on top of the people below and on to the pitch. The match had to be abandoned, a signal that not all the hooligan elements had been flushed down the cistern.

It wasn't as if football had rid itself of some of its own dodgier elements closer to home. The word 'bung' became synonymous with financial impropriety in the game, one that was now awash with more money than it had ever seen before. Temptations were everywhere.

The England coach himself had come a cropper in his already decaying relationship with Alan Sugar by suggesting when he wanted to buy Teddy Sheringham from Nottingham Forest in 1993 that the deal would only happen if Brian Clough got a bung (i.e. a brown envelope payment to sweeten the deal).

Sugar went apoplectic, saying he would never consider such a thing. Frank McLintock, the former Arsenal captain, then came into the story, acting as an agent to persuade Sheringham to move, but he, too, according to Sugar, wanted £50,000 in cash for the deal to go through. Sugar demanded a proper invoice for services rendered plus VAT.

Two years later, George Graham's nine-year career as Arsenal manager ended abruptly when an FA inquiry declared him guilty of taking a £400,000 payment from the Norwegian agent Rune Hauge as part of the deals which took Danes Pål Lydersen and John Jensen to Highbury.

Graham said these weren't illegal payments but 'unsolicited gifts'. He was banned from football for a year but would return to manage both Leeds United and, remarkably, Tottenham where he was appointed by Alan Sugar.

* * *

The signing of Rob Shepherd raised the *Mail*'s football coverage to unparalleled heights. As a trio at the top of the writers' pyramid, I thought Shep, Powell and I had promoted the paper to the one that *had* to be read. As we prepared for Euro '96, this was hugely significant.

David Walker led the northern writers expertly, my pal for the best part of 20 years John Richardson was based in the north-east and knew everyone, Colin Wood was still eminent on Merseyside, Ray Matts was now our Midlands man. We all needed to be at our sharpest with a major tournament approaching.

In the summer of 1995, England staged the Umbro Cup, an event endorsed by the FA for the benefit of the country's kit sponsors and the head coach who was able to pit various selections against Japan, Colombia and Brazil, who included an 18-year-old striking sensation named Ronaldo.

There was a sense that Venables was getting closer to the squad he wanted, as much by a process of elimination as picking his perfect side all the time. The Southend supporter in me wanted to see former Shrimper Stan Collymore given an extended run in the national team but for whatever reason Venables wasn't charmed.

Stan played alongside Alan Shearer against Japan at Wembley but was never picked to start a match again. A month after the Umbro competition, Liverpool broke the British transfer record and paid £8.5m for Collymore from Nottingham Forest. Roy Evans obviously saw something that Venables didn't.

Anfield was the stadium from where I enjoyed reporting on football most (St James' Park was a close second). There was a genuine and appreciative warmth in the greeting, the fact that players, press and directors walked in through the same front door, the cosy mingling, sharing the main staircase before the directors and their guests went to the left and us to the right. The press box was 20 rows from the pitch and you were emotionally invested in every match all the time.

I worked with three managers there: Kenny Dalglish all too briefly, Graeme Souness with whom I had good relations – he gave me an exclusive interview before the 1992 FA Cup Final against Sunderland from his hospital bed after his first heart attack – and finally Evans, the most genuine of people.

Liverpool were unable to string one huge season together in my period at the *Mail*'s helm but did win the best match I had the privilege to cover, the 4-3 victory over Newcastle when both clubs had an opportunity to deny Manchester United another title in 1995/96.

Kevin Keegan had become Newcastle's manager in February 1992. When he departed from the club as a player eight years earlier, the journey had to be undertaken in a helicopter because the city's roads were awash with supporters literally weeping into their brown ales. Keegan was persuaded back to Tyneside by Newcastle's new chairman Sir John Hall who, confronted with 'horrendous financial pressures' had to set things right on the field too. Manager Ossie Ardiles was the sacrificial lamb.

Kevin once told me, 'The chairman called and said that whatever had gone wrong with the club only two people could save it and they were talking to each other.' Exactly four years on from the appointment, Keegan and Sir John had Newcastle exactly where they wanted. They were top of the pile by four points with a game in hand over Manchester United.

On 5 March, the Reds went to St James' Park and won by a single goal from the otherwise anonymous Eric Cantona. Newcastle could have scored half a dozen. I wrote, '[Peter] Schmeichel was unbeatable. He saved three times in the first ten minutes, twice from Les Ferdinand whose confidence is in danger of drying up like the service he's been receiving and then from Peter Beardsley. You sensed one of those had to go in.'

By 3 April and the visit of Newcastle to Anfield, Keegan's men were three points adrift of United but had two games in hand. From first to last on this most enthralling of nights, the Premier League paraded the very best of its wares. Each second buzzed with intent and potency, there was electricity in the air, adrenalin surged on the field and in the press box.

Liverpool led 1-0, trailed 2-1 and 3-2 and won the affair two minutes into added time when Collymore – who set up Robbie Fowler's opener with the best left-footed cross of his life – scored the second of his two goals at the Kop end. Newcastle were in anguish. Keegan almost collapsed in a heap. Playing a part in perhaps the best Premier League match of them all was scant consolation for losing it.

Two weeks later, Manchester United defeated Leeds by a single Roy Keane goal at Old Trafford. Leeds had played much of the match with ten men and Lucas Radebe, their centre-half, in goal after Mark Beeney had been sent off for handling outside the area. It was the moment for Alex Ferguson to ratchet up the psychological warfare.

Ferguson was asked to assess the extent of Leeds' resistance. 'These players have put their manager [Howard Wilkinson] in trouble and after seeing that tonight, I can only say they're cheating him. Why are they not in the top six? For some of them it's more important to stop Manchester United winning the league than anything. When it comes to playing Newcastle, you wait and see the difference.' A classic Fergie wind-up.

Newcastle would win 1-0 at Leeds 12 days later and we awaited the post-match summaries with bated breath, not to know Keegan would deliver the most astonishing tirade any of us would witness. In the Sky studio, Richard Keys and Andy Gray were pressing Keegan, who was in the Elland Road tunnel wearing a pair of headphones. Writing our reports on high in the press box, we had one eye on the lone TV screen in one corner.

Kevin was trying to control a seethe. 'You've got to send Alex Ferguson a tape of this game, haven't you? He went down in my estimation when he said that [about Leeds]. We haven't resorted to that. We're still fighting for this title and he's got to go to Middlesbrough and get something. Honestly, I'll tell you, I'll love it if we beat them. Love it.' Keegan was now jabbing a finger at the camera for added emphasis.

There was an audible gasp in the press seats. We'd need to file a new story for the back page after completing our considered match reports. I was seated in the back row of the box next to Steve Curry who had finished his rewrite and was reading it through before pressing 'send'.

At the back of the box re-emerged those reporters who had been downstairs for Keegan's conference. One such was Martin Lipton of the Press Association, a right eager beaver. In his rush to get to his phone, one of Lipton's legs became entangled with Curry's electrical lead, yanked the plug out of its socket and Steve's copy disappeared line by line as he frantically pushed every button to try to stop it. I sensed I was about to witness my first homicide.

I consoled Steve with the fact that I was sure most of the report would come straight back to him and he told me I could fuck off as well.

* * *

Steve was back to his jaw-jutting best a few days later when United indeed won at the Riverside against a Middlesbrough side now managed by Bryan Robson and with the superlative Brazilian Juninho in their ranks. These were changing times on the Tees but, for United, their domestic irresistibility was secured.

They completed the double with a 1-0 victory over Liverpool in a dire FA Cup Final, summed up in that there was more focus on the dress sense of the Liverpool players than their contribution to sport's state occasion.

Had we mistaken the occasion for a Mr Whippy convention? Into the glare of the ritual pre-final pitch-stroll walked a group of players dressed in cream suits and wearing sharp shades. I would love to have been a fly on the wall when Alex Ferguson first spotted them. It was either brazen self-confidence or brazen stupidity.

Liverpool may as well have played in their suits given their utter lack of contribution to the match itself. Cantona scored the only goal, squeezing a shot through five players after goalkeeper David James, an Armani model in his spare time, flapped at a corner.

Once the catwalk had been removed from the Wembley pitch, it was time to prepare for Euro '96 as England was readied to host a major football event for the first time in 30 years. We now knew Terry Venables wouldn't be in charge after the tournament regardless of whether England won it or not.

The official explanation was that the head coach didn't want to be distracted by the continuing morass of legal complications – including a lingering case for unfair dismissal from Tottenham. In late 1995 I'd written a piece with Noel White of Liverpool, chairman of the FA's international committee, whose admission he was reluctant to commit to any extension until he'd seen what a Venables's England could produce caused much chastening of egos.

Venables saw this as a slight that generated an apostolic fervour among his media supporters and many more across the country. Terry met White, FA chairman Sir Bert Millichip and chief executive Graham Kelly in Birmingham on the eve of the Euros draw but White, in particular, wasn't for budging.

Just before Christmas, Rob Shepherd secured a major exclusive with Venables who said he was opening talks with Kelly about a two-year extension to his contract. He had come back from a holiday to Oman over Christmas to reiterate his preference for an immediate decision or he'd be seeking alternative employment. The FA wouldn't bend.

White received unwarranted vilification from many of my colleagues. England would be looking for a new manager after the Euros while Terry spent more time with his lawyers.

* * *

The final stage of preparation for the tournament involved a trip to China and Hong Kong, ostensibly to build camaraderie in the squad and give Venables the opportunity to come closer to his definitive side. It all went a little further than anyone had anticipated.

Initially all was chilled, the weather being a humid exception. We walked a decent stretch of the Great Wall – most of which seemed to be upwards – and were delighted to stop now and again for a swig of water and picture-taking. England won 3-0 in Beijing with two goals from the talented Middlesbrough striker Nick Barmby and one from Paul Gascoigne, who was now playing for Glasgow Rangers.

The dentist's chair re-enacted – Paul Gascoigne drinks in the euphoria of his brilliant solo effort against Scotland at Wembley in Euro 96 ably assisted by Steve McManaman, Alan Shearer and Jamie Redknapp. June 1996

So near and so far. Gazza is an inch away from connecting with Alan Shearer's cross and scoring the 'golden' goal that would have sent England to the final of Euro 96. Germany, inevitably, won on penalties.

The Prides of Leigh-on-Sea – David Lloyd [right] and his brother John as captain and coach of the Great Britain Davis Cup team.

So near – Tim Henman lunges for a volley in the 2004 French Open semi-final against Guillermo Coria of Argentina at Roland Garros. Tim should have won the title that year.

A second Wimbledon – Rafael Nadal accepts the congratulations of Wimbledon chairman Tim Phillips and LTA president Derek Howorth on his 2010 victory at the Championships. Rafa and I shared a great bond.

The golden boy – Andy Murray in perfect poise as he strikes a forehand on his way to Olympic glory at Wimbledon in 2012.

Standing tall – Andy is full of emotion as the national anthem is played on Centre Court after his victory over Roger Federer [left] in the final. Argentina's Juan Martin Del Potro [right] took bronze.

The first person he saw – Andy Murray has just won his first Wimbledon. He looks up to the press box where I was pumping my fists. He did the same.

A must read – Murray takes in the thousands of words on his Wimbledon success. The Times *comes first, of course.*

Back home – Murray is greeted at home in Dunblane, Scotland after his Wimbledon victory in 2013. The crowds turned out in their thousands.

A doomed relationship – Rory McIlroy and Caroline Wozniacki at Eastbourne in 2013. I was the only journalist to interview them as a couple.

They had been deeply in love – Caroline caddied for Rory at the par-three warm-up event at the 2013 Masters at Augusta. She clearly did a fine job.

Splendid isolation – Wycombe Wanderers manager Gareth Ainsworth in typically energetic pose on the Wembley touchline at the League One play-off final in 2020. Wycombe beat Oxford 2-1 and were promoted to the second tier for the first time.

Glory days – Joe Jacobson, who scored the match-winning penalty for Wycombe, leads the celebrations. I enjoyed a fabulous season with the Chairboys and wrote Close Quarters *to document it.*

On to Hong Kong where the opposition was a motley crew of ex-professionals and expats, Venables complained about the length of the grass, England won 1-0 and the players were glad to get it over with without getting hurt. The headline on my match report was 'England a joke before the off'.

The players chilled at a race night at the famed Sha-Tin course (Gascoigne stayed at the hotel to have his hair dyed blond) and then, on the final night of the trip, Gazza and a few others were told they could let down their combined hair, whatever its shade.

A couple of the younger pros, the common-sense Gary Neville included, went to David Platt to ask his advice on whether they should join the fun. Platt said he would be resting in his room and it might be best if they did the same.

A few of the press lads went out for a drink and late on, a tired and emotional Alan Shearer walked in to where we were with the Umbro rep Martin Prothero. I moved across to chat with them. The word was that in a different bar a few streets away there had been some shenanigans but nothing too serious.

Our flight home – different from the FA's – was in the air when photographs emerged of raucous scenes with Gazza (on his 29th birthday), Teddy Sheringham, Steve McManaman and Steve Howey in a bar which housed something called the dentist's chair, where you could relax and have alcohol poured down your gullet with no need for lidocaine to dull the pain.

Not long after we'd gathered our breath back in England, it emerged that airplane equipment had been damaged on the players' journey home.

For good or evil, Gascoigne copped the lion's share of criticism. The press was demanding a sacrificial lamb. I wrote that he should be dropped from the tournament.

This was becoming really serious. The FA, whose PR was now determined by ex-BBC man David Davies, tried to draw a veil by citing 'collective responsibility' – a clever means of not offering up the lone culprit. This circling of the wagons that worked so well to Alex Ferguson's advantage at Manchester United became the national mantra.

As ever, what mattered was results on the field rather than miscreant behaviour away from it. Pitting writers who longed for English success as the 'enemy' was a discredited but oft-used method of stoking the squad to raise their game and bringing the public who mistrusted the press further onside.

The nation was beginning to flirt with irrational optimism. Skinner and Baddiel's ditty about three lions on a shirt and 30 years of hurt went to the top of the pop charts. The team did its part to douse the fires, performing feebly in a 1-1 draw in the opening group match against Switzerland at Wembley.

The Scots would now descend on the Empire Stadium, always an occasion to bring out the worst in the tabloids and our dafter brethren. Man for man I didn't think there was much to choose between the two sides. The match would swing on a penalty save by England's David Seaman from Gary McAllister after Alan Shearer had headed his country into the lead.

Seaman thrust up a left arm, the ball struck his elbow and ballooned clear. Moments later the goalkeeper cleared his lines, Darren Anderton prodded the ball forward and Gascoigne, flicking it up and over Blackburn's Colin Hendry, volleyed home past Andy Goram. He raced behind the goal, pointed at the water bottles and demanded a re-enactment of the dentist chair-follies. You had to give the boy bloody credit.

Now it was the return of the Dutch. Three years earlier, England had scored in the first minute, led 2-0 and were hauled back. This time hype exceeded hope but there remained a sense that this team had a very special performance in it.

Venables's team made the *Oranje* pay for the liberties they had taken against Graham Taylor's selections. Gascoigne was irrepressible, Paul Ince rock-solid, Steve McManaman darted and probed and Alan Shearer and Teddy Sheringham fused to devastating effect. Holland were spellbound, as were all of us inside

Wembley as England won 4-1 (the goal they conceded near the end robbed Scotland of a place in the quarter-finals).

There could be no resting of laurels, for Spain awaited the following weekend and, if truth be told, they were comprehensively the better side but couldn't score though they had two excellent shouts for a penalty and a blatantly fair goal ruled out for offside. The match went to a penalty shoot-out.

Venables had set great stall on the practising of spot kicks but with an unorthodox twist. At the end of a training session, he would take his prescribed penalty takers along with Seaman to a secluded spot at Bisham Abbey. Shearer, Gascoigne, Stuart Pearce and David Platt would have to tell Seaman where they were going to place their kicks and not vary from that spot.

The coach wanted the taking of penalties to become routine and such an approach found immense favour with the players. 'It was genius really,' Platt said. 'I had my set routine, I always believed that taking a penalty meant the kicker needed to be in control, not the goalkeeper. Making us have to pick a target and not deviate from it added to my confidence when the penalties had to be taken for real.' Gareth Southgate had not been included in this routine.

Against Spain, Shearer, Platt, Pearce (whose reaction to scoring was such I thought he'd burst blood vessels) and Gascoigne all scored, two of the Spaniards erred and so it was England who went through to face Germany in the semi-finals.

By now the red-tops were in a state of unrestrainable jingoism. It was so blatant and so depressing. The *Daily Mirror* editor Piers Morgan wanted to drop pro-England leaflets over the German training camp using a retired Second World War bomber and was reined in on that act of stupidity, though he did write a front-page piece 'declaring war' on Germany under the headline 'Achtung Surrender', which was equally moronic.

We had a shedload of headlines using words like Fritz, Herr, War and many more that made us look right idiots. Fifty years after the end of the Second World War and still we couldn't restrain ourselves. I couldn't wait for the match itself and an end to this nonsense.

The Germans were dressed in their normal white shirts and England plumped for grey. Why not red, like 1966, which would have made us look elegant and poised? Grey suggested dullness and a lack of identity. I never got a straight answer to why that was the FA's choice. When Alan Shearer thundered England into an early lead, heading in from a Gascoigne corner, it seemed not to matter as much.

BBC commentator John Motson – a great chap – had his tail pulled after a commentary on the Germans when he talked about having had two players substituted and recalled only one of their names. He said 'Kuntz' emphatically which only went to enamour him more with the football-watching public. But Stefan Kuntz it was who drew Germany level against England, taking the match into extra time.

In their wisdom, UEFA had initiated a new rule for the tournament, a 'golden goal', by which the team scoring first in extra time won the match there and then rather than playing a full 30 minutes. It was done in the hope of rewarding enterprise and energy.

England certainly had both of those. Darren Anderton struck an upright when falling off balance and immediately, Shearer crossed low from the right, German goalkeeper Andreas Köpke missed it and Gascoigne slid in from two yards but was never close enough to the ball to divert it into an empty net. The nearest England player behind him was David Platt.

'If I had been in Paul's position, I know I would have scored,' he said. 'It is having an instinct. I'd have read Alan's mind and moved a second sooner and been there. Paul was brilliant from further out, but he didn't score many scuffy tap-ins.'

The inevitable penalty shoot-out started with ten brilliant finishes – Venables's training ground nous working again – and it was only when Gareth Southgate stepped forward for England's sixth kick that Wembley was gripped with unease. He shot straight at Köpke, then Andreas Møller scored for Germany. In 30 seconds England were out and Venables's leadership of the national side had ended.

* * *

I was six months older than Glenn Hoddle, we were both Essex boys, me Southend, him Harlow. I revered him as a player, as good as I'd seen in England. To work with him as a journalist wasn't what I had expected. Glenn was aloof, in keeping with how he'd been ever since he knew he could get the football to do his talking for him. He was never that good at talking for himself.

He had done a terrific job at Swindon Town, taking the club from the depths of the Second Division into the Premier League via an astounding 4-3 play-off final victory over Leicester at Wembley in 1993.

Hoddle scored the first goal with a typical flourish, watched his team toss away a 3-0 lead and then win the biggest match of the club's life through a dubious Paul Bodin penalty late on. The Swindon champagne had barely lost its bubbles when Glenn moved to Chelsea where I was granted a couple of interviews, at which I sensed neither of us felt really comfortable.

I didn't know what to expect of him when he was anointed Terry Venables's England successor but recalled asking David Davies, the FA's communications chief, for Glenn's private number and the request was declined. 'But that was never the case with Graham or Terry,' I said. 'It's the way it's going to be with Glenn,' Davies replied.

Hoddle's task was to pick up where Terry had left off and secure a place for England in the 1998 World Cup in France. The draw placed us in a group with Italy, Poland (again!), Georgia and Moldova. Before Euro '96, Hoddle and assistant manager John Gorman decided to watch the Moldovans first-hand and walked on to a TAROM flight from Heathrow to Bucharest, a plane that had three rows in business class to fund the four seats in row one occupied by Steve Curry, Martin Samuel of *The Sun* and Harry Harris of the *Mirror* and me. Glenn wasn't amused.

At Bucharest airport for the flight home, we bumped into West Ham's CEO, Peter Storrie, who had been to Romania in a hush-hush attempt to secure Ilie Dumitrescu's transfer from Tottenham which had as much to do with sorting out the quarantine arrangements for his dogs than persuading Dumitrescu himself. Storrie wasn't amused that we'd tumbled him either.

When it came to qualifiers proper, Hoddle made a huge decision. He chose to give a lad named David Beckham of Manchester United his international debut in Chișinău, as well as a first cap for Everton's Andy Hinchcliffe. England won 3-0, in a state of relative comfort against a nation that had only recently been formed as an independent republic.

Economically and structurally, Moldova was in a parlous state. There had been -30 per cent growth the year before England set foot on its soil and I wanted to see the levels of poverty for myself. With photographer Ted Blackbrow in tow, I ordered a taxi to take us to Hîncești, the location of an infamous orphanage I'd read up on.

The owners were given no advance warning, so couldn't spruce the place up. I doubted they could have done much if they'd wanted to. I had never seen children in such appalling surroundings; lice-ridden, fed little more than gruel, forced to lie for hours in their own faeces, the lack of hygiene was simply too awful for words. Ted told me he'd never seen a sadder sight in his life.

He was almost too physically sick to want to take any pictures but there was one that, when we saw it later on his roll of film, of a little girl, probably four years old, with the brightest blue eyes you ever did see, we knew that if they ran the story, the *Mail* had to use it. They did and letters poured in from our readers asking if there were adoption procedures they could follow.

If I did anything decent in my writing career, the thought that a little girl may have been taken out of this ghastly apology for a life to be raised with some degree of love and consideration made me happy. I often wonder what became of her and the others from that hellhole. If alive, she would be in her early 30s.

* * *

Newcastle United opened the 1996/97 Premier League season in rude form and by November sat top of the table. They had signed Alan Shearer from Blackburn, a messianic return to his homeland for the striker who had lost not a scintilla of pace, strength or finishing power. I was at his investiture at St James' Park and couldn't recall seeing anything quite like the fervour his appearance on a makeshift stage generated.

When they defeated Manchester United 5-0 in October – a rout completed by Philippe Albert, the central defender, lobbing Peter Schmeichel from 20 yards – this was overindulgence at its finest. The Geordies were flying.

In what felt like a cruel twist, Newcastle suffered their first defeat of the season at home to Arsenal just as Steve Curry and I – now a Morris Man splinter group – had secured a sit-down interview with Kevin Keegan, planned for the next afternoon.

The loss was shit timing and we were convinced Keegan would call it off. Instead he rang to say that rather than meet at the planned location on the A1, we should come to his local, the Three Tuns in Osmotherley. He'd gladly do the interview there.

It was a lovely pub in a rural location near the North York Moors. Kevin was tucked straight-backed into a corner of the bar when we walked in. We ordered lunch, a pint of local brew and started to chat. A further round of drinks was requested, then another.

By late in the afternoon and the atmosphere very convivial, Keegan said why not move on to his house ten minutes away, the drive to which was almost vertical, with him at the wheel.

We were supposed to be catching the evening flight from Teesside to London and time drifted on. The karaoke machine was getting a decent bashing, Steve and Kevin were highly proficient at snooker (I still hadn't mastered it at all), there were a couple of video games machines I was also crap at, so further sampling of the Keegan wine collection was called for.

Kevin took us back to the Three Tuns, booked rooms for the night, paid the bill and re-booked our flights. I had to tell Maureen I wouldn't be home and called her. Before she answered, Keegan demanded I handed over the phone.

'Hello, Maureen, it's Kevin Keegan here, your husband's a bit pissed and he's staying another night up here. Don't worry, he's in good hands, you won't miss him. Ta-ra.'

The Newcastle manager stayed for another couple of pints and around ten o'clock I was cogent enough to ask Steve to check he had recorded the interview from seven hours earlier. He fumbled about, found his contraption, played back Keegan's voice and we stumbled up to our rooms, put our heads down and were awoken at six the next day for our 6.30am taxi to Teesside airport.

What neither Steve nor I had an inkling about was that Kevin was seriously doubting his position at the club. He seemed so content. I was stunned when, two months after our day in his life, he announced his resignation saying he had taken Newcastle as far as he could.

There were tears in the streets of the city and convulsion pretty much everywhere else. Two weeks later, Kenny Dalglish was installed as the new manager.

* * *

We reflect on life and wonder why a certain person with whom we had no defining affinity became, dare I say it, a friend. What could Kenny Dalglish and I possibly have had in common, someone from the north end of Glasgow and the other from the west end of Southend?

As I reminded myself of the hundreds of articles I wrote as the *Mail*'s chief football writer, one name occurred more than any other. From his resignation as Liverpool manager the day after

I tried to make sense of the 4-4 draw against Everton in the FA Cup at Goodison Park, his move to Second Division Blackburn, their 1995 Premier League title, his immediate move 'upstairs' to become the club's director of football, his departure from the club to his appointment at Newcastle United, Kenny is there, first and foremost.

I can't quite get it. Maybe my appreciation of Scotland's architecture, first realised in that amateur golf championship at Troon in 1978, had spread to its people more than I understood. Many in my business found Kenny's manner intimidating. He could cut people off with an abrupt word or sentence but my respect for him as a person and what he had achieved in football overrode these elements of his personality.

In 1993 he played a round of golf with Sky's Richard Keys in a *Meet the Boss* documentary series. Without saying a word, he watched Keys address the ball and hit a beauty straight down the middle, then said, 'I don't fancy your second.' 'Why not?' Richard asked.

Kenny placed his ball on the tee, selected his driver, and fired it in the opposite direction. 'Because the hole's that way,' he said, creasing up with laughter. Richard corpsed too. You had to.

Dalglish gave me an exclusive interview when his remarkable period at Blackburn came to an end. He told of a recorded delivery letter sent to his home when the club knew he was on a golfing holiday and how it lay unopened on his front mat for five days.

Kenny rang his house and asked his son Paul to open the letter. 'It's my dismissal from Blackburn,' he said to Paul, who thought his dad was pulling his leg. When he was appointed as Rovers' director of football after the club won the Premier League title, he said he was left high and dry, 'Not consulted, not involved, not asked for my opinion. It was useful to have my name on the letterhead but that was about it.'

What rankled Dalglish more than anything was how Blackburn let Alan Shearer slip away without due care and attention. 'I wasn't informed about his move [to Newcastle] by Blackburn although

Alan came to see me before he flew to Jersey to see Jack Walker to tell him face to face of his decision. The next thing I knew it was announced on Teletext. I sat down in my living room in a state of disbelief.

'I had told him I still thought Blackburn was the better option, and not just financial considerations but other choices. I can't say exactly what I mean because that wouldn't be fair on the lad. And how could a player of his stature lose?

'Alan was only ever comfortable if he was happy with the surroundings where he worked, it didn't matter how much he was being paid. The transfer money won't bother him whether it's £15m or a fiver. He'll just be wanting to win. That's him, isn't it?'

* * *

I never did ask Kenny what he thought when I christened Liverpool as 'the Spice Boys' in the spring of 1997. It wasn't pre-planned but came as a flash of inspiration in the middle of a considered piece on the team. It hadn't meant to belittle but perhaps explain the club's consistent inconsistency. Several years later, in football publication *The Blizzard*, writer Rob Smyth recalled the occasion:

'Neil Harman's description in the *Mail* of Liverpool as the Spice Boys was made primarily because of Liverpool's lifestyle and the role of agent Simon Fuller, who managed both Steve McManaman and the girl group. As a consequence, a few of Liverpool's players attended the Brit Awards in 1997.

'It's sometimes forgotten that Harman's nickname was not given until long after the cup final white suits. The Spice Girls emerged in the summer of 1996 and it was not until March 1997 that the Liverpool team were first called the Spice Boys. It was almost a posthumous sobriquet. "We all hated the tag, but the truth always hurts doesn't it?" said [Liverpool defender] John Scales. "I know I could have done more to avoid it. All the boys could have."

'A few days after Harman coined the phrase, the tag was used to describe Manchester United. They beat Sheffield Wednesday 2-0 at

Old Trafford, a match watched by Melanie Chisholm and Victoria Adams, who met her future husband David Beckham for the first time that day. "Cole powers the Spice Boys" was *The Independent*'s headline. It was Beckham who actually got the Spice Girl.'

I didn't take the slightest umbrage at this 'theft' of my description by *The Independent*. I regarded it as the sincerest form of flattery.

* * *

An indelible image formed of the day Bryan Cooney walked into the office as our new boss. He was wearing a raincoat so white it felt as if you were either witnessing a transfiguration or had stumbled into a Daz commercial.

Cooney had been employed to turn the sportsdesk around and saw it as a chance to tear the team apart. I knew from the outset that I was high on his hit list. He had called me arrogant in my tennis writing days and I'd never seen him as anything other than a complete chancer.

Frankly, I despaired at the choice Paul Dacre, the new *Mail* editor, had made. If the sports department required a shot in the arm, if we'd fallen asleep at the wheel (a charge I bitterly resented), was there not someone out there to inspire us with a better track record of distinguishing fact from fancy?

Cooney's idea of sports editing was to lay as many mines as he could across the landscape and see how many his staff stepped on. He proclaimed to know all that was needed about certain sports and we should write what he demanded.

One by one, the departures began. Michael McDonnell, the doyen of golf writers, Nick Townsend, a terrific all-rounder, David Walker, first-rate in everything he did, and Rob Shepherd, the best young football writer around decided that the Cooney way wasn't the way for them. Shep was tempted to stay by being offered my job while I still had it, which was Cooney all ends up. He turned it down.

Into the office came a slew of red-top bods, not least my old sports editor on the *Evening Echo*, Phil Osborn, as sports news editor. Osborn hadn't changed from the rogue he'd been in Basildon. Nigel Clarke, the *Daily Mirror*'s ultimate Beastie Boy, was employed, as was Cooney's mate from the *Star*, Bob Driscoll. All of them owed allegiance to one man for finding them a place on the Kensington bandwagon. I didn't know whether to laugh or cry. Very soon it didn't matter anyway.

I'll admit the pages livened up with a widespread use of WOBs (white headlines on a black background rather than the other way about), which lent stories drama and emphasis. It was the content and Cooney's malevolence towards those who didn't see it his way that was really disturbing.

Something must have happened when he was a reporter in Scotland that led to his particular dislike of Alex Ferguson and Kenny Dalglish, two people central to my work. The trouble was that I now had a much better relationship with Alex than I ever had and Kenny and I got on really well too. Maybe Cooney was jealous of such liaisons.

The chief football writer's task was demanding enough without being constantly undermined from within. The atmosphere in the office was terrible. Cooney had a few supporters afraid to raise any doubts but most of the lads kept their heads down and got on with it. A wrong look in his direction could cause all sorts of grief.

He loved to stoke an argument where none existed and began a series of Yes/No features. 'Is Schmeichel losing his touch at United?' Yes says Neil Harman, No says David Walker. I'd be asked (told) to write 750 words saying Peter Schmeichel was showing signs of fading when it was demonstrably untrue. Cooney wanted antagonists rather than journalists.

Ferguson had a sense of what was going on when a pal of his dining in a London restaurant overheard Cooney disparaging me to those with him in the most disgraceful terms. Fergie told me all about it and I made a mental note but didn't take it further.

The straw that broke the camel's back came on Newcastle United's trip to play Croatia Zagreb in the qualifying round for the 1997/98 Champions League in August 1997. Newcastle had won the home leg 2-1 and the second would be arduous. I sent my preview and checked in with the office for any queries after finishing my first course at dinner.

The subeditor who had dealt with my copy said that the back bench needed a word. The message was that they'd been trying to get in touch at my hotel because Cooney had changed my first two paragraphs so they now read, 'Newcastle chairman Sir John Hall last night issued a European war-cry to chill the blood of manager Kenny Dalglish as much as tonight's Champions League opponents Croatia Zagreb.

'Though Newcastle teeter on the brink of elimination from the big-money European challenge, Hall was adamant that though a consolation prize of a place in the UEFA Cup awaits the losers, the Champions League is his preferred option.' The headline was 'Dalglish hit by Sir John battle cry'.

I asked to speak to Cooney but he'd left the office with specific instructions that the piece went in as he'd rewritten it. The first paragraph was pure downmarket tabloid shit (his level) and the second was stating the fucking obvious.

I said I wanted my name taken off but Cooney had insisted it stayed. He didn't have the guts to come on the phone himself. This was unconscionable.

I rang Sir John at the Newcastle team hotel and read both my original piece (sadly I don't have it anymore) and what would appear in the next day's *Mail*. He thanked me for letting him know and said his lawyers would be on the case. The minute Cooney discovered that, he flew into a red-faced rage.

We weren't going to get anywhere like this. Cooney had his agenda of which I wanted no part otherwise what reputation I had would be trashed with the paper itself. My last match as the football correspondent was a rousing 4-2 win for Liverpool over Chelsea at Anfield on 5 October 1997. Ignoring the odd protestation from colleagues that I should stay the course, I resigned a few days later.

I made an appointment with Dacre who said he was sorry to lose me but felt obliged to support his newly appointed sports editor. He said I could send him the bill for my farewell 'do' which was about a tenner as Cooney banned anyone from the sportsdesk from attending it.

A couple of members of staff refused to abide by his sanction and I thanked them sincerely though I didn't want them to suffer retribution for the sake of a pint and a handshake.

* * *

I had never resigned from anything and now here I was with two daughters – Kathleen had been born the previous October – and no income. The peculiarity was heightened the following day when the home phone rang at 7.30am. Maureen answered it and shouted up that Alex Ferguson was on the line. I wasn't particularly in the mood for nuisance calls.

I lifted the phone, heard the click and said, 'Hello, Alex?' A familiar voice came down the line. 'What's happened?' he asked. I told him I couldn't take any more of Cooney and had quit. What followed was five minutes of half anti-Cooney rant, half pep talk. I thanked him for his courtesy, that he was the first person to call and quite frankly, I hadn't taken it all in.

'You know where I am if you need me,' he said and replaced the receiver.

Alan Sugar called soon afterwards. He, too, was sorry about what had happened and, rather more menacingly, added that if I'd like him to do anything, he was available. I formed a terrible image of Alan hiring someone to give Cooney a nudge on the platform as a train arrived at High Street Kensington tube station.

In his autobiography, Sugar wrote of the press, 'Basically they are glorified fans, in awe of people like Venables, Graham and Clough. In the eyes of these hacks, chairmen and directors of football clubs are the devils, while the players and managers are angels.

'Before I alienate the whole of the sports reporting industry, I will make the point that in some serious newspapers there are great journalists who are balanced and honest – Neil Harman, Patrick Collins and Oliver Holt for example.'

The week after my departure, England qualified for the 1998 World Cup thanks to a sterling performance in Rome against Italy, where they secured a goalless draw with a performance of real courage under Glenn Hoddle. I was sad for myself that I wouldn't be there to report on the finals, but so pleased for a lot of the lads I'd grown to know fondly over the previous seven years.

Then France was back on the timetable again. Len Gould, my old sports editor at *Today* and the *Mail*, had been recruited by Mirror Group Newspapers to work on plans for a sport-only daily paper based on the concept of French publication *L'Équipe*, a hugely respected paper that sold more copies than some national dailies.

Len wanted me to be the main football writer for the paper – we never got around to naming it – and help recruit the best names from Fleet Street who might relish a role. I had the odd surreptitious tea and sandwich with Paul Hayward, one of our finest sports writers, and Lee Clayton, the best of the young Fleet Street bunch, about moving and both were intrigued.

We had the whole enterprise where we wanted it when, without warning, the plug was pulled. Kelvin MacKenzie was a hugely controversial, unlikeable former editor of *The Sun* who had been employed by the *Mirror* to run L!VE TV, a new and zany attempt to appeal to a youthful television audience.

He was in charge of our operation as well and on a whim said the whole thing was being dropped. I took it upon myself to go into his office and persuade him of its merits but he told me to fuck off. What a contemptible arsehole. L!VE TV was a useless shambles, which I was very pleased about.

* * *

The thought of writing a book had never entered my head until I received a call from Tony Stephens, the former commercial manager of Aston Villa. Tony was an astute businessman who had initially helped David Platt navigate his way through his move to Bari in 1991 and realised that even the brightest of footballers didn't understand the minutiae of contract negotiations.

On the basis of the success with Platt, Alan Shearer had decided to allow Stephens to oversee his contracts and David Beckham was similarly engaged. As one of the components of building the Beckham brand, Tony wanted someone to help David write a book on the story so far. He asked me.

I spent a day with David's parents Ted and Sandra at their semi-detached in Walthamstow in which one bedroom was a homage to their son. Ted was as careful with cuttings of David's progress as my dad had kept them for me; he recounted stories of Bobby Charlton summer camps and talked of his pride at David making his debut for United and earning his first England cap. It was all precious stuff.

The parents' stories were one thing, the player's quite another. By this time, David was dating Victoria Adams, a member of the Spice Girls. She was Posh Spice, the one who was ridiculed for making up the numbers as she had no discernible singing voice. She had David in her thrall, even if she couldn't hold a candle to Whitney Houston.

I presumed David's story could be concluded in a couple of decent interview sessions. We met for the first time at a flat in Leigh, Lancashire, some ten miles outside Manchester. I was invited to the second-floor living room where the predominant colour was a blinding white and the windows were protected by white steel railings.

'Did you see them out there?' David asked. 'Did I see who?' I answered. 'The photographers,' he said. 'They're all out there.' I had to tell him I didn't see anyone. We were both a bit hungry after a couple of hours of talking and he asked if I might go to McDonald's to pick up something for the pair of us. I returned with a couple of Big Macs with extra ketchup for him and did get the sense that when I rang the bell there was the sound of leaves rustling and plodding movement which suggested snappers in the vicinity.

It didn't take an awful lot of time to put the book – *My Story* – together and if truth be told it would sell more for pictorial than editorial content. David was pleased with it though, as was Tony Stephens. I made a few quid, though nothing life-changing.

15

A Sunday Man

MY CAREER was about to take another twist thanks to the ever-gregarious Morris Men team leader Colin Gibson. In four years, first as football editor and then sports editor of the *Sunday Telegraph*, Mr Big had had a transformative effect.

While its daily sister paper remained staid and grey, the Sunday upstart was sharper in news sense, dramatic in design and represented a real threat to the *Sunday Times*'s arrogant presumption that it was the only Sunday broadsheet worth reading.

In fairness to *The Times*'s sports editor Alex Butler – once of the *Evening Echo* – he had offered me a football match or two plus the odd feature opportunity in my time of need after quitting the *Mail*. Kenny Dalglish was happy that I should spend a day at Newcastle United with him for *The Times*.

I climbed into a large taxi with Kenny, chairman Freddy Shepherd and CEO Freddie Fletcher for a very acceptable lunch and interview. My positive reflection of Newcastle's manager didn't go down too well in a city that was beginning to tire of him. Even local reporters were contemptuous of the piece.

Gibbo then called to offer me the tennis job on the *Sunday Telegraph*. Ron Atkin was writing the sport as well as he had done but he was a prickly character and team spirit meant a lot to Colin. He was happy to keep Ron, who didn't want to stay once he heard I was coming in, which was perfectly understandable.

The *Sunday Telegraph* had a terrific first team. Patrick Barclay was the football columnist, Colin Malam the chief football man, Steve Curry had left the *Express* and happily reacquainted with one of his best pals, and Clive White was a stylish wordsmith. Scyld Berry wrote imperiously on cricket, Derek Lawrenson knew golf inside out, there was no more informed racing writer than Brough Scott and it didn't take long for me to pick up the threads of tennis.

Mr Big had an unexpected ace up his sleeve. Bill Bateson had spent 34 years at the *News of the World*, the last 12 as the sports editor, and was regarded as a superb craftsman. When he retired from the paper, Gibbo snapped up Bill to become a consultant on the *Telegraph*. It was a masterstroke.

Every Tuesday the lads would gather in the sports office on Canary Wharf to debate weekend prospects. Gibbo's deputy Simon Hart and the number three Paul Newman brought talent and wisdom to the debates, we'd plan meticulously and then head off to Davy's wine bar to settle our bodies.

It was there, especially, where Bill was in his element; his journalistic know-how, a sense of how to bring the best out of reporters and his sheer enthusiasm that made you feel ten feet tall. It helped, too, that Gibbo was unrestrained when it came to travel. The *Sunday Telegraph* sports writers journeyed well.

For the tennis correspondent there was added value in that the paper had concluded a ghostwriting deal with John McEnroe. I never asked how much it cost and was glad I wasn't told.

I knew from way back that there was nothing about tennis on which John didn't have an opinion. Shutting him up was the problem. Our conversations would last at least an hour and the *Telegraph* usually only wanted around 800 words. There were times when one call with Johnny Mac emptied three columns.

He was certainly more than brilliant value as we moved into a new century. John was appointed as the US Davis Cup captain in late 1999, a choice not without more than a chorus of dissent. The first female president of the United States Tennis Association

(USTA), Judy Levering, was taking a heck of a gamble because John's undeniably short fuse and the need for diplomacy in the captain's chair made for an uncomfortable combination.

What could not be denied was Mac's love for an event of unabashed patriotism where personal glory was sacrificed on the altar of national success. Could John persuade the likes of Andre Agassi and Pete Sampras, not always enthused Davis Cuppers, that they should give their all, especially as the first tie on the agenda was in Zimbabwe, immediately after the Australian Open of 2000?

Agassi was in breathtaking form. He had won the 1999 French and US Opens, trailing by two sets in the Paris final to Ukrainian Andrei Medvedev and coming from behind to beat fellow America Todd Martin in New York. Andre won in Melbourne, too, his most sparkling form coming in a five-set semi-final victory over Sampras.

Gibbo said I could make the trip to Zimbabwe, for all the understandable reasons. The route took us from Melbourne via Sydney, Perth and Johannesburg to Harare. I was upstairs on the Qantas jumbo where the other snug seats were taken largely by ITF officials, including the two umpires, Bruno Rebeuh of France and Australia's Wayne McKewen.

Agassi, who confirmed he would play, was downstairs with his coach, Brad Gilbert. Sampras had bruised a hip in Melbourne so the unheralded Chris Woodruff, a Davis Cup rookie, was a late call-up to play second singles.

The draw took place in the back garden of the palatial home of Zimbabwe's despotic ruler, Robert Mugabe, who was tiny by comparison to the power he exuded. You could see the top of his head and his glasses above the rostrum when he made his welcoming speech but not much more. I had never seen so many bodyguards in one place in my life.

It became, as expected, a tumultuous tie in a stadium little more than an expansive tin hut in which any pocket of fresh air was greatly appreciated. Agassi, despite the exertions of his Australian triumph and the 17-hour flight to Africa, won his first singles against Wayne Black, the younger brother of Byron Black, who was also representing the hosts.

The press seats were in the front row opposite the umpire's chair and the moment captain McEnroe felt compelled to have a rant, Rebeuh looked across at me and rolled his eyes. By the end of the second day the US were 2-1 down, a situation that encouraged groups of jubilant locals in the crowd to perform impromptu dance routines at each change of ends. The captain's hotseat was getting decidedly hotter.

Agassi's resolve, though, was unshakeable. He vomited at the side of the court during his sweatbox three-set victory over Byron Black but refused to buckle and brought the tie level. Best of all was Woodruff's performance in the final rubber, a victory of enormous courage against Wayne Black that went against all rationale. McEnroe had his winning start.

We landed in London the next morning in various states of disrepair after much clinking of champagne glasses on the flight from Harare. John mumbled a few indecipherable words at the luggage carousel and staggered away to catch the Concorde to New York.

If the sporting panoply, the Meikles Hotel that hosted us and Harare itself had been special enough, one memory abided. During the stay, a group of us clambered into the back of a minivan, McEnroe to the fore with Levar Harper-Griffith, a black teenager who was in the side to gain experience as a hitting partner.

We were taken to the Chitungwiza township where a tennis court, in pretty decent shape considering, was filled with black kids who from the moment we arrived, surrounded us, tugging at our clothes, hoping there was something we might offer them. One boy, around ten or 11, wouldn't move more than a foot from me all the time we were there.

'Please, sir,' he begged as we were about to climb back into the van, 'take me home with you.' I told him I wished I could, but I couldn't. It was too hard to look back out of the window as we pulled away.

* * *

There was a momentary opportunity to move back into full-time football in 2000. Adam Crozier, a Scot who had moved up the ranks at the advertising agency Saatchi & Saatchi, was a surprise choice to be the new chief executive of the Football Association when Graham Kelly stepped down.

David Davies had manoeuvred himself into a senior role at the FA and was ostensibly Crozier's right-hand man. The role of communications director became available. I applied.

I thought I had a decent chance. The football boys surely looked upon me with respect, I knew their role and had been at the sharp end of FA relations for seven years. In the anteroom before the last round of interviews I bumped into Paul Mace, a well-respected freelance from Leicester, so I knew I was in for a battle.

I didn't like Davies's sniffy attitude throughout the process. Steve Curry said Davies wouldn't recommend me because he knew I'd do the job better than he'd done it. I didn't take to Crozier at all – far too up himself.

When the FA appointed Paul Newman – a news reporter and BBC man like Davies – I knew they'd made a mistake. He had no experience of top-level football and lasted a little over two years.

* * *

On 10 September 2001 I was leaving New York City the day after the US Open. The ritual on a recuperative day in the city was lunch at the Oyster Bar inside Grand Central Terminal, an iconic Manhattan venue.

It was a 15-minute stroll from my hotel to 42nd Street and if you timed it right, you'd get a seat at a long bar, sample a dozen Cuttyhunk oysters with a Bloody Mary of Curry proportions, order the day's catch, hopefully a bluefish filet washed down with a Kendall Jackson chardonnay. All very nice if you weren't paying.

Lleyton Hewitt, a precocious youngblood from Australia, had won the men's singles the previous day but the story of the tournament was an all-Williams sisters final, won by Venus over the younger Serena. These girls could really play ball and the American public was seized by their extraordinary talent. I admired their athleticism but found them tough going in journalistic terms.

I was booked on the final BA flight from Kennedy airport to London at 9pm, about the time local weather reports indicated a major storm would be bearing down on the city. We barely had time to stow our hand luggage when the plane began to move.

The pilot said that if we didn't go that instant we'd be trapped because he couldn't take off given the expected ferocity of the incoming storm. The plane thundered down the runway and as I looked back across the skyline of Manhattan, it was covered by an eerie shadow of forbiddingly deep red.

The following afternoon I was half asleep on the couch when Maureen said there were reports of a plane crashing into one of New York's iconic World Trade Center towers. I tuned to CNN. The storm had gone through the previous night to leave a cloudless blue sky and perfect flying conditions. The horrors that unfolded that day need no further elaboration here.

My immediate task was to track down John McEnroe to see if he would contribute a *Telegraph* column way outside his usual remit. John had visited fire and police stations in the nearest precincts to the now destroyed Twin Towers on the evening of 9/11 to thank the workers for their life-saving efforts in distressing circumstances.

It took a couple of calls to persuade him to write for us but in the end he did so, recounting highly charged tales of heroism, his tears, denouncing the savagery of the attacks and just being, well, John McEnroe from New York City. The article was used across the top of the Sunday front page. A sports column had never received such prominence.

When I left the paper a few months later, John sent a lovely signed poster thanking me for making him appear so erudite. I had just let John be John.

16

The Times Comes Calling

THE CALL came out of the blue. Keith Blackmore was head of sport at *The Times* and asked if I fancied lunch with David Chappell, the sports editor, and him. Oliver Holt, a young writer I admired, was departing as the paper's main sports writer to join the *Daily Mirror*, quite a leap of platform.

All sorts of machinations went through my head and I ended up preparing myself to say yes to returning to football, my true sporting passion. The conversation instead was all tennis. Ollie, bless him, had recommended me strongly to the sporting top brass who were keen to make a change in the role.

The current correspondent was Alix Ramsay who wrote in a distinct style that verged too often towards the cynical for my taste. There had been a falling-out between her and Holt at the 2001 French Open when a mix-up over who was writing what about which match ended with Ramsay calling Ollie 'sunshine', which wasn't meant to suggest he brightened up her day.

Rumours quickly spread that I was party to some malign conspiracy to bring about Alix's downfall – and they were total bullshit. There was no conversation about the role prior to my lunch with Blackmore and Chappell. It was they who turned the subject to tennis.

Once I'd accepted their offer, there wasn't much the *Sunday Telegraph* and their new sports editor Jon Ryan could do about it. I was only a contract writer so had a minimal notice period and Jon didn't kick up a fuss which was really good of him.

I recall asking Blackmore if there was anything about my style he wanted me to change for *The Times*. 'We wouldn't have asked you to come if we wanted you to do anything differently,' he said.

The crusty formality of an interview with the editor of *The Times*, Peter Stothard, remained to be negotiated. The sports chiefs may have been eager on my appointment but if the big boss took a dislike to me, the whole process could come to a jarring halt. Having read up on him I formed the impression that Stothard wasn't particularly passionate about sport. I would not have the opportunity to test that theory out.

Stothard's stewardship of the paper was coming to an end. The man chosen by Rupert Murdoch to lead the most prestigious of his global newspaper titles was Robert Thomson, an Australian who had been working in the far east for the *Financial Times*. Robert arrived in post a couple of days before my scheduled interview and saw no reason to postpone.

It was the first time I'd been in *The Times* building in Wapping and was shown into an office lit by a single bulb with no decorative shade, whose main desk had not one adornment and where the bookcases were bare. It did have two straight-backed chairs though. Stothard had at least left those behind along with a thin coating of dust.

'Not much to see is there,' said Thomson, an awkward, slight, stooping figure wearing a thin, dark tie and a tight-fitting suit. He didn't look like an editor was supposed to look but having chatted tennis and more with him for half an hour, I found him exceptionally bright and disconcertingly knowledgeable about my particular sport. He said I was his first appointment so it would always be special for him and, he hoped, for me.

Leading for *The Times* was an honour and at Wimbledon – only a couple of months away – it meant conducting a team of many talents gathered from across the department, the most flamboyant and gifted of whom was Simon Barnes.

The chief sports writer really was much more than that. He was a wordsmith *par excellence* blessed with an ability to paint pictures, evoke emotions and – how can I put it? – be so damned good, he lifted our content to a different level.

Simon's big thing was ornithology; he could distinguish a lesser-throated warbler from 50 paces. He despised golf and when sent to cover the Open once, wrote his entire piece about the local wildlife in Sandwich, then went home.

Fortunately for me and our readers, he loved tennis. In *The Times*'s row at Wimbledon, I took the desk nearest the window, between which was a walkway where reporters could pass and stop for a chat, to pick brains and have theirs picked in return.

Players and coaches would often venture in, sit on the windowsill and gossip away and a lot of times there would be a rap on the window and a gesture from someone outside who wanted a word but not where everyone could hear it. Barnes sat to my immediate right and beyond him were such diverse talents as Owen Slot, Alyson Rudd, Patrick Kidd, Ben Smith, Rick Broadbent and Giles Smith, backed by the very best sports photographers in Marc Aspland, Graham Hughes and Gill Allen. We were a brilliant team.

There would be an early morning huddle to talk through the plans of the day, decide on who did what and then we'd venture our separate ways, always mindful of having to react if something occurred that we hadn't prepared for.

The first day of that first Wimbledon would become another unforgettable baptism. Goran Ivanišević was the defending men's champion but had declined to play because of shoulder problems, leaving the way for Roger Federer to take centre stage. Federer was playing Mario Ančić, Ivanišević's fellow Croatian and an 18-year-old qualifier.

Ančić was tall, distinct and commanding. His qualification for the main draw was completed by a victory over Byron Black of Zimbabwe, a formidable athlete on any court, especially grass. Ančić won in straight sets as he had his other two matches.

'When the draw was made I felt confident,' Mario said. 'I was not going to be fazed by the Centre Court though it was my ultimate dream to play there. I knew I had the game to cause Roger problems and that was the way it happened that day. The first set was incredibly important and once I had that in my hands, I really believed the match was mine.'

Ančić's startling victory was clearly the lead story and therefore my responsibility. I stared at a blank screen. What the hell was I going to write? Next to me Barnes was bashing at his laptop as only he did. He had an eccentric style in this as in so much else. The minute he hit a wrong key he would emit a cascade of 'fucks', an utterance so much at odds with someone who could write poetry at 100 miles an hour.

I saw his paragraphs flowing. It was nearing 6pm and I hadn't written a word so girded myself to tap him on the arm and ask a question. 'Might I see what you're saying, Simon, so we don't write the same thing?' He took mortal offence. 'My dear chap,' he said, 'we *won't* be writing the same thing,' before returning to his keyboard and thumping away to a further flurry of fucks.

Barnes didn't hang around for friendly chit-chat once he'd finished his piece and cleared it with the office. He would rise swiftly from his chair, fiddle with his cravat, don his headgear – not unlike the Sorting Hat in the Harry Potter stories – bid a wavy, jovial farewell and disappear, job done.

Whatever I did write that afternoon was the following day's back-page lead with Simon's eloquence alongside it. From that day I never asked to see his copy and we would form what I considered an unbeatable duo for the next dozen years at Wimbledon that's not been bettered since.

* * *

Pete Sampras remained prominent among those whose life I was intrigued with. In 2000 I interviewed him for the *Sunday Telegraph* at the Intercontinental Hotel in Stuttgart. It felt like a covert operation. He wouldn't say what room he was in. I was to go to the front desk, ask the receptionist to call ahead and then take the lift to his floor and knock on his door.

I made my way along the corridor, tapped lightly and the door opened though I couldn't see inside. I did hear a voice. There was a single small lamp lit, otherwise the room was completely dark. Pete said he didn't like lights on in his room at night, even if guests arrived. It was eerie. The contents of the interview have rather passed me by.

Pete was ostensibly a private man who neither courted fan worship nor was unduly concerned if he didn't get much. It may have been his on-court demeanour, that of a player who though blessed with many talents had a going-through-the-motions manner (massive serve, smooth volley, fine-tuned groundstrokes if required), walked with shoulders hunched and possessed a desire to constantly monitor the state of his feet.

He would just about look a ball kid in the eye when he wanted the ball while expecting them to keep him under permanent surveillance.

He was pissed when the order of play for his second-round match against George Bastl of Switzerland placed him on the old No. 2 Court, the 'Graveyard of Champions', where the finest had been cursed. Sampras thought it an insult to his standing to be despatched to such a relative hinterland.

Bastl, blond, squat and a decent athlete, was in the main draw as a lucky loser, a player who had been beaten in the qualifying competition and earned a reprieve when a main draw player had to withdraw, in this case the Spaniard Félix Mantilla.

This was a match that – through experience – required making sure you were in the vicinity of the press seats at least half an hour before you anticipated the match might start. And you might be sticking around for quite a while. The front row of the seats on No. 2 offered a stunning view, knees pressed against the canvas court surround and if you extended your arm, it almost reached the tramlines.

Bastl, astonishingly, led by two sets to love before Sampras dug deep and recovered the deficit. This would often be the time the lesser player would fold or, at the very least, start to doubt. Bastl wouldn't go away. Sampras was winning games yet didn't seem to have the requisite verve to win the match. Then, midway through the fifth set, at each changeover, he'd dig into his bag, take out a couple of sheets of paper, read for a few moments and then fold them back up.

Gill Allen, *The Times*'s photographer, was in the row directly behind Sampras's chair. She wrote this for the paper a few years later, 'I saw Sampras pull out and read a note. Before I knew the content, it seemed incongruous.

'Normally all that the players have on the court is water and bananas – and rarely does Sampras show signs of emotion and weakness. I was so intrigued that I switched lenses and trained my Nikon 300mm on the white paper. It was only when I could read the first sentence that I realised what it was. The lettering was girly and the opening words were, "To my husband."

'I felt I was intruding on an extremely intimate moment. But it showed the human side of sport, and the vulnerabilities of a sporting legend. I was in the one seat from which it was possible to capture the words. I had an exclusive. There were moral questions. I used a telephoto lens – how intrusive was it? Is Wimbledon, with all its spectators, TV cameras and journalists, a private place?

'Did we need permission? I left it to my editors to decide. The next day the note appeared on the front page, but with just the first line visible. The editor told me that he'd spent the afternoon agonising over its use.

'Three months later, at the US Open, Sampras met Neil Harman, *The Times*'s tennis correspondent, and thanked him for the paper not disclosing the letter's contents. Neil asked, "What if you won the Open, Pete, would we be OK to use it then?" "Yeah, that would be cool," he said.'

There was indeed much agonising about Gill's image after Sampras's defeat as to whether we should use the letter without permission. He had been crushed once that day. I approached Pete, told him what we had and asked if we could print it.

He said he'd rather we didn't. In an increasingly frantic to and fro of calls I suggested to the desk we might use the first couple of lines and blur the rest. Pete said he was OK with that, so that is what we did.

As Gill said, it was front-page material and a *Times* exclusive.

* * *

Tennis was a lovely sport to cover. I'd make no bones about it. Who in their right mind would turn their nose up at annual stops in Paris, Melbourne, New York, Monte Carlo, Madrid, Rome, Indian Wells and Miami with Wimbledon mixed in?

The touring regulars hadn't changed much from my time at the *Mail*. John Parsons was still demanding more words from the *Telegraph* than they were willing to give him, John Roberts pored over his copy for *The Independent* and though David Irvine had retired from *The Guardian*, the coverage was in safe hands with the excellent Stephen Bierley who I knew from covering football in the north of England.

I had been at *The Times* for a year when I was voted in as chairman of the Lawn Tennis Writers' Association, a venerable institution formed in 1951 and to which a majority of us had a strong emotional attachment.

Parsons had been secretary since Rod Laver was in short pants and the chairmanship was handed down on a rotational basis every two years. Muggins had his chance in 2003.

The kudos of being an LTWA member was being able to fight for improved press facilities at home tournaments, engaging especially with the LTA and Wimbledon and, as far as the Championships were concerned, the guarantee of an allocation of tickets for Centre and No. 1 Courts as a quid pro quo for our devotion to the sport. The association members voted annually for the recipient of an award for 'services to British tennis' presented at our festivity in December.

In 2003, Georgina Clark was our nominated award-winner. I was particularly fond of Georgina, the first woman to umpire a Wimbledon final and latterly a prominent referee on the WTA Tour. Her talents were to the fore, notably at the 1999 French Open Final between Martina Hingis and Steffi Graf, one that became an irresistible addition to the sport's folklore for reasons both joyous and infamous.

Graf was supposed to be on her last legs. Hingis, the Swiss Miss, was rampant in 1997, claiming three of the four grand slams and had won her third consecutive Australian title heading into Paris, the only slam she had not won.

The final lived up to and exceeded expectations. With a 6-4, 2-0 lead, Hingis only had to keep her characteristically nerveless self-control and the title would be hers. Then she lost it. The first point of the third game was called for Graf but an aggrieved Hingis was sure the lineswoman was mistaken. French umpire Anne Lasserre descended from her chair, pointed to the mark and affirmed the call.

The simple thing would have been for Hingis to reluctantly accept and play the next point. Instead she insisted she knew where the right mark was and committed the cardinal tennis sin of walking around the net to her opponent's side to point it out. A point penalty was called on Hingis, who promptly returned to her chair and refused to play on.

The referee was summoned and Georgina was at his side walking on to court. They talked Hingis around, but her mind was frazzled, she lost the second set 7-5 and as the crowd roared Steffi's name, the German won the final set for the loss of two games. Hingis even served underarm in her last service game, which got the French in a right state. Hingis was inconsolable and walked off in tears. Away from public glare, Georgina was at her persuasive, forceful best. She said Hingis had to go back out on court whatever her emotions. A few moments later, on the arm of her mother Melanie Molitor, Hingis reappeared and was given a generous reception.

* * *

I wanted to make the LTWA night as memorable as possible for Georgina, especially as it was staged at the All England Club. HRH Birgitte, Duchess of Gloucester was a fervent tennis fan and a delightful person. Wouldn't it be a bit of a coup if we could persuade her to come? I wrote to her lady-in-waiting and received a positive response.

Who to have as our guest speaker? The golden oldies tour reached its finale at the Royal Albert Hall at this time of year and perhaps John McEnroe, with whom I had an enduring relationship, might look kindly upon the occasion. He said he would.

There were all sorts of protocols to follow. A two-page foolscap letter arrived with the details of how the Duchess would travel to the venue, timings down to portions of a minute, how to greet her and what form of words we should use thereafter. It only just stopped short of saying how we should lay out the cutlery and where to stick our pinkies.

As the car carrying the Duchess neared the entrance to the debenture holders' lounge on a frosty evening, Maureen and I were accompanied by Wimbledon chairman Tim Phillips and the LTA president Charles Trippe as we made our way down the stairs to greet her.

The proper behavioural procedure was to welcome her as 'Your Royal Highness', which was how you would introduce her to other guests in the room as you walked through towards the top table. Touching was not allowed, only guiding.

Once the initial YRH was out of the way, it was in order to call her 'Mem' as opposed to 'Ma'am', the unique preserve of Her Majesty The Queen. I had Mem-ed a few times when she whispered, 'Please just call me Birgitte.'

I did have a rumble in my tummy as Johnny Mac approached the dais. I needn't have worried. He realised the sensitivity of the occasion and gave a heart-warming speech, full of lovely anecdotes and with just the right balance of humour and ironic outrage.

Mem applauded warmly. We waved HRH off into the night with a satisfying sense that everything that could have gone right went right. Three days later I received a handwritten note from her lady-in-waiting, with a Kensington Palace letterhead.

> *Dear Mr Harman,*
> *The Duchess of Gloucester has asked me to write and tell you how delighted she was to attend your annual dinner dance at the All England Club.*
> *Her Royal Highness thought there was a very happy and relaxed atmosphere and she could not have enjoyed it more.*
> *She was so pleased to meet you and your wife and would like to thank you both for looking after her so kindly.*
> *Yours sincerely,*
> *Louise Wigley*

As a postscript to the event's main course, the LTA awards were well received, especially when the Junior Player of the Year was announced. Sixteen-year-old Andrew Murray from Dunblane was the recipient, having risen 640 places on the ATP Tour. What would become of him, we wondered.

17

Goodbye JP

THE WEATHER was unfailingly perfect in Indian Wells in March. There was rarely a cloud in the sky, the dewpoints were non-existent, we were surrounded by the greenest of greenery and more golf courses than you could shake a nine iron at. Heaven on earth.

John Parsons, Barry Flatman and I made up the British national paper contingent in 2004 and for my hire car, usually a bottom-of-the-range job to suit *Times* finances, the man behind the Avis desk pointed on his sheet to a rather extravagant yellow, open-topped sports he said was in the budget range. It would be fun to be seen gliding down El Paseo in this little beauty.

Though the sun beat down consistently in the desert, JP was never one to let loose in the sartorial sense, preferring a rather faded blue blazer with buttons on the cuffs and long pants. As a small concession to temperatures approaching 100°F he would take off the blazer and wind his long-sleeved shirt to his elbows, which was a bit daring.

John never willingly slowed down, even though he operated on a single kidney that had been damaged when he was struck by a soldier's rifle butt in the midst of a *coup d'état* in Nigeria in 1975. He had to be careful with his lifestyle and diet and I used to watch on in abject horror as he would tip a disgusting cereal-like concoction over his orange juice at breakfast before stirring it into a disgusting paste he had trouble swallowing.

Heading to the site this particular year, JP climbed into the back seat of my yellow sports, taking in the clear desert air. He often had to hold tight to his wide-brimmed straw sunhat for fear it would lift off and go hurtling back down Route 111.

The tournament was one we enjoyed more than any other for quite a while. Tim Henman reached the final, dropping a single set en route to a meeting with Roger Federer. Here was a gig we set our hearts on whenever we pursued our selfish holy grail of a Brit lasting an entire week. Might Tim actually win?

The answer came rudely in a 6-3, 6-3 loss to the Swiss, a savage reverse for their Wimbledon quarter-final meeting 18 months earlier. At least with the eight hours of time difference against us, the swiftness of the match meant we could report Tim's loss in our first editions. However much JP tried to hide it, he never did take a Henman loss well.

In the calmest of retrospect, both Flatters and I had noted a distinct and troublesome weakening in both John's steps and enthusiasm during the week. But, as ever, he had to be at Palm Springs Airport at the crack of dawn on Monday morning for the flight to Miami so he was in position for the draw for the next event, in Key Biscayne. To JP a tournament wasn't real unless he was there from first ball to last.

Call me unprofessional but I preferred to unwind and concentrate fully on the arduous journey on Interstate 10 from the desert back to the hire company in Los Angeles. There was enough time for a chilled beer at some cheerless airport hotel to rise at 5am on Tuesday for the 9am flight from LAX to Miami on American Airways – often a turbulent few hours across the Gulf of Mexico.

In the diary that first evening in Miami was a dinner for the British press at the Intercontinental Hotel with Ian Wight and Chris Kermode from the Queen's Club tournament. Henman had been invited along for a convivial couple of hours. JP was there but didn't last the first course before saying he wasn't feeling great and wanted an early night.

We woke next morning to the news that John had been taken to Mercy Hospital in Coconut Grove after collapsing in his room. It was too early to know what was wrong but it appeared he had caught an awful infection in the desert, which was drilling down on his one functioning kidney. I don't know why but the whole thing didn't feel good from the outset.

The two British freelancers, Alix Ramsay and Eleanor Preston – doing what they thought was right – took it upon themselves to organise minibus journeys from the tournament to the hospital, which was 20 minutes away if the traffic wasn't snarled on the Rickenbacker Causeway that linked Key Biscayne to downtown Miami.

I declined each time a seat on the bus was offered, instead choosing a couple of times when I could be on my own with John and only if the nursing staff felt I wasn't getting in the way.

On the second visit, which would be the last time I saw JP alive, the mobile phone resting on his pillow rang. It was Heide Cohu from the LTA hoping to chat. I picked up the phone and had a brief word saying it didn't look good at all. John was terribly weak and appeared to be shrinking into his bed.

I read him the day's results so far, said the *Telegraph* wanted 1,000 words and that he'd better be back at the tennis soon. At that, with tears in my eyes, I said goodbye.

We had to leave on our appointed flights at the end of the tournament and waited at home for developments. In April, a month after his initial collapse, came the heartbreaking news that JP had passed away from acute kidney failure. The whole repatriation process was a nightmare. I so felt for his sister Heather and her husband John, who had to deal with the paperwork and US Customs intransigence. Finally, they brought our man home.

John's memorial service was held at St Margaret's Church, Wimbledon, from where the All England Club was visible and in which every pew was replete. Tim Henman, on whom JP doted as a fellow Oxfordian, read from John's Gospel, chapter 14. 'In my Father's house there are many dwelling places. If there were not, would I have told you that I am going to prepare a place for you? And if I go and prepare a place for you, I will come back again and take you to myself, so that where I am, you also may be.'

John Roberts delivered a touching eulogy. As chairman of the LTWA, I was both obliged and very honoured to read 'Death is nothing at all' by Henry Scott-Holland, which ends:

'Life means all that it ever meant. It is the same as it ever was. There is absolute and unbroken continuity. What is this death but a negligible accident?

'Why should I be out of mind because I am out of sight? I am waiting for you, for an interval, somewhere very near, just around the corner.'

And then, in glorious sunshine, the congregation walked just around the corner and down the hill for drinks and sandwiches to prepare for another day of championship tennis with JP somewhere very near.

* * *

In the interregnum between John's passing and the memorial service in his honour, I had been asked if I would assume the role of Wimbledon yearbook author and Tim Henman exceeded all expectations – especially his own – by reaching the semi-finals of Roland Garros.

Tim wasn't regarded as a clay-court specialist. I'd seen him play fabulously well on the surface many times because he was stupendously light on his feet, approached the net more than opponents were prepared for and could end a rally both instinctively and with panache. When he was in the zone, he was a sight to behold.

To suspect he might put himself in a position to win the French and break his grand slam duck in Paris really did extend credulity to unanticipated heights.

In the first round on Court Suzanne Lenglen, Henman trailed Cyril Saulnier, a Frenchman then ranked 79 in the world, by two sets to love. We were metaphorically packing our bags. Tim then noted that Saulnier was in a bit of physical distress and thought it might be useful if he stuck around. The match slowly turned as our boy pushed Saulnier deeper and deeper into the court and won the final three sets, 7-6, 6-4, 6-3.

Astonishingly, in the fourth round and on the same court, Henman trailed by two sets and 0-30 in his first service game of the third set against Frenchman Michaël Llodra – exactly the same position he'd faced against Saulnier. He couldn't produce another piece of escapology, could he? But he did, from match point down just to accentuate the occasion.

For *The Times*, I wrote, 'The only time that Henman had recovered from match point down to win a grand slam encounter was against Jim Courier in 1999 on Centre Court at Wimbledon, his favoured patch. This is a foreign field that had once been totally foreign to him but Henman has become the first Englishman to reach the French Open quarter-finals since Roger Taylor in 1973, though Henry Billington, the British number one's maternal grandfather, made it in 1939 when this was a 64-man draw and the quarter-finals were a round sooner. This was in the genes all the time.

'The final set ebbed and flowed and Llodra, egged on by the entire France Davis Cup squad, was cavorting across the court each time he confounded Henman with an outrageous winner – and there were plenty. The tenth game proved critical, Henman double-faulting three times and missing a backhand volley to stand match point down.

'Llodra, rightly, chose to chip and charge behind a backhand approach, but Henman ran around his backhand and found a tiny opening. "For an hour and 50 minutes I was playing the wrong way and it wasn't a great sign," Tim said. "To find a way to win is character-building."'

Tim was now in the last eight in Paris, a lone attacking player in the company of those steeped in the lore of baseline attrition, the Argentines Gastón Gaudio, David Nalbandian, Guillermo Coria and Juan Ignacio Chela; former champions Carlos Moyá of Spain and Gustavo Kuerten of Brazil, along with Lleyton Hewitt of Australia. The Brit was the outsider by a country mile.

He was scheduled late on Court Philippe Chatrier against Chela on Wednesday evening and won at a straight-sets canter. We rubbed our eyes at such a disdainful performance. Henman would now face Coria, who had despatched Moyá with equal ease. Oh well, it had been fun while it lasted.

Except that on Friday afternoon, taking the game to an opponent regarded as the clay court 'future', Henman led by a set and 4-2. To use a boxing analogy, he had Coria on the ropes and one more punch, flush on the jaw, would finish him. One might argue, given his ultimate record in grand slams, that the one element Henman lacked was a killer instinct. There's no doubting that here, against Coria, he backed off.

The young Argentine suddenly sensed nervousness in his opponent and ran off 13 games in succession. If the match hadn't inextricably turned – Henman served for the fourth set at 5-3 – it was never quite the same contest again. Tim said au revoir but what memories his challenge evoked.

Coria raced into a two-set lead in the final against his compatriot Gaudio – the first an embarrassing 6-0 – and twice stood a point from the title but was similarly betrayed by the shock of what he was about to achieve.

I wrote, 'Something can happen in the head of a player who sees his opponent rocking and rolling. In the fifth set Gaudio lost his focus, double-faulted a couple of times and was 4-2 down. From then Coria could not hold his serve, though he will see forever in his mind those two match points at 6-5, a backhand wide on the first, a stuttering forehand on the second. What a terrible way to lose.'

18

The Davis Cup

THE SPAN was 28 years, six continents and too many ties to tell of them all. Telford was the first, Naples the last and at various times with various colleagues I was present in such places as varied as Bucharest, Geneva, Harare, Mexico City, San Diego, Seville, Sydney, Tel Aviv, Umag, Vilnius, a whore house in Odessa and a gay bar in Luxembourg (the last two weren't venues for the ties, more improbable diversions).

The Davis Cup formed an indelible element of my days of tennis reporting and contained so much political intrigue, team insurrection and diplomatic faux pas there was barely time left to play the matches.

The event could transform a non-entity into a hero and reduce a hero to a non-entity. A lot of players thrived in Davis Cup theatre while others shrank from it. And all of this was played out, of course, in a format wildly distinct from any other event on the calendar. It was team v team, nation v nation, home and away, singles and doubles combined. Beautiful.

What had initially begun at the start of the 20th century as a bit of hit and giggle between college types from the US and Britain turned into something quite marvellous, with barely a corner of the globe not touched by its magic in some form or another.

The choice of a nation's Davis Cup captain held as much kudos in tennis as that of a national manager in football. The scrutiny of them could be harsh and often their choices were only as good as the players allowed them to be.

Trying to persuade your best players that their country needed them often fell on deaf ears. Then there were the players who didn't want to be on the same side, in the same locker room or on the same court with another player of the same nationality.

Then there were those who changed nationality freely and others tempted with non-too-subtle inducement to change nationality but wouldn't do it. Then there were players who wanted to be captain but who certain players wouldn't play for. And all this was just in Britain.

It had appeared so straightforward in the spring of 1986 admiring on at a tennis centre in Telford as Jeremy Bates and Leigh-on-Sea's own John Lloyd gave GB a rollicking 2-0 lead against Spain in a league called the World Group, which seemed marvellously grand. When Lloyd and Colin Dowdeswell won the next day's doubles, Britain had won the tie.

That meant Britain would play Australia in the second round at Wimbledon, which wasn't at all like Telford. Pat Cash, a dashing upstart from Melbourne, and Paul McNamee, noted more as a doubles player, kicked the backsides of Bates and newbie Andrew Castle. The doubles and the tie were lost and therefore Britain would return in the 1987 first round of the World Group, starting the process all over again.

Paul Hutchins was team captain, a thoroughly nice man of easy-going temperament who accepted defeat and loss in the same stoic manner. He didn't go for expansive emotion if the team won or sulk disagreeably if they lost. Such equanimity would be tested to the full when Britain drew Mexico as their first opponents in 1987.

The tie was to be played in Mexico City the week after the Lipton tournament in Key Biscayne. Castle was Britain's only participant in the singles in South Florida and lost in the first round, which was hardly a happy portent.

Rex Bellamy, *The Times*'s correspondent, and I were in the same row on the flight from Miami to Mexico. As the plane careered down the runway, there was such wailing, praying and signs of the cross being made it was clear that hardly a single economy passenger was confident our Pan Am 727 – which did look ready for the knacker's yard – would make it.

Circling Mexico City, I had never seen so many buildings stacked, it seemed, one on top of the other for as far as the eye could see. You could only imagine how many people this mass expanse housed and in what state they lived. I was only to see the real Mexico City from the air. The British team and press were housed in relative opulence.

On the eve of the tie, Hutchins appeared at a top-table event with Bates and Castle, his nominated singles picks. The usual niceties were followed before we gathered at a 'Brit' sidebar. It was at this where Castle, when asked a relatively innocuous question about potential crowd influence, used the word 'animals'.

There was much clearing of throats and penning of notes. We had a diplomatic incident on our hands, as well as the potential for some lively headlines. The captain's head was spinning. Chris Martin, a freelance radio reporter, was preparing to send the quote across the international airwaves and probably earn himself a decent few more quid than he had initially bargained for.

Hutchins asked for a meeting and for the first time in my experience – before or since – pleaded with the press to ignore the 'animals' quote. We had to come to a pretty quick decision and agreed – more reluctantly in some cases than others – to his request.

We'll never know what would have happened had we said no, and Castle – free of the shadow of that incident – has gone on to greater success in radio and television than he achieved on the court. Britain lost the tie 5-0 and the crowd was rowdy but didn't overstep the bounds of decency.

Hutchins, who had captained Britain to the 1978 final in Palm Springs where a certain John McEnroe made a startling debut for the USA, had decided to retire after the 1987 World Group relegation play-off against Yugoslavia in Zagreb. The great Fred Perry was chief guest for the tie, a marvellous man in every respect, charming, eloquent and a good laugh.

I lucked out by getting the biggest room in the team hotel – massive wrap-around balcony and all – a stone's throw from the splendid main railway station. Rather than take us all to an expensive restaurant, Hutchins asked me if we could hold his farewell reception chez Harman.

There we were in my quarters the night the tie ended, after another drubbing, spilled out on to the balcony – Fred Perry and the LTA hierarchy swelling the throng – toasting Paul's retirement and wishing him all he wished for himself.

* * *

The LTA had their Sven-Göran Eriksson moment and appointed a foreign captain to replace Hutchins. Warren Jacques from Australia was a gritty pro whose international chances were limited because he was in the same age group as Rod Laver, Fred Stolle, Neale Fraser and Roy Emerson. Jacques had made his name as the coach who inspired South Africa's Kevin Curren to the 1985 Wimbledon final.

The task was to restore Britain to the World Group, a daunting prospect given our limited playing resources. A happy home win on grass against Finland was followed by a crushing reverse on clay in Zell am See to Austria, who possessed in Thomas Muster and Horst Skoff two competitors far too ferocious for the British boys.

For the opening European zonal encounter of 1989 Britain again drew Finland, and a whopping 4-1 win in Helsinki meant that when Argentina came to Eastbourne on grass a couple of weeks after Wimbledon, a formality was expected, especially as neither of their chosen singles players, Alberto Mancini and Martín Jaite, had played in SW19.

Instead – as the Davis Cup was wont to do – the favoured nation was given a slapping and in Mancini, the Argentines discovered a young player of immense character, given that the surface was entirely foreign to him. Argentina won the tie 3-2, Mancini taking the first-day scalp of Chris Bailey in five exhilarating sets as light faded.

Which led us in May 1990 to Bucharest, my final tie as the *Mail*'s correspondent. The capital of Romania was in a state of simmering unease five months from the summary trial and execution of the former dictator Nicolae Ceaușescu and his wife Elena, so any time a noise vaguely akin to gunfire was heard, you were tempted to duck under the nearest table.

The walls and glass-fronted balcony of my room at the Intercontinental Hotel – where the foreign press had been billeted during the previous winter's revolution – were riddled with bullet holes. We were told it was better for our well-being to eat in the hotel and only leave on official transport to the Club Sportiv Progresul which hosted the tie.

There were nightly demonstrations, some of which went on until three in the morning, so sleep was hard to come by. We were taken on a tour of the presidential palace, the structure of which was disfigured by signs of violent struggle and whose sheer size and opulence in a country bedevilled by economic hardship went to the heart of the uprising against the old despot.

The tie was stage-managed by Ion Țiriac, a former Davis Cup player and shrewdest of businessmen who was making hay in the financial free-for-all after Ceaușescu's assassination. The arrival of a team of Britain's diplomatic standing was the perfect opportunity for Țiriac to showcase a new, free and appealing Romania.

Țiriac had once suggested to me that he should run British tennis, a sport he said was bedevilled by professional privilege and amateur administration. He wasn't wrong in either case but the thought of having someone so unpredictable in charge sent shivers down what passed for an LTA spine.

The official dinner for the players, press, bigwigs and our Romanian hosts was staged at a picturesque restaurant chosen by

Țiriac. Imagine his horror when Jacques said thanks but no thanks to the food because the team had already eaten the tinned corned beef and baked beans they brought from London.

Țiriac had copious amounts of the finest Black Sea caviar to shift and raged at what he perceived as an unforgivable slight. The visiting press could be relied upon both to make sure all the food was consumed and to devour the story too, quoting his angry reaction at length. 'It is the British team's privilege not to eat my food if they don't want it, I can't educate them,' he said.

The tie itself almost became an irrelevance as Corned Beef Gate continued. Jacques – usually a jovial chap – wasn't happy in the slightest with the coverage, even turning on John Parsons of the *Telegraph*, telling him to grow up. The normally unflappable JP had never been so insulted.

One could understand the captain's dismay at the headlines, especially as his team produced a remarkable victory in such strenuous conditions. Danny Sapsford, called in for his debut on a blisteringly hot day, won the first singles in four sets over George Cosac and though Jeremy Bates lost the second rubber, he combined with Andrew Castle to win the doubles easily and then excelled in his first reverse singles, defeating Cosac in four. The tie was Britain's.

When it came to filing our reports, all was not so successful. There was a lone lady in an office at the tennis club with one phone from which the wiring was visible. Those of us who had thought to pack a few dollars were able to catch her attention when pleading it was our turn to be put through to the copy takers back home. The queue of hot and bothered British writers stretched a good 20 yards.

The story didn't end at the back of that line. As a parting gift, each of the visiting press was presented with a 3ft-long inflatable pencil to remember Romania by. We stacked them in the overhead compartments for the flight home, which stopped over in Vienna from where a couple of colleagues and I diverted to Rome for the Italian Open.

The remainder of the party landed at Heathrow and, as they waited for the baggage carousel to churn into action, some indignant team members began to raise their voices at the media party in anger at the tenor of the coverage.

There is no filmed evidence of the press lads waving their inflatable pencils in the face of some aggravating tennis players, though I was assured the arguments were protracted enough to cause one of our group, Ron Atkin of *The Observer*, to suffer worrisome chest pains.

* * *

Eight years later with the *Sunday Telegraph*, I would pick up the Davis Cup baton where I had dropped it in Bucharest. Even better, my Leigh-on-Sea chums David and John Lloyd were now captain and coach respectively.

The team had moved on from Bates and Castle to Tim Henman and Greg Rusedski, who were a whole different can of worms but just as afflicted by personal ambition and political infighting. Lloyd had helped discover Tim when – with financier Jim Slater in the mid-1980s – he started a scheme to nurture young talent while offering a first-class education at Reed's School in Cobham. Tim was one of the initial intake and thrived.

Rusedski arrived a decade later amid much fanfare and plenty of raised eyebrows from Canada to the country of his mother's birth. There was jealous antagonism from those in the British system who didn't want an interloper diverting their money supply, a view at variance with the LTA's desire for a ready-meal potential champion.

Lloyd had no qualms about Rusedski's status and relished the thought of having a doubles team holding their own with any in the world. 'They weren't great pals,' Lloyd said, 'but in the '60s Mike Sangster and Bobby Wilson hated each other and were superb together. I told Tim and Greg that if they played as a team at Wimbledon they'd win it for sure, but it never happened.'

Lloyd's tenure as captain pivoted on two ties within the space of ten months. In April 1999 at the National Indoor Arena in Birmingham in the World Group, Britain hosted the USA, a rebirth of the competition's original challenge. Henman and Rusedski led for Britain; the Americans selected a former number one player in Jim Courier along with Todd Martin in singles and a world-class doubles team of Martin and Alex O'Brien.

What followed was three days of magnificent tennis that came down to a single-point difference. Britain were trailing 2-0 on the first day whereupon Tim and Greg were mesmeric in defeating Martin and O'Brien in five sets, keeping the dream alive. Henman, who had extended Courier the distance on Friday, then beat Martin in the fourth rubber which meant the tie would be decided between Courier and Rusedski. There had never been a tennis match in Birmingham – or many other British cities – like it.

Twice Rusedski recovered from a set down to take the match into a fifth. The tennis was truly exceptional, the courage of the two players phenomenal. Courier just had that little bit more quality on the big points. 'If Greg had won that match, I think there could have been a gigantic change to tennis in Britain,' Lloyd said.

The captain wasn't so bouncy at the turn of the century when he paid his own fare to watch his team's preparations for the Australian Open, with a Davis Cup tie in the Czech Republic directly after the grand slam. 'I was shocked at what I saw,' he said. 'Tim and Greg aside, the players were totally unfit. There was absolutely no excuse for any athlete not being 100 per cent fit. I decided to train the arses off them.'

The positive response was such that Lloyd decided to upgrade all the contenders for his side to business class for the journey home. 'They took their punishment and I decided they should have a reward, that's the way it should be,' he said. 'You know what a bloody long way that trip is and the boys had a tie a week later.'

Lloyd went to meet LTA president Malcolm Gracie and John Crowther, the chief executive, who had arrived in tennis from

Vickers defence systems – 'a bloody tank builder', Lloyd rather disdainfully described him. The LTA were not only unhappy with the extra expense of business class fares to sign off but faced a fiery personality in Lloyd fed up with working to a 12-week contract who said the job of Davis Cup captain ought to be one part of a full-time role running the men's game (the system that now operates).

Gracie and Crowther turned that idea down and after a 4-1 loss in Ostrava, Lloyd resigned to discover later on Teletext that he had been sacked. 'How could they sack me when I'd already resigned?' he said. In British tennis nothing was ever quite what it seemed.

Roger Taylor succeeded Lloyd in time for what should have been a cakewalk tie. If you could hand-pick your debut, Taylor would have been hard-pressed to better Ecuador at home on grass a week after Wimbledon. Well, that was the theory.

Nicolás Lapentti defeated Rusedski in five sets on the opening day, teamed with brother Giovanni to win the doubles that gave Ecuador a 2-1 lead and then, in the final rubber, Arvind Parmar squandered a two-set lead to 17-year-old Giovanni, and Ecuador triumphed 3-2. A public post-mortem was required and perhaps a scapegoat or two as well.

You could hardly fire Taylor after one tie and the LTA's French performance director Patrice Hagelauer, only 15 months into the job, couldn't have worked out how to fix the endemic problems in the game, so Richard Lewis – the head of men's international tennis – became the fall guy.

Crowther said Lewis would become 'a media agenda item'. Tim Henman spoke to one of his favoured writers and in a ghosted column agreed with the decision to show him the door.

In the following week's *Sunday Telegraph*, I wrote, 'There were whispers when Lloyd lost his job in February that Henman was not exactly unhappy, even though it was from a private scheme backed by Lloyd in the mid-'80s that a teenaged, toothy Tim first emerged.

'Since Lloyd's departure much has been made of Rusedski's "friendship" with him to the extent of an invitation to the players' box for his Wimbledon bid. Rusedski made a fool of himself by prevaricating over whether he'd continue playing Davis Cup in the wake of Lloyd's dismissal – which has begun to look like froth and fuss over nothing, given his failure to come through for his adoptive country when the chips have been down in the competition.

'I understand Rusedski – through his agents – heaped pressure on the LTA to come up with a contract involving a lump sum payment to their client in return for his help in promoting the sport, guaranteeing his availability for the Davis Cup and other British tournaments and getting out among the public, to pump the virtues of a tennis career. No such agreement has been signed and there is a lingering resentment at Rusedski's attitude.

'There are conspiracy theories everywhere. A number of newspapers have been pestering Henman and his wife Lucy in an attempt to stand up a rumour that she is pregnant (she is not). Their families were receiving calls during the build-up to the Ecuador tie and there are those at the LTA who think someone is trying to get at Henman through mischievous rumour.'

* * *

Great Britain won three of their next four ties but in 2003, as I was getting my feet wet at *The Times*, Taylor's reign came to an end. A defeat in Australia the week after the Australian Open was not unexpected as the home nation laid a slow clay court at the Sydney Olympic Tennis Centre at Homebush Bay and Britain's two singles players were Alan Mackin and Alex Bogdanovic.

Neither Henman nor Rusedski was fit and though the rookies tried their hearts out they were out of their international depth. The craic from the Aussie crowd was typically robust. They mocked Mackin's ghostly white skin and as Lleyton Hewitt, the Aussie number one, was frontman for a particular brand of toilet paper, called for him to 'wipe the floor with the Boggy-boy' Bogdanovic.

Britain were thumped 4-1 and a further loss later in the year in Casablanca, Morocco, was deemed to be the time to change the occupant of the captain's chair once more. In came Jeremy Bates at the same moment as David Felgate, his good friend and Henman's former coach, was named as LTA performance director. Hagelauer yearned to be back in France and who could blame him?

Bates's first tie was against Luxembourg in a middle-of-nowhere town called Esch-sur-Alzette. The opening day was my 47th birthday and did not begin well as Arvind Parmar lost another five-set match, this time to a giant left-hander named Gilles Müller. Blushes were saved as Henman paired successfully with Rusedski in the doubles and then won the first reverse singles.

That evening a group of press boys and LTA coaches ventured out for a drink. We couldn't find anywhere half decent and I strode on ahead insisting that the next place we found open we'd stop. Without pausing to check the signage, I walked purposefully to the bar, turned and saw everyone else was backing out.

It was only when I realised the clientele were all male, tattooed, wore biking gear, head scarves and were moving in on me in a rather-too-expectant manner that I, too, decided retreat was the preferred option and we'd have to go thirsty.

* * *

Our next stop on this magical mystery tour was Tel Aviv, quite a mesmerising place. I'd never set foot in Israel and its tennis association was in our profound debt for organising a trip to the holy city of Jerusalem the day before the tie.

We walked the steps of Jesus in the Garden of Gethsemane, entered the church of the Holy Sepulchre which stands at the location of Christ's crucifixion, placed a prayer request in the Wailing Wall and spent time submerged in the cultures of the Old City where one minute you were in the Arab sector, and with another step – without a sense that you had crossed a border – had passed into Jewish territory.

For the entire day we were escorted by an armed guard whose duty was to round up those dawdling too long in the market's treasure troves and make sure we stayed together as a group. It was hard to reconcile that in a city beyond one's imagination and of such beauty, a single false move, even an unknowing one, could spark something that might require the threat of gunfire. A bit like relations between the LTA and the British press.

I really wanted the partnership of Jeremy Bates and David Felgate to thrive. I had known them for 20 years, reported on their playing careers, we were near-contemporaries and could enjoy each other's company, albeit with the degree of tension that always stirred when LTA and press mixed, even with a pint in our hands. They thought we were too quick to snipe whereas our attitude was that something always came along to thwart our not entirely unreasonable hope that we might win some matches here and there.

One evening I became embroiled in such a fierce debate at the hotel bar about something or other in British tennis that Martin Bohm, a chain-smoking Swede recruited by the LTA to bring more fire and technical nous to the leading players, punched me hard in the stomach. It certainly extracted the wind from my argument, even if I can't remember what it was.

The tie itself saw the Davis Cup introduction of two very distinct personalities as a doubles team. David Sherwood was the son of John Sherwood, the 1968 400m Olympic bronze medallist. David seemed to find it hard to dwell in the shadow of such parental excellence. He never let his shield down.

Bates chose to partner Sherwood with a 17-year-old named Andy Murray and it proved a masterstroke. By walking on to court for the opening ceremony with iPod attached, Murray gave tennis the street credibility it required for more youngsters to treat it as a serious sport of choice.

Murray – without his iPod attachments – and Sherwood played with astonishing maturity to defeat the long-established Israeli partnership of Jonathan Erlich and Andy Ram and set up a British victory. I wangled a seat home in business class and drank the champagne of victors that had not been a regular sensation heading back after Davis Cup ties.

The taste of sparkling success in Israel was to be short-lived. Six months later, in a play-off to win a lucrative World Group spot, the British team were thrashed 5-0 in a large tin shed next to Geneva airport by a Swiss side who called upon a couple of decent players, Roger Federer and Stanislas Wawrinka.

The following April a team from Serbia and Montenegro landed in Glasgow, parading a confident young chap named Novak Djokovic who spoke perfect English. Behind the scenes, negotiations had begun that might have altered the course of British tennis history entirely.

* * *

'The talk was serious to be very honest with you.' Novak Djokovic and I were discussing for the first time the extent to which Great Britain was prepared to go to turn a Serb into a Brit. As far-fetched as it seems now, Djokovic and Andy Murray were mighty close to becoming team-mates.

It was only Djokovic's devotion to Serbia – a country struggling with its identity in 2006 and which could not match the splendour offered to a starry-eyed teenager and his family by the British authorities – that prevented what would have been the liaison to end all tennis liaisons.

That year, the destiny of the almost 90-year union between Serbia and Montenegro was at a crossroads and a referendum had been called as to whether the two states would remain locked or go their separate ways. By a small margin, independence won the day and so Serbia went out on its own for the first time since 1918.

The LTA seized on this nationhood uncertainty to bend the ear of the Djokovic family and suggest that a move lock, stock and barrel to Britain was worthy of careful consideration. Look at how Greg Rusedski had prospered. 'Britain was offering me a lot of opportunities and they needed someone because Andy was the only one,' Novak said. 'That had to be a disappointment for all the money they invest.

'But I didn't need the money as much as I had done. I had begun to make some for myself, enough to afford to travel with a coach, and I said, "Why the heck would I?" I am Serbian, I am proud of being a Serbian, I didn't want to spoil that just because another country had better conditions.

'A lot of athletes had been misunderstood in Serbia and it is still not easy always to be appreciated. But hope was there. If I had played for Great Britain, of course I would have played exactly as I do for my country but deep inside, I would never have felt that I belonged. I was the one who took the decision.'

No one inside the LTA would confess that the discussions with the Djokovic family went as far as they did. Novak would have had to live in Britain for two years, another would be required to fill in all the paperwork, but it would have been worth the wait. No one did anything wrong. It was left to Novak to do the right thing by himself.

Djokovic, playing to the local Glaswegian audience, wore a Scottish football jersey to Serbia's pre-tie press conference and subsequently won both his singles against Rusedski and Parmar in a tie staged in Scotland for Andy Murray's benefit before Dunblane's own was declared unfit to play singles.

When Israel came to Eastbourne later that year and defeated the British on grass in a humiliation as great as that inflicted by Ecuador five years earlier, Jeremy Bates decided to resign the captaincy and John Lloyd of Leigh-on-Sea was on his way in.

* * *

The changing rooms for the away team in Odessa, Ukraine in September 2007 had once housed a brothel. There was a rather ingenious positioning of mirrors, several of which were on the ceiling. Captain Lloyd's first task was to explain to one of his players what crabs were.

For some reason, I'd been separated from the rest of the press group and was housed on the waterfront in a huge-ceilinged, repressively ill-lit and cold hotel I discovered was once the KGB headquarters in the city. I didn't take a single meal there, preferring to leg it to a local coffee shop for sustenance. Who knew who was listening, even to *my* copy?

There was quite the GB entourage – Lloyd, the Swede Peter Lundgren who was Roger Federer's former coach and long-time friend of the captain, Andy Murray's coach Brad Gilbert, and Ron Yu, one of the world's leading racket stringers. Britain had better win to afford to pay all the bills and stave off relegation to the competition's Euro/Africa Zone Two. League One, in other words.

Greg Rusedski had an affinity with the host nation as his father Tom was part-Ukrainian, part-Polish. There was no better occasion to give Greg his head and he responded with a bravura opening-day performance, defeating the home side's number one player Sergiy Stakhovsky across five demanding sets, 9-7 in the fifth.

The appearance of Gilbert in the British locker room was causing a bit of angst. The American wanted to have his say as to whether Murray should play singles and doubles in such a demanding tie. Lloyd wanted him to get lost. As it happened, John selected Murray for both and he was required to play the first singles on the final day, responding with a straight-sets victory over Stakhovsky to confirm Great Britain's success.

The great story behind the ties at this period centred on the conundrum of Murray's form, fitness and dedication to the cause. Andy wasn't always the easiest to deal with. John Lloyd not only had this particular political hot potato on his plate but had his older brother David going on at him about remaining a BBC commentator while captaining the team as if it somehow reduced John's ability to say what he thought in match analysis and not know who to pick a couple of times a year. The brothers had a falling-out about that one.

The years of 2009 and 2010 weren't exactly golden. Britain lost two home ties, first against Ukraine in Glasgow when Murray wasn't fit (again) and Lloyd blooded babes Josh Goodall and Chris Eaton who found the exposure just too much. The second setback was a 3-2 defeat to Poland in Liverpool in September when Murray chose to play but Dan Evans lost both his singles matches. Britain were thus relegated to Euro/Africa Zone Two, from which there was little further to drop before we fell through the floor. In the first tie of 2010, GB would play in Vilnius, Lithuania, a first-time opponent.

There were four press boys on the trip: Jonathan Overend of the BBC, the *Mail*'s Mike Dickson, Mark Hodgkinson of the *Telegraph* and me. We were a stoic quartet. It was snowing outside but the Lithuanians were wonderfully warm hosts and their tennis centre was every bit as good as any I'd seen.

On the eve of the tie, the four of us were heading out to eat with LTA press officer James Munro. As we assembled on the steps of the hotel, Munro said we'd be joined by chief executive Roger Draper and the head of performance, Steve Martens, a Belgian recruit who was supposedly dynamite with statistics. Munro knew how much I, in particular, disapproved of Draper's tenure and had no time for Martens's madcap theorising.

What occurred was one of the least enjoyable free meals I experienced in all my time in reporting. None of us really knew what to say. Three days later the pair had to come to our hotel to explain away a 3-2 defeat to Lithuania that humbled Britain. It was pretty much the same old tripe.

I discovered the LTA had tapped up Greg Rusedski for the captaincy with Lloyd still in the post and wrote it for Monday's paper as an exclusive. The shit really hit the fan. Rusedski was not exactly popular with the majority of his fellow players. If Murray didn't want him, the appointment would be stymied.

Lloyd had offered to resign once before but the players wanted him to stay. The LTA were worried more about the press, the public and the perceived state of the game. Draper announced that an inquest was being held into the Lithuania debacle, something Lloyd discovered on the TV's text service in his hotel room.

There was much legal toing and froing about how much the LTA would pay Lloyd and Paul Annacone, the American who had been brought in as Davis Cup coach – a role he once held with Tim Henman – so they might go quietly. Did Lloyd and Annacone go of their own volition or were they ejected? We were never quite the wiser. A settlement was agreed, though Lloyd and Annacone felt they had been harshly judged.

And Rusedski didn't get the job after all that. From out of absolutely nowhere – though he had been Andy Murray's coach as a junior – Leon Smith became the new captain.

19

The Making of Andy Murray

THERE WERE a privileged few at the US Open who, by dint of superstardom, breeding or seeding, were guaranteed an official tournament Mercedes to and from Flushing Meadows and their posh hotels in Midtown Manhattan.

Everyone else with a pass, the lower-ranked, juniors, press, TV, officials, American hangers-on with loud voices and booming indifference to protocol, took one of the Greyhound buses that left every half an hour, hither and thither.

The first time I came into contact with Andy Murray was midway through the junior event that year when he clambered aboard – his tennis bag clumping against those passengers now wishing they hadn't preferred an aisle seat – for the journey back into the city.

Andy was pale and gangly, hair all over the place and entirely indifferent to the likes of me. His fellow Scots competitor Jamie Baker – neat hairstyle, neat game – had a fascination for reporters and their jobs and took the next seat to mine. Andy was in the row behind. Jamie and I chatted away before he introduced me to Andy who shook my hand and grunted something I assumed to be 'hi'.

A few days later, Murray was junior champion. I climbed to the top of the Arthur Ashe Stadium with Andy and his mum Judy as they posed for pictures with the Manhattan skyline as a perennially magnificent backdrop. Top o' the world, ma!

This was a kid worth getting to know although my sense was that he would take some persuading to open up. He was a typical shy teenager but with an atypical experience that shaped his attitude to life and an understandable suspicion of those in it.

Andy and elder brother Jamie had been pupils at Dunblane Primary School in 1996 when Thomas Hamilton, who had run a boys' club in the town that the brothers frequented, chose to go on a shooting rampage in the school. Hamilton shot dead 16 children and one teacher, an abomination that the brothers survived as they hid, protected, from the gunfire.

No one who hadn't endured something as awful as this could appreciate how it affected human emotions. Andy, I suspected, was a quiet soul anyway and my attitude towards him was as someone who wanted to know him and never pressed too firmly in that regard.

I warmed to him even if his attitude was cautious to the point of obstreperousness. When he collapsed on the centre court at Queen's Club in 2005 while playing Swede Thomas Johansson, I was as pissed as he was that my 'colleague' Matthew Syed wrote 'you're nae fit laddie' in an article about his physical strength. I thought it was a bloody stupid thing to say.

I needed to work to regain Andy's confidence in *The Times* and there were significant roadblocks along the way. Patricio Apey, his agent, had been a particular pest, blocking all requests for an interview until at Indian Wells in 2006, he relented. I'd be allowed half an hour in Andy's hotel room, tape recorder off, to keep it relaxed and informal.

The pair climbed into the back of my relatively tiny hire car and Andy gave me a ton of crap for my easy-listening musical tastes. It was like driving with my daughters. We decamped to his room at the Grand Champions Hotel and he laid back on his bed.

We'd been chatting for about ten minutes when he stopped me, opened his computer and started to read out my articles about him. Why did I say this? What prompted that comment? Then he said I didn't watch enough of his practice sessions.

The talk turned to ambition, 'I said at the end of 2004 I wanted to be in the top 100 by the end of the next year. I had a couple of bad tournaments at the start and people said "he should keep his mouth shut". What would people prefer, someone who said they wanted to be inside the top 100 and finished 120, or someone whose ambition was to get inside 300 and finished 280?

'Greg Rusedski has believed in himself more than anyone on the tour and that's why he's had such a successful career. I don't know if other players haven't been ambitious or good enough, but when a 17-year-old says what I said, why can't people just be happy that there's someone who wants to do well, rather than wanting to be mediocre?'

He asked if I thought Alex Ferguson would be interested in tennis. 'Probably not, but he'd be intrigued by you,' I said. 'That's because we Scots have a fierce pride in the things we do that others can never appreciate. I am the British number one, but I would prefer to be the British number one from Scotland every time.'

* * *

Greg Rusedski needed to believe in himself more than at any other time at the start of 2004 when he was enmeshed in a doping story that threatened to bring his British dream to a crushing end.

A routine urine sample taken during the previous summer's tournament in Indianapolis contained low levels of an anabolic steroid called nandrolone which, in one of its forms, could enhance performance.

At that same time the ATP was having to deal with the case of Czech Bohdan Ulihrach, who had been banned for two years for ingesting nandrolone then raised suspicions that it may have been administered by the ATP's own trainers in the form of electrolyte (salt) tablets. There was a potential link to the cases of six other players, whose names remained secret.

Rusedski would have to clear his name at a tribunal in his home country Canada in February 2004. He was adamant he would never knowingly take a performance enhancer, railed against the 'biggest scandal in world sport' and was delighted that elements of the British game rallied round. David Lloyd, for one, helped Rusedski beat a path home from Australia and then housed him at his home on the banks of Loch Lomond to shield him from prying press lenses.

My information was that the tribunal may well find against Rusedski's attempt to link his failed doping test with the seven the previous year. He would have to prove to the judges' satisfaction that he took the drug unknowingly and had acted responsibly at all times. I wrote an article in the paper suggesting he may well lose the case.

Before the edition was on the newsstands, the front page was featured on Sky News's paper review. My phone rang. It was Lloyd in a vituperative rage, 'I'll fucking have you, your paper, everyone, we're going to sue, you'll lose your job over this.' I couldn't get a word in edgeways and my hands were shaking.

A month later, the tribunal found in Rusedski's favour. The exoneration was utterly complete. 'The ATP could and should have taken steps to notify players in a meaningful and direct way of its decision to cease distributing the electrolyte tablets that it had previously handed out so freely,' was the most prescient of its final analysis.

Lloyd and Rusedski didn't sue me, *The Times* or anyone else and a few years later had fallen out themselves over a property deal in Thailand and don't speak to each other anymore.

* * *

The LTA went out on an expensive limb in the summer of 2006 and employed the boisterous American Brad Gilbert to become a travelling coach at an annual cost of £750,000. The job was to take care of Andy Murray full-time and if any other British player happened to pass by, he might give them an hour of his well-remunerated time.

The contract was regarded as one of the most remarkable agreed in world tennis – a national association with a remit to build and sustain the sport would pay the wages of a coach who was ostensibly working with one player. Gilbert readily accepted the deal; the rest of the sport looked on in disbelief.

The pair would work together at only three grand slams, the last of which was the 2007 Australian Open, which began in furnace-like conditions. The heat of Melbourne was like none other for sporting competition. Summer in New England could be bloody hot but it never felt as if your skin was being seared. In Australia, you took a deep breath and your throat was parched.

These hothouse conditions suited a Spaniard over a Scot, certainly one as pale as Murray, now the 15th-best player in the world. He had drawn the diminutive Alberto Martín in the first round and was relieved when the match was transferred to the Vodafone Arena (the second show court) and played beneath a closed roof.

Murray won the first 17 games and was about to whitewash his opponent when Martín's backbone stiffened enough for him to gouge a single game. Murray reached the last 16 before losing from a 2-1 lead in sets against Rafael Nadal in the match of the tournament. A couple of us raced around to the coach's box at the end and found a teary Gilbert unable to say more than a few words – a rare treat.

I had wondered how long the pair might work together before Gilbert got on Murray's nerves. By the autumn I knew it was all over and when I called Brad at 5am on the west coast of the USA (he said he always had his first coffee at that hour) and his opening line was, 'I don't really want to talk about it,' this was verification. It was a back-page lead exclusive in *The Times* the following morning.

It was my second major story of the year. While on holiday in the US just before the Open, an impeccable source told me that Tim Henman was to announce his retirement in New York, a story confirmed by different contacts.

As a journalist you were often on the horns of more than one dilemma while writing any story. I could have called Tim and asked him to confirm or deny its veracity. In my gut I sensed that in doing that he would tip off those in the British press closer to him than I was and tell them what I was up to.

Did I just go ahead and write it and take the consequences, knowing that it had been verified by different people? No one wanted to be quoted directly. I played a hunch and chose to write the story.

The Times published it on the front page and Tim was unforgiving. This was a man whose career I had followed near enough ball by ball since 1998, who I stoutly defended in print when many others condemned him and shared perhaps half a dozen cross words with in the best part of a decade.

The retirement article changed it all. Several years down the track from its publication – when he had become a political bigwig considered potential Wimbledon chairman material – we might shake hands and exchange the odd pleasantry but that was all.

It is easy for me to say he should have been bigger than that, but I'll say it anyway. So much written about him in his career was both visceral and unsubstantiated and here I was, seen as 'on his side', condemned because of a story that was absolutely correct.

Paul Annacone, his coach at the time, took me to one side at Flushing Meadows and said how hurt Tim – and he – had been because I didn't call to check the story with him first. I thought they should both grow a pair.

* * *

A couple of months after the Henman revelation, while covering the Masters tournament in Madrid, Keith Blackmore, the head of sport, said he wanted a word. Would I be interested in becoming *The Times*'s football correspondent? I was pacing up and down a wooden walkway outside the tennis centre for hours on end taking it all in.

Surely lightning wouldn't strike twice, from tennis to football in one fell swoop? There was a lot to consider. Tennis was in a good place, there were stories everywhere, the travelling was overseas for the most part and to fabulous places. I saw in Andy Murray a potential champion whose career would be fascinating to follow. If I said yes to football it would be back to a largely domestic grindstone though it was a more prestigious position. Maureen and I discussed the pros and cons.

Being football correspondent of *The Times* was as good as it got in our profession so why did I turn the job down? It was the first time in my career that I rejected a forward step. I came to regret my decision the following month, the following year and every year thereafter, especially when my end came. Whoever heard of a tennis writer losing his job unless they were a habitual drunk?

In March 2008, in the midst of the Indian Wells tournament, I was summoned home by the office to attend the Sports Journalists' Association (SJA) awards evening at The Brewery on London's Chiswell Street, which seemed a long way to come on the off-chance of a decent meal and a few pints with known associates.

It turned into an incredible night for *The Times*. Martin Samuel was the Sports Writer of the Year, Matthew Syed the Columnist of the Year, Marc Aspland took the Best Sports Picture of the Year, Simon Barnes was co-winner of the Columnist of the Year and I won the Sports News Reporter of the Year award for the Henman and Gilbert stories as well as being highly commended as a specialist correspondent at a time when every sport was included in the one category. Jeff Stelling of Sky Sports presented the award and was extremely complimentary at the after-dinner drinks.

The paper said I could fly to Los Angeles business class the next day. Arriving back in the desert, I went straight to my favourite restaurant, Shame on the Moon in Rancho Mirage, for a reflective evening. They had set aside the prime seat at the bar, baked me a cake and it seemed every patron knew of the award and wanted to shake my hand.

* * *

Covering tennis meant having to deal as best you could with the players and, because many competitors were fresh out of nappies, with their parents too. The days of crossing swords with Stefano Capriati and Peter Graf and laughing along with the delightful Karolj Seles had long passed when I arrived at *The Times* but as a new youthful cream rose to the top, so did their mums and dads.

Many were happy to let my attempts to establish a rapport pass with a smile, a handshake or other acknowledgement that they knew who I was but weren't keen to engage beyond that. Those who couldn't converse in fluent English, such as Sebastian Nadal, Robert Federer and Srdjan Djokovic, confided with a nod and wink.

Tim Henman's parents, Tony and Jane, solidly stoic in the players' box whenever they watched their son play, would say hello but the minute you broadened the chat which might lead to a comment on Tim's play/chances/demeanour they dashed for the nearest enclosure where the press weren't granted access.

There were the rather irritating ones. Helen and Tom Rusedski used to stay at the same hotel in New York, the Elysee on East 54th Street, and if they spotted me at breakfast, there would follow a half-hour diatribe on their son and the fates befalling him. I resolved to stagger my breakfast arrival time or peer around the corner, snatch a coffee and retreat to the sanctuary of my room.

The more intriguing and initially approachable were the Aussie parents, notably Glynn and Cherilyn Hewitt and John Tomic (I never met Bernard's mother), although in time I lived to regret being as engaging as I tried to be.

At the US Open in 2001, Lleyton Hewitt had defeated American James Blake in the second round and courtside it was clear that there was a degree of tension in the air. You couldn't pick up on everything if you were in the press seats diagonally opposite to the players' support area amid the interminable noise-fest that was Arthur Ashe Stadium. A sixth sense just kicked in.

The upshot was that Hewitt had some rather unsavoury things to say about the similarities between Blake's colour and that of a linesman who twice foot-faulted him. In the seats just above their son, Mr and Mrs Hewitt weren't exactly helping calm his mood.

Darren Cahill, Hewitt's coach, had been incommunicado with the parents for a while over a desire to bring his wife and infant daughter to tournaments with him. The Hewitts believed he should be concentrating solely on their son and his tennis.

Even though the player would break his grand slam duck five matches later, including a devastating performance in the final against Pete Sampras, there was no bridging the disagreement. Cahill chose to leave a couple of months later.

The following year, my first for *The Times*, Hewitt became Wimbledon champion defeating Argentine David Nalbandian in a one-sided final. It was glory, glory Aussie, I wrote the script for the official Wimbledon film but something in the family still festered about the Cahill incident.

On top of this, Lleyton had refused to participate in a TV interview for ESPN in Cincinnati in August 2002 for which the ATP, the governing body, fined him $105,000, sparking widespread debate and, eventually, legal action.

When we reached Shanghai for the Tennis Masters Cup – the year-ending men's showpiece – Glynn Hewitt was broiling. I was sitting in the foyer of the Intercontinental Hotel having a coffee one morning when Kelly Wolf, Hewitt's agent at Octagon, made her way over. There was a distinctly nervous tone in her voice, 'Um, hi Neil, Glynn Hewitt would like a word.' 'Not a problem, Kelly.'

Over walked Glynn and Cherilyn who sat together on the sofa across from my armchair with not a hair's breadth between them. Wolf moved to another single chair. What followed for the next ten minutes (though it felt longer) was a haranguing of such four-letter word venom from Glynn I really couldn't believe my ears.

Wolf's cheeks reddened, as did mine quite possibly. I did thank the Lord that most folk around us were Chinese and therefore not quite getting Glynn's drift. My feeble attempts to stop the onslaught simply loosened his tongue further. Finally, he ran out of names to call me.

Now, I'm not a coward but Glynn Hewitt in full flow took a bit of resisting. I replied with one thought, 'Your son is the number one player in the world and I work for the number one newspaper in the world. I suspect I'll be around in that position longer than him so we should try to get along.'

In the circumstances, where my head felt like mush, I thought I'd done rather well. His response was along the lines that I could fuck off.

I don't know whether sticking up for myself struck a chord but when Lleyton's legal dispute with the ATP grew more serious into 2003, Glynn became my best mate and secret supplier of information on the case. Notes were pushed under the door of my hotel room with the latest developments. Funny old game, tennis.

In everything he did, Lleyton was an awesome competitor and I liked him immensely. He had his faults – haven't we all? – but I would want him on my side in a scrap. I wish he'd won his home Aussie Open.

* * *

Bernard Tomic was the tall, lean, complex Aussie boy wonder. He had won the prestigious Orange Bowl (the unofficial world youth championships staged in Miami) at under-12s, under-14s and under-16s, a set of successes previously unheard of. He had also been sent home from the French Open for an unacceptable level of commitment when just 14, so he could be a bit of a slouch.

Wanting to get to know more about Bernard – as any self-respecting tennis writer would – meant having to deal with his dad John, a towering figure about whom there was a degree of menace made more so in that he spoke strangulated English to which you had to listen hard to pick out the best bits.

The Tomics were of Croatian stock and their desire to fit in with the Australian establishment was complicated to say the least. John would demand more funding from the authorities and yet be wary of the coaches Tennis Australia sent to work with Bernard, a really precocious kid.

John was grateful for a couple of my articles suggesting his son had the hallmarks of a future champion, so much so he invited me to dinner with him and Bernard at a Melbourne steakhouse as a thank you. I remember it for two things: the biggest steak knives I ever saw and a display of Bernard's incredible sleight of hand.

We had ordered our meal and John instructed me to touch one of the objects on the table while Bernard looked away. I should hold it for five seconds and then put it back down. I picked up the pepper pot, counted to five and replaced it. Bernard's massive right hand floated across the top of the table, resting momentarily above each implement and he picked up the pepper pot.

The same was true of a knife, a fork, my wine glass, the pepper pot again thinking I'd outwit him and he got every single one right. 'He has something special in his hands,' John said. 'He is a magician.' Bernard looked both embarrassed by and proud of his talents in equal measure.

As time went by, the family's relationship with the Australian authorities soured with accusation and counter-bouncing back and forth, usually concerning how much money the Tomics wanted and how much TA was willing to give them. The player's form was like a rollercoaster and John's attitude worsened.

It reached the stage where Bernard demanded his own father be removed from the environs of the court when he was playing. When I arrived in Madrid in May 2013 for the clay-court Masters, I was told that John had been involved in a physical altercation with Thomas Drouet, a French hitting partner who had been working with Bernard, the latest in a long line of assistants who could stomach neither the player's *laissez-faire* attitude to his career nor his father's aggressive persona.

Drouet was pictured with injuries to his forehead and nose and his neck was in a brace. The police had been summoned and took Tomic into custody. I wrote this for *The Times* the next day:

'There are many times I have taken John Tomic's side, I have listened to his stories, he has confided in me more perhaps than with any other journalist, we have had debates and discussions about Bernard, he has shaken my hand, he has ignored my hand when I have offered it, that is the way it has been.

'He has blown hot, he has blown cold. Whether or not we shall ever speak again – his wish, not mine – time will tell. I actually hope that I do not see him at another tournament.

'John Tomic does not deny headbutting Thomas Drouet and for that alone, tennis has to make a stand. Can it possibly tolerate having someone who would turn violent in this extreme – whether defending himself or not – present at its tournaments?

'The ATP, the WTA and the ITF have not often acted in concert but here is an opportunity for the sport to put on a united front and say that it cannot allow Tomic to be present at any of the events that has their sanction. The grand slam tournaments, too, have a duty to prevent him from gaining admission.'

I received texts from John saying I should make sure to look behind me whenever I was at an event. I couldn't believe he was allowed access to Queen's in June. I saw him sat at the back of the stand watching Bernard lose to the German Benjamin Becker and, worse, he saw me. If looks could kill, I was a dead man.

I snatched a few backward glances all the way to the car park that evening and for a good few evenings after that.

* * *

I felt in Judy Murray a kindred spirit, though the protection and promotion of her sons – and herself as an extension – was her paramount concern. The successes of Andy and Jamie offered her a platform on which to speak on a multitude of subjects affecting the present and future of British tennis.

She was not enamoured of much that happened at the LTA and there we shared a common bond. We were both consummate supporters of the County Cup, an event at which spectators' golden anniversaries were announced during play and the contestants dropped their rackets to join in the applause.

The LTA County Cup was a one-off annual doubles-only event played in five days across the nation's grass courts two weeks after Wimbledon. If your county was in Group One – the tennis equivalent to the Premier League – you played at Devonshire Park in Eastbourne and the whole thing was a lovely, occasionally overindulgent party.

One evening in 2009 at the Grand Hotel – where much of the overindulgence took place – Ian Conway, the delightful North of Scotland president, tipped me the wink that Andy and Jamie Murray would be playing for the county the next day. I told the office to get a photographer down to Eastbourne pronto. I was the only journalist on the spot.

The LTA found out about the Murrays and suddenly Roger Draper, the CEO, and his media officer arrived saying they were taking over the day's press interviews. I politely told them to get stuffed.

Judy drove a Volkswagen Polo up to the pavilion (Andy was taking his driving test the next day) and out slid the brothers, complete with tennis bags. How they managed to squeeze in I'll never know.

All of a sudden a few more tennis writers appeared, tipped off by the bastards at the LTA. But the matches were over, the boys had left – having lost 6-3 to Hertfordshire – I'd spoken to Andy, got the quotes I needed and had already filed. I decided to give the late arrivals a few, not all, of the quotes and they had to make do with that.

This was the kind of Fred Karno silliness that rendered the LTA such an amateurish organisation. Draper, trying to impress the press soon after his appointment, booked a five-star restaurant in the centre of Rome for a group meal, forgetting the fact that Tim Henman was on that night's order of play, so we weren't able to leave the grounds and make it at the appointed time.

The booking was hastily switched to a drab pizzeria near to our hotels and, as we wrote at different speeds, we arrived in ones and twos, no one knowing which conversation had started and which had finished and the whole thing was an entire waste of time that probably cost the LTA £500 once we'd drunk the place dry of vino rosso.

Judy was a close confidant. She called me the 'Harmanator'. We set the world to rights many a time on email where she would happily feed me the latest bits of information, usually but not exclusively about her boys, and I'd keep her informed of developments as I saw them. These were a constant and valuable source of amusement and instruction.

It was a bit like the reincarnation of Pat Rafter on the touchline in the old Southend United youth-team days. I was trusted with a lot more than I probably should have known but only ever used the bits that helped shape a story. What I didn't use would remain our little secret.

20
Courting Popularity

ETIENNE DE Villiers was dying in 2005. No one quite appreciated the extent of his illness; the cancer to his prostate had become horridly advanced and yet, at the age of 55, having stepped out of the Disney Corporation he accepted the chance to become executive chairman and president of the ATP Tour.

De Villiers admitted he was angry with life, angry with the medical hand he had been dealt, angry at the world. It was not the time to enter the maelstrom of tennis politics demanding every element of his body was functioning properly. Tennis was in a terrible state and he was being asked to repair it while facing the prospect that no one might be able to repair him.

He was introduced to a sceptical world that wondered how a Disney executive might possibly transform a moribund men's sport that had been overseen for the best part of the previous decade by Mark Miles, a US lawyer who somehow had managed to protect the status quo without really doing anything definitive.

The ATP was stymied by its own procedures, which gave the tournaments and the players equal representation at board level, with three members apiece and a chief executive who, if an impasse was reached, had the power to make a deciding vote. This led to atrophy, deadlock and compromise.

De Villiers arrived with little pomp. Andre Agassi had been the number one player in the world, was still in the top ten and remained a hugely influential personality. Agassi's best friend and agent Perry Rogers was a player representative on the ATP Board. Agassi asked De Villiers if he was going to make decisions based on what benefitted the player or what was best for the sport. De Villiers replied that his entire concentration was to do what we felt was right for the sport.

Agassi's response was to tell him that he was right but ought to be prepared for a torrid time, sleepless nights, and daily battles with those who would never take to change. Never was a truer set of words spoken.

The men's game was in a real state of flux. New heroes were emerging. Good people played it. In 2005, I was seated on a balcony of the tennis centre at Key Biscayne in Florida chatting to Benito Perez-Barbadillo, a former ATP media manager who had decided to throw in that lot and work exclusively for a young lad named Rafael Nadal. The kid appeared, tennis ball at his feet, which I failed abysmally to try to take off him. We had been formally introduced the previous year and he was relaxed in my company considering I was his parents' age.

Nadal was charming, polite and with his pidgin English, delightfully endearing. I was building a rapport I wished to enjoy with Andy Murray. That spring, Rafa reached the Miami final and then won Monte Carlo, Rome and the French Open at the age of 19 and tennis had a teenager with a physical presence not felt since Boris Becker's days.

Four days after Wimbledon (Nadal lost in the second round to Gilles Müller of Luxembourg), 52 innocent people were killed in a series of ghastly terrorist bombings on London transport, on buses and on the underground. My phone rang the next morning. 'Hi, Neil, you ho-kay? So sorry for London.'

I recognised the voice immediately. It was Rafa wanting to make sure I hadn't been injured. If I looked upon his successive achievements with a small sense of favouritism, I hope anyone would understand why.

I became a confidant and dare I say friend of De Villiers who was approachable and shrewd. There was no US corporate bullshit, he told it as it was. I admired that, if some of his staff and players found it a touch unnerving. Tennis needed him badly at that time.

There had been threats to drop doubles as an element of the men's game from the ATP Tour. Tournament directors felt the drain on their resources was too insistent to keep paying for doubles players who couldn't draw a crowd, having to pay their accommodations and *per diems* too.

It wasn't possible to simply scrub doubles from the game but neither could those who play doubles exclusively just expect to keep turning up and taking the cash. De Villiers sought compromise, 'Doubles is like water – it has to find its own level. We have to discover what will make it a more attractive proposition for everyone, because if you have a product that's not desirable, obviously you have to improve it. It is totally inappropriate to talk about removing doubles from the ATP Tour. But we have to make it better.'

In time, a shortened doubles format of two sets and a tie-break to settle the match if a decider was required was introduced and in the end-of-season ATP Tour Finals – moved with such incredible success to the London O2 arena – the doubles was played as the *hors d'oeuvres* at both sessions, a simple yet brilliant concept.

The All England Club invited SP (I knew him as Super Prezz) to the Royal Box just once after he stepped down. He may have worked at Disney for a long time but he wasn't quite showbiz enough for the new regime at Wimbledon.

* * *

In his period at the helm of men's tennis, De Villiers had many conversations with Rafa Nadal. 'The first time Rafa was a new kid on the block and was very much, "You do it your way, I'm happy with what you decide,"' De Villiers said. 'But he soon became very forthright in his views about where the sport should go and what we should do.'

By early 2007, Nadal was already twice the Roland Garros champion, a Wimbledon finalist and a signature performer. We arranged a round of golf at Indian Wells in March, a chance to relax and at the same time chinwag about the sport he played professionally while engaging in one he played for fun – well, that's what I thought.

The evening before our tee time, a group of 20 clay-court specialist players met to debate the threat that tournaments in Monte Carlo and Hamburg might lose their noted Masters status, something proposed by the ATP. Nadal was dead against it and told De Villiers so.

I had thought of raising the subject of tennis politics in the splendid isolation of a round of golf but he was having none of it. Golf was golf. It demanded all his concentration. Then he leapt back in to the buggy and hurtled towards the hotel before a ball had been struck. I thought he'd decided to drop me.

Within a couple of minutes, there was a second deafening screech of tyres as he returned. Rafa had forgotten to have the tips of his fingers taped as he did before every tennis match. He couldn't play golf without the same anal attention to preparatory detail.

I was decidedly nervous. Rafa wanted me to drive the buggy we had been allocated to play the Celebrity Course at the Hyatt Grand Champions (where Maureen and I had honeymooned) and I realised that any errant piece of steering could be calamitous for the future of Spanish sport.

'This is pressure,' I said, to which he replied, 'No, pressure is if *I* driving.' On one precipitous slope he chose to put his foot on the accelerator while my hands were on the wheel as he wanted to get to his ball quicker than the pedestrian pace I was setting. We zig-zagged aimlessly. I said I'd prefer to be the passenger.

Nadal, a 12 handicap, played golf right-handed, hit a brute of a ball, especially with his five wood, occasionally took great tufts of earth with his wedge – refilling divots as fastidiously as he screwed back the tops of water bottles at tennis changeovers – and did it all with the glorious lack of inhibition one expected of a 20-year-old who attacked sport with an uncomplicated relish.

When he missed a putt – some of the pin positions must have been set by Roger Federer when he learnt that Nadal had a tee time – he leapt in the air emitting yelps of despair in the fond imagination that he should sink them all regardless of degrees of difficulty.

There were the abiding memories of him knee deep in beautifully manicured flower beds searching frantically for his ball (he pushed the timekeeper's patience on the golf course too) or just clobbering the white chap out of sight and intuitively flexing his very muscly forearms.

* * *

Roger Federer against Rafael Nadal would become the signature tennis match-up of my period at *The Times* and two matches that stand out for their enduring brilliance both ended with success in a fifth set for the bull from the Balearics. Lest I fall foul of those who prefer the luxuriant skills of Federer to the more blood-and-guts approach of Nadal, I was never less than fulsome in my praise of Roger, the most elegant of champions.

But both in Rome in 2006 and on Centre Court at Wimbledon two years later, Nadal exuded extraordinary defiance and duly lifted the silverware. Put another way, he was the only player who consistently planted uncertainty into the mind of Federer even if the Swiss was poised for success with the ball on his racket and the court at his mercy.

When else did Federer lose a match in which he won a tie-break 7-0, didn't serve a single double fault, led a final set 4-1 and had two match points which both fell to his usually inimitable forehand? Nowhere but in Rome, to Nadal.

If Rafa wasn't exercising inside Roger's head, his coach uncle Toni was toying around with it. Federer never liked what he regarded as Toni's blatant coaching of his nephew and how often the sport looked the other way. 'I caught him in the act today,' the normally uncontroversial Federer said, though the Italian umpire Romano Grillotti, a bit of a cult hero on home territory, neither saw nor heard anything awry.

The Masters final in the Italian capital was best of five back then and the press were thankful that the tournament had seen fit to build a little shaded box in the top corner of the main stand on Campo Centrale, otherwise we'd have fried.

We ought to have known the best would be saved for last when we had no more sweat to give. A cameo in the fifth set summed the Majorcan up. Trailing 4-1 and with the first point of his next service game pocketed, Nadal enticed Federer into a mis-hit attempted lob that landed a yard long.

The reaction of most players would be to grit their teeth and gleefully collect the next ball to serve. Nadal instead leapt up and punched the air. It was hard to believe he suspected at that moment, with the finishing line so distant, the tide had turned but you never knew with him.

Nadal held serve and broke back in the seventh game. At 6-5 behind, he served a first double fault and was two match points down as Federer appeared content to roll the ball over the net and entice errors. In his dreams, Federer would want a match point against Nadal on his forehand. He would give up a Wimbledon title for two.

Federer had led the second-set tie-break 3-1 and failed to hold on, so when he was ahead in the final set sudden death by the same score, a sense of *déjà vu* descended. At 5-3 ahead, Roger hit those errant forehands that cost him extended rallies and, as a matter of course, the title.

In London just over a year later, with the Centre Court roof in its construction phase, Federer had won the Wimbledon title for a fifth time in succession, beating Nadal in five sets. He had defeated Nadal in the 2006 final as well. In 2008 the world number one had not lost a set before the final; Nadal just the one. Nadal had won the French Open and the grass-court tournament at Queen's the following week for good measure, having caught the Eurostar from Gare du Nord to St Pancras International rather than hop on to a private plane as many of his status would.

Nadal, in full piratical top and billowing shots extending below the kneecap, took the SW19 citadel by storm, winning the first two sets of the 2008 final. Federer inched slowly back into the final, edging two phenomenal tie-break sets, the second of them 10-8.

For many of us long in the tooth, this was tennis beyond belief, a level untouched before. The thrust and counter-thrust, not an inch given, was rare genius. By quarter past nine the natural light was quickly fading and when those in the inner sanctum were switched on, their glow could be seen from just above the canvas backdrop. Federer was beginning to resent being made to play on.

It was from the roller end, looking towards the lights and at 9-8 down in the deciding tie-break, that the great champion would take on a three-quarter-length ground stroke and plop the ball into the net. Nadal was on his back, halfway to heaven. He had won 6-4, 6-4, 6-7, 6-7, 9-7 in what I called the Match of a Generation.

We guests at the Champions' Dinner were well into the dessert course when Nadal and an ecstatic entourage arrived in the early hours of Monday for an event scheduled for Sunday evening. They stayed for all four courses. We emptied into the streets well after two.

Across the globe, reaction to the manner of the championship decider was a mixture of disbelief, joy, thankfulness for having been able to witness it and a respect for its two protagonists, which should have dissuaded Federer from carrying out any of the darker thoughts that crossed his mind in its aftermath.

Novak Djokovic, the world number three from Serbia, watched the final while on holiday in Italy and at its climax sent a text to Benito Perez-Barbadillo who was his PR manager as well as Nadal's. 'I still have a lot to learn,' it read.

* * *

In 2010 there was a changing of the guard in SW19. The rules stipulated that no chairman should stay in post for more than a decade and so it was time for the admirable Tim Phillips to stand down.

Phillips had overseen the club's increasingly extraordinary progress, the final act in the open and shut case of the Centre Court roof, the No. 1 Court redevelopment, and had done it all with no grand gestures, no need for posturing, no overt flexing of power, but an old-school charm and collaborative nature.

There were two things he should have tackled more decisively. The club had dragged its feet over equal prize money for the women players for years, closing the gap by minor fractions without levelling the playing field. I had a conversation with Carlos Fleming, Venus Williams's agent, suggesting a first-person piece for *The Times* in which Venus would offer her views on the subject that I knew to be very tasty. The article, published just before the championships in 2006, was quite devastating.

Under the heading 'Wimbledon has sent me a message, I'm only a second-class champion', the three-time Wimbledon title holder wrote, 'Have you ever been let down by someone that you had long admired, respected and looked up to? Little in life is more disappointing, particularly when that person does something that goes against the very heart of what you believe is right and fair.

'The decision of the All England Lawn Tennis Club yet again to treat women as lesser players than men – undeserving of the same amount of prize money – has a particular sting.

'I'm disappointed not for myself but for all of my fellow women players who have struggled so hard to get here and who, just like the men, give their all on the courts of SW19. I'm disappointed for the great legends of the game, such as Billie Jean King, Martina Navratilova and Chris Evert, who have never stopped fighting for equality. And disappointed that the home of tennis is sending a message to women across the world that we are inferior.'

The following year, prize money parity was attained. I felt I'd played a small part in securing it.

* * *

It may seem absurd but Tim Phillips and I were in our grey change-into Qantas pyjamas on the way home from the Australian Open – I had managed to wangle an upgrade – standing at a business class stewards' service area debating the Wimbledon profits and why I believed the LTA shouldn't be handed the surplus from the Championships without the need to prove they had earned it.

It stuck in the craw that the club should deliver such annual bounty for the LTA and not have any say in how the money should be spent. Tim, not raising his voice, simply said that their remit was to make a success of the tournament and shouldn't go poking their noses elsewhere.

I appreciated what he was saying but I didn't agree with him at all. We begged to differ and had another G&T.

The three chairmen of the club I had worked with, Buzzer Hadingham, John Curry and Phillips, were largely cut from the same cloth; top-quality people who didn't take themselves too seriously and had an easy-going manner with the media we hoped their successor would replicate.

Philip Brook adopted a sterner, more standoffish tone. I sensed someone who liked the trappings his new role afforded in the world game and intended to make the most of them with no particular desire to engage with people irrelevant to his ambitions. His wife was similarly taken with her own importance.

Never again would a Wimbledon chairman walk through the British ranks at a foreign grand slam and place on each desk a copy of the appropriate paper he'd brought from England or just hang around in our space for a chat. The Brooks weren't the cosying-up type, well not to the likes of us. We weren't royalty.

* * *

I stupidly missed out on a major story at the end of 2011. Ivan Lendl was going to become Andy Murray's new coach and the tennis world would reverberate to another tectonic shift in the Scot's career. I'd have a bloody good exclusive.

A prominent coach told me the deal was agreed three days before Christmas Day but said I couldn't use it yet otherwise the Murray camp would know where I got it from.

He rang twice more during the holidays to confirm the tale and each time told me to keep it to myself a little longer. This was infuriating but I was as good as my word. As often happened in these circumstances, the story leaked out and I could only write it at the same time as everyone else.

I flew to Australia on New Year's Eve, changing my plans at the last minute to take in Brisbane – a debut destination – where the Lendl and Murray partnership would have its first outing. I did steal that particular march on my British colleagues.

It was the perfect occasion to celebrate new beginnings with plenty of time in the air to consider how the partnership might work. The two men had similar ethical approaches to life; they would leave no stone unturned to bring the best from each other and as a pair that much was certain.

I took myself back to 1986, my debut year as a full-time tennis writer on *Today*. I wouldn't say we became mates – that would definitely be stretching it – but I believed Lendl appreciated my diligence in taking time to try to get to know and understand what made him tick. Too many in the press chose to pigeon-hole him as dull and robotic, closing their minds to anything other than his grinding efficiency on court and deadpan performances off it.

When he got to know you better – and the other way around – a mutual trust developed. He'd happily take the piss out of you in front of an audience, a sure sign of grudging affection. But he never let you know *everything*. That would be to let down his guard too far.

'You were one of the very few in the media I would speak to,' Ivan said. 'I immediately knew that you did your homework, you knew about the subject and you were interested in what I had to say, not the other way around. And I trusted you as I had to trust my coach and the player I coach has to trust me.'

On court, Lendl was as good as I saw. When the US sporting bible *Sports Illustrated* greeted his success at the 1986 US Open with a front cover 'The Champion That Nobody Cares About', it gained international approbation. It was a devastatingly insensitive headline and its accompanying article demeaned everything Ivan had worked so hard for.

'I heard about the article from my agent but never read it myself,' he said. 'I was told that the main editor was off that week, they put a younger guy in charge and he wanted to make a name for himself.'

* * *

Murray's team (bar Lendl who was on his way from Florida) were waiting at the Brisbane site, sniggering like crazy. They had known all about me knowing all about the liaison but being forced into silence.

Murray adeptly won the Brisbane title, so the partnership was off to a flying start. The next stop was Melbourne where Lendl wanted to meet the British press, those he already knew and the rest he'd have to acquaint himself with smartly. He was sharp, witty and frank.

'I admire Andy's guts for hiring me because he had to know that it's not going to go unnoticed and be a quiet thing,' Lendl told us. 'It ups the ante a little bit and that just shows me that he wants it. It would have been very easy just to hire someone, just another coach, and not get a high-profile person.'

Lendl kept his own counsel on the self-defeating tendency of Murray to go into a grump on court if things weren't going his way, 'I don't mean to be evasive. There has to be a relationship between player and coach and if that's violated, it's wrong. It's like doctor-patient privilege. Whatever is said between Andy and I will never come from me anytime, even after Andy retires.'

Lendl won eight grand slam titles, a man who outwardly did not take much notice of what was written about him, hurtful or otherwise. Murray's skin wasn't so tough that he hadn't been affected by some of the press he had received. In the past, he had preferred that his coaches didn't speak to journalists.

Lendl said, 'I'm going to do whatever it takes to help Andy, if it's talking to you guys every day to take pressure off. Every match is a tough match, even for the top players. If they don't play their best, they could lose, whereas in our era if you didn't play your best, maybe you lost a set in the first or second round and it was a huge surprise already.

'I do have a philosophy about how the game should be played. However, that does not necessarily mean that Andy has to play that way. I also have a view about how Andy should play – and those two don't have to match.'

It was clear that Lendl's words – we had to guess what they were – had immense effect. There was concert too between the pair and Murray's long-time pal, Venezuelan Dani Vallverdú, who was part-coach, permanent-confidant. Murray reached the final of Wimbledon in 2012, where only the brilliance of Roger Federer denied him the crown. Murray broke down during his live TV interview.

There wasn't much time to wallow in grief. The London Olympic Games were on the horizon. Murray was selected for the torch parade, collecting the flame at the front door of the All England Club, running it up St Mary's Walk past an applauding press contingent and on to the next beneficiary. From carrying a torch to burdened by the nation's hopes.

From an initial 64-man draw, the semi-finals pitted Murray against Novak Djokovic and what became the finest three-set men's match I was privileged to report on as Federer locked horns with the loveable giant from Argentina Juan Martín del Potro.

The purple backdrop on Centre Court had taken getting used to, the country colours of the competitors likewise, the surface was caked hard on both baselines and thus gave the perfect track for indulgent talents, the touch and fluency from The Fed countering the flat, pounding groundstrokes of Delpo.

There were to be four hours and 26 minutes of this masterpiece of a match-up before the Swiss triumphed 19-17 in the final set. Murray's victory over Djokovic, 7-5, 7-5, was delightfully straightforward from a domestic viewpoint.

Whether or not Federer was exhausted from his semi-final endeavours, he was swept aside as Murray became Olympic champion, 104 years after Josiah Ritchie had won Britain's previous gold in the men's singles, also in London. Andy added silver to his collection when he teamed in the mixed doubles with young left-hander Laura Robson where they were beaten in a 'golden' tie-break final by Belarusian pair Max Mirnyi and Victoria Azarenka.

* * *

It had to happen that Sir Alex Ferguson would walk back into my life one day but I didn't expect it in a press conference room at Flushing Meadows. I hadn't a clue he was in the crowd on the day his compatriot defeated Tomáš Berdych of the Czech Republic to earn a spot in the US Open men's singles final.

The weather was much as Alex would have remembered it at Aberdeen's Pittodrie stadium, a gale-force wind blowing straight down the ground (or court in this case), so composure was hard to come by, self-control vital and an ability to put the conditions out of your mind essential. Andy did it all spectacularly.

Murray was midway through his explanation later when the side door to the interview room burst open and in strode Sir Alex and Sir Sean Connery, the original and the best James Bond. The room was stunned to silence except for some swooning female American journalists when they recognised 007.

Alex looked along the front row and spotted me at the far end. 'Neil!' he exclaimed. 'Hi Alex,' I replied. 'There are some right ******* in here,' he responded. I couldn't hear exactly what he said but it drew a wide grin from Andy so it was definitely derogatory.

I sneaked out of the back of the conference room and collared Alex in the corridor. He had downed a few. We had our arms across each other's shoulders again, 19 years on, him more pissed than me this time.

He scribbled his mobile number on a bit of paper ripped from my notebook and said he was staying in New Jersey near the home of Michael Dickinson, the racehorse trainer. He thought he might be back for the final against Novak Djokovic on Sunday.

There he was indeed, in Andy's player box no less. The men's final in New York historically started in the late afternoon, so very late evening UK time. We yearned for a swift finish. The first set went to a tie-break of almost 25 minutes, the longest in tournament history. One rally in the set extended to 54 shots. The British press was already staring at the bottom of a production no-hoper.

Murray led 4-0 and 5-2 in the second set but Djokovic fought back only for the Scot to recover and win it 7-5. Two sets to love. History beckoning. Djokovic won sets three and four. History straining. Murray took himself off court and into the gents', not for a loosening of his bowels but a pep talk. He won the final set 6-2 and a title beyond even compare with his gold medal.

When asked about his impromptu toilet break, Murray said, 'I was thinking about the situation I found myself in, after I guess nearly four hours of play by that stage. I went to the toilet and had a think and said to myself, "It's just one more set. Give everything. You don't want to come off this court with any regrets. Don't get too down on yourself. Just try and fight."

'I got a bit fortunate to get the break at the beginning of the set with a net cord on the slice backhand. I settled down a bit after that. When it does happen, you think in terms of the training you've done, the physical suffering, the stuff you put your body through on a weekly basis to try and prepare for these moments so you can play for four and a half hours at a high intensity. I'm very fortunate to be able to do this for a living.

'But, when you get so close to achieving the last goal I had to achieve in tennis in winning a grand slam, and when you have been there many times and not done it, it is easy to doubt yourself.'

At the moment 'game, set and match' was called, the British press guys pressed the button to send their reports. It was one in the morning in the UK. I left it a couple of minutes and made sure my report had landed. Yes, it was there, but the presses had stalled. Bloody hell. Another call. Still not gone to print. I was shouting down the phone now. A historic victory and *The Times* was fucking it up.

Finally, about 20 minutes after the words had arrived in London, the presses rolled again. We managed to get British tennis's greatest day for 35 years into around 150,000 copies.

* * *

Andy Murray had become used to his fitness levels being debated and dissected ever since his dying swan act at Queen's back in 2005. He now cut an impressive physical specimen, honed and chiselled.

At the end of 2012, he set the British press a bit of a challenge. Why not see how many of us could endure his regime and live to tell the tale. What macho man could resist?

All we had to do was get ourselves to Miami and he'd organise the rest. Jez Green, Andy's fitness trainer, prepared the sessions and – as a reward for this piece-of-piss endeavour – we'd get to interview Murray after what had been a significant breakthrough year.

Lendl thought the whole idea was hysterical as he rather enjoyed seeing fellow human beings – especially those in the press – suffer physically. We first gathered at Key Biscayne, the old tournament venue, and the coach invited us on to court, one after another, where he set a test.

He would strike the ball as high as possible into the air and we needed to catch it, without letting it bounce.

What we – or certainly I – had forgotten was that even in December, the sky was so brilliant in that part of the world it was impossible to follow the ball when you were half blinded. I was spinning around like a demented top and missed the ball by at least a yard. Lendl was gleefully filming it on tape which he said he'd keep as a piece of blackmail if ever I was disposed to write negatively about Andy. He's still got it on his phone, all these years on.

Next it was down to the Crandon beach and some short sprints on the sand – bloody tough – before a less rigorous mile-and-a-half jog. Kevin Mitchell of *The Guardian* trailed off at the back but he was the oldest and no disgrace. We were each allowed to pose with Andy for a picture so it looked as if we were having a private running session.

Bikram yoga was next. Fucking hell. I had never done ordinary yoga, was not the most pliable of people and thought I was going to die. Simon Briggs of the *Telegraph*, a bit of a geek where this stuff was concerned, didn't bat an eyelid as the rest of us slumped sideways or forwards into puddles of sweat around him.

Lastly to the gym and the versa-climber – 'the total body vertical cardio climber' – I'd seen Andy on many times before. It looked like a tortuous piece of equipment and so it was, with your arms and legs pumping in some kind of unison as you 'virtual climbed' against the clock. I had to be helped down from it.

Then we completed an exercise round which included leaping from the floor on to a two-feet-tall soft-plyo jump box in a single bound. I tottered on the edge for about three seconds before falling backwards into the arms of the US Open champion. Thankfully he didn't drop me.

As part of the agreed interview, I wrote, 'Gone are the days when tennis was a genteel pastime. In a five-set match, Murray will run five miles, much of it staccato: stopping, turning and twisting. The effort he puts in is brutal, and yet he does so without a flinch.

One wonders if those who still deride him – more for his accent and perceived manner than anything else – could last ten minutes.

'And yet, only now, with Olympic Games gold and the US Open title in his treasure chest, does the 25-year-old Scot feel able to stroll down a street with his head held high. "I've found it much easier to go out and about, just to walk around," he said. "I've felt more confident, maybe, as a person, to walk with my head up, whereas before I was a bit like … (he drops his head deep into his shoulders). I never wanted anyone to say anything to me."

'"To be honest, I don't really like getting pointed at, I still feel a bit uncomfortable with that stuff, but it's something you learn to deal with. I just feel a bit better about myself."

'"Having lost in so many close finals and in a lot of tough matches, I felt as if I had let people down, in that I was reminded of the fact that we hadn't won anything big every day for the past five years. There was a part of me that felt some kind of responsibility for that."'

What would 2013 bring for this big, honest, gifted lad, we wondered.

* * *

For the best part of a decade I was considered part of the BBC radio commentary team, which was a wonderful sideshow and got me away from the press room – often a blessing. Stuck in there for most of the day with a large number of fruitcake people drawn to cover tennis would drive anyone potty.

I was grateful for an opportunity to spread my wings and join a great group of commentators, summarisers and producers who made the whole experience a joy. My role was largely confined to the grand slams, bar Wimbledon where there were so many ex-players jostling for their turn behind a microphone there wasn't room for an actual storyteller.

Jonathan Overend had become the BBC's tennis correspondent the year after I had assumed *The Times* role. He was a terrific broadcaster, making the whole process appear so slick and controlled, even if there was occasional mayhem behind the scenes.

The main commentary booths at Melbourne Park and Flushing Meadows were up in the Gods; indeed, in New York, it seemed impossible to deliver the ball-by-ball description on which the BBC prided itself, yet 'Overs', with fellow commentators David Law, Alastair Eykyn and Philip Studd, rarely mistook the flight of the ball. Theirs was a real gift. I just filled in the bits around the edges.

At Roland Garros, the Beeb had a shoebox booth into which two people could squeeze at a pinch and if a third voice was required, the provider would have to stand in a corridor two feet wide and crouch down to see the ball at all. On a warm day it was like commentating from a sauna.

In 2013 the BBC team provided wall-to-wall commentary for the Indian Wells tournament at the request of the tournament owner, the Oracle founder Larry Ellison, and once again I was ready and willing to offer my services. There would be a steady stream of personalities invited into the booth to talk tennis and life.

Studd and I were commentating on some match or another when the great Gladys Knight arrived to be interviewed. She was a devoted tennis fan and an utterly delightful person. Phil sensed I was itching to ask her for a song and when the opportunity presented itself, Gladys and I delivered a chorus or two of 'Midnight Train to Georgia' live on air. I got to do the 'woo-woo!' bit.

She declared me an honorary Pip, befitting her backing group. Every time I hear that song I'm reminded of glorious days in the desert.

* * *

Rory McIlroy and Caroline Wozniacki gave only one interview as a couple during a courtship that mesmerised golf and tennis and a few more sports besides. To me. The three of us sat in the players' restaurant at Devonshire Park, Eastbourne on 21 June 2013, two days before what would become my penultimate Wimbledon as a working journalist.

To be fair to them, they had promised it for at least a year and my persistence was rewarded. I hustled them to a table as far away from the restaurant entrance as possible so that if on the off-chance another journalist wandered in, he or she probably wouldn't spot us. I didn't want this secret to be disturbed.

Rory had been to Indian Wells a couple of times, taking a break from his professional duties to watch Caroline play. He'd often ball-boy at her practice sessions and carry her bags back to the locker rooms. He invited me to a table on the patio at the tennis centre one afternoon to meet Fred Couples, a real hero of mine.

Caroline was delightfully warm and natural. Her father Piotr, a former professional footballer from Poland, had moved to Denmark to further his career and was Caroline's tennis coach. He and his wife Anna were never far from their daughter's side. Although Piotr didn't speak much English, we understood one other and Caroline would translate the bits I didn't quite catch.

She didn't play in a particularly eye-catching style; it was her obduracy from the baseline and incredible work ethic that earned the successes that would eventually send her to the top of the WTA rankings. She ought to have won the 2009 US Open but was out-thumped in the final by Belgium's Kim Clijsters, although Wozniacki eventually became a grand slam champion nine years later, winning the Australian Open having been match point down in the final to Romania's Simona Halep.

I was chuffed with the Eastbourne coup. Piers Morgan, the ex-*Sun* pop columnist and *News of the World* and *Mirror* editor, who had moved to the USA, was desperate to get them on his talk show on CNN but couldn't twist their arms. The bosses at *Hello!* or *OK!* would have loved this one.

Critics of the Wozniacki/McIlroy relationship suggested that the reason she had slipped to number nine in the WTA Tour rankings and he was number two in the golf standings (behind

Tiger Woods no less) was that they'd fallen so completely for each other, they had taken eyes off their respective balls.

'There are always people that want to talk and make a story,' Wozniacki, then 22, said. 'The thing is when Rory was winning everything last year I was the lucky charm. Now, when he misses a cut, I'm a bad person.

'It has nothing to do with this [their relationship]. He's a great support and there are so few people who know exactly how it is to feel and be in the position I am in and have been in. Rory is young, he's been number one, he's won many tournaments. You don't find many people who can relate to it.'

McIlroy, the Northern Irishman who had won the 2011 US Open and the following year's US PGA, said, 'Everyone knows how it feels to be in love and want to make something work. That's where we are.'

I asked them to recall how they met – who said hello to whom first – at which they giggled, interrupted each other and became a touch red-faced. The 2010 US Open was their first touchpoint.

Wozniacki was playing Carly Gullickson of the USA in the night session as McIlroy returned to his guest seat. He said, 'I liked her tight black dress. My caddie would confirm I went on about her for weeks. I admired her from afar. Then I was invited to the Royal Box on Wimbledon ladies' quarter-final day.

'One of the matches was expected to be Caroline against Maria Sharapova and I thought, "Oh, perfect," but she lost a round earlier and that was a real disappointment.'

Four days later Vladimir Klitschko was fighting Britain's David Haye in a world heavyweight boxing championship bout in Hamburg and through her friendship with the Ukrainian and his manager, Caroline had been invited and noticed Rory ringside, 'He was in the third row staring and I thought it was at someone behind me but literally he couldn't stop looking at me [McIlroy pulled his cap down over his eyes at this revelation]. He had a pretty dark-haired girl on his left and a friend on the other side. I was thinking it was pretty rude to be staring at me when he had his girlfriend with him.'

Feeling the burn of McIlroy's eyes in her back, Caroline took the initiative, introduced herself and offered congratulations for his victory at the US Open. It turned out the pretty dark-haired girl was the girlfriend of the British boxer Carl Froch. The next moment, McIlroy asked to have a picture of he and Caroline together.

McIlroy was due back at Wimbledon on Sunday for a Royal Box seat to watch the men's final. It was his intention to have an early night for an 8.30am flight, 'I said, "I follow you on Twitter so I can send you a direct message and let you know if we're going to do anything [later]." And she said, well, take my number if you want – if I want!' They went for a drink.

'We found a table in the corner, ordered a drink and hardly touched it as we just talked hours. The next thing I know a guy tapped me on the shoulder. I said, "What's up?" and we realised it was light outside. I flew back to London and at every change of ends of the Wimbledon final, I was going into the toilet and texting Caroline, then going back to watch the tennis. Two years later we are together, in love and in a great place.'

Wozniacki was the driven one: unrelenting on the practice court. Yet McIlroy was the epitome of someone who had a gift and, if not taking it for granted, knew it. 'Since meeting Caroline I've had a renewed desire to work hard,' he said. 'I always felt I was a pretty hard worker in comparison to other golfers and then I saw how she goes about her profession, how dedicated she is and it made me think I can work that little bit harder.'

Wozniacki replied, 'If I say something, I'm going to get it done. I'm very pushy and Rory is laid-back. As for our relationship, I guess if you really want something, it's not difficult to make it work.'

* * *

I took a seat in the press tribune on Court 2 at Roland Garros in 2014 to watch a first-round match between Caroline Wozniacki and Yanina Wickmayer of Belgium. It was a lovely, intimate arena that held around 1,000 fans and where the press seats were tucked into a corner at the junction of tramline and baseline.

Caroline walked out dressed all in green, the colours of Ireland, which I thought was utterly bizarre.

She somehow managed to find the heart to spend two hours and seven minutes competing, but then she wanted to be as far away from the place as possible. Her world had been torn apart the previous week, the reason for which she still had no rationale.

McIlroy had left the apartment they shared in Monaco to fly to London for the BMW PGA Championship at Wentworth. When his name appeared on her phone half an hour later, she answered in anticipation of a lover's exchange. When she put the phone back down, it was in a state of absolute shock. McIlroy had called the engagement off. The call lasted for a few minutes.

Caroline and I met two weeks later at Eastbourne where, a year earlier, we were ducking Cupid's arrows. The defeat in Paris to Wickmayer had been banished the minute it occurred though I recalled her tottering aimlessly – someone shouted that she was walking off the wrong way – back to a world changed from the beautiful one she had planned it to be.

To get away from it all, she flew to Florida the next morning where Serena Williams met her. 'Serena has always been there for me. We had something different to talk about, a new energy. She's an unbelievable competitor on the court and I admire her for all she's done and the role model she is. Off the court she's such fun to hang with,' Caroline said.

'Sometimes you get caught up in what I should be doing rather than why I do it and the love of the game and the passion we all feel. It's impossible not to have passion for the game and get so far. I think we all agree that to become a great player and great champion you have to love the game.'

The word 'love' did not stick in her throat. 'I'm not a victim,' she said. 'Everyone has ups and downs, hard times, terrible times, incredible times, it's just a part of growing up and learning.'

* * *

In my final throes as *The Times*'s correspondent, John McEnroe senior became a real friend – a real astonishment. He had once waved articles in my face when his son was at his recalcitrant worst but had become a tennis elder statesman and often attended Flushing Meadows as a USTA guest.

One evening I was loitering around the players entrance when John appeared. 'OK, Neil,' he said. 'We're off to Bill's. I've got a car.' Mr McEnroe didn't actually have the right credentials for a tournament vehicle but blagged his way into the queue and once I'd retrieved my gear, we were off.

The Mercedes dropped us outside my favourite bar, John was in there like a shot, had the microphone in his hand, taken the stool next to the pianist and was belting out all manner of rebel Irish songs. He was tolerated because of who he was. I was very content to be in his company, especially when he thrust the microphone in my direction and insisted I sang a song. It was something from *My Fair Lady*. I miss him.

21
Murray's Wimbledon

ONE LATE afternoon in February 2013, I was sitting at the All England Club with Ross Hutchins. Somehow Wimbledon and February didn't go together, much like Hutchins and cancer.

Ross was one of Andy Murray's biggest buddies, two diverse personalities who instantly hit it off. When Andy discovered three months earlier that his 27-year-old pal was diagnosed with Hodgkin's lymphoma, he burst into tears.

The evening that Murray, having reached the Australian Open Final once more, landed home from Melbourne, he insisted he and Ross went out for a meal with their contemporaries Colin Fleming, Jonny Marray and Jamie Baker. The subject of hair was bound to come up in the conversation because they had long ribbed each other about their respective, ever-so-slight follicle loss.

'I think Andy's going to win the contest in a few months' time,' Hutchins said, preparing for the intensification of his chemotherapy course.

Ross had dismissed weeks of back pain as wear and tear on a young athlete but it grew to become excruciating and he was sent home from a training camp in La Manga, Spain, when he was told what may be happening to him.

Ross said, 'I think of this cancer in tennis terms, like being on a bad run, which is a strange thing to say, I know. We've all lost a load of first rounds, I lost 11 in a row once; a tough time. If you try and hide something and push it away, you end up thinking about it more and worrying about it more.

'You try to lie and start kidding yourself but I am open about it – there is a very high cure rate and yes, I have a brilliant team. I'm feeling good and feeling positive.'

The story of the first week of the men's singles at the tournament was the second round, four-set loss of the favourite Roger Federer to Ukraine's Sergiy Stakhovsky on Centre Court, a sporting once-in-a-lifetime. Murray cruised through the first four rounds without losing a set. His quarter-final opponent on a gorgeous Wednesday evening was Fernando Verdasco, a Spanish left-hander built a little like Rafael Nadal.

When Verdasco won the first two sets, the worse was being feared before Murray dug into his enormous depth of self-belief and willpower to force his way through. Two days later, he would face Jerzy Janowicz, an almost maniacal competitor from Poland. I went to see Jerzy the day before the match and disturbed him having a nap in the players' lounge.

He said, 'All I want to do tomorrow is to bring my best tennis, nothing more. I don't really want to think about the match at all, I am a strange guy like that. I know the crowd will try to help him but I hope they will not try to disturb me. Now I need to go and get some more sleep because I didn't get much last night.'

Janowicz blazed the first set with an abandon that unnerved the home crowd but didn't seem to worry Murray unduly. He fought his way back with a ferocity that woke the Pole up to where he was and what he was trying to do. Though Janowicz led 4-1 in the third set, Murray was not to be denied and won in four.

The final was staged on a sunshiney day, nothing Dunblane about it. The toffs had all come out. Novak Djokovic was triple break point down in the first game and yet held, the kind of pugnacious, draining, athletic rally that would mark this match out for posterity. Murray would win the first set but Djokovic led –

we thought decisively – in both the second and third. Murray kept finding a way back. Djokovic looked tired.

We came to the tenth game of the third set, Murray 5-4 to the good. I wrote, 'The tenth game, the bloody tenth, went on and on. Murray raced to a 40-0 lead triple championship point which left as soon as they had come. Three break chances for Djokovic. Angst and hellfire. Another match point for Murray, a serve, a couple of half-hit groundstrokes, a backhand into the net. Story told.'

Murray let the racket drop from his hands, flicked off his cap and started to pump his fists. He was looking straight up at the press seats, indeed straight at me. Miguel Seabra, a long-time friend and colleague from Portugal, was a row in front, turned to me and said, 'Neil, he is looking at you.' To think, after all Andy had done to turn himself into a Wimbledon champion and I was his immediate focus. It was quite something.

To be fair, I was pumping my fists straight back, losing the decorum for which the British press were recognised especially as our players went out of tournaments in various forms of disarray. Bugger decorum.

* * *

The Harman family headed to Turkey a week after the tournament and while I was floating off the coast of Marmaris, I could see my daughter Kathleen signalling from the beach that my mobile was ringing. It was Mahesh Bhupathi, the former Indian doubles player who had joined Andy Murray's team as an adviser. Would I be interested in writing a book about his Wimbledon success? If so, I had a month to do it.

No sooner had we landed home than I was on my way to Ohio where I could have a couple of sit-downs with Murray and get as much in the can as I could by way of interview material. We did our first hour in a Whole Foods restaurant in the middle of nowhere while he devoured a whole chicken, which did make for a frustrating time when trying to make head nor tail of his words when I replayed the tape.

I'd not been to the Cincinnati Masters before and I had to give the tournament full marks for its presentation and friendliness. I had rarely encountered a more convivial, helpful bunch in a press room anywhere. Then I bumped into Jimmy Connors.

It had been quite a while since I'd seen Jimmy and hadn't expected to find him in the players' lounge on my tour of the site. He dropped a bombshell. He was Maria Sharapova's new coach. A *Times* exclusive at a tournament I'd had no intention of attending.

I had a front-row seat courtside directly opposite Jimmy for the first match of an intriguing liaison, against Sloane Stephens, an up-and-coming young American. I'd watched a lot of tennis in my time and I could tell from the first game something wasn't right. Maria barely looked at Jimmy, who seemed detached from the whole affair. Sharapova lost and two days later the partnership ended, something to do with irreconcilable differences. Another exclusive. I could honestly say I'd seen it all.

The Sharapova story that year wasn't quite complete. Climbing aboard one of the tournament buses at the US Open two weeks after Cincinnati, I was beckoned to the seat next to him by Max Eisenbud, Sharapova's long-time agent at IMG. 'Listen up, Harman,' he said in a whisper. 'I've got a scoop for you.'

He told a story I really couldn't believe, nor could *The Times* when I relayed its content but it was used on the front page and went like this:

'Maria Sharapova, the richest female athlete in the world, is planning the most audacious move of her career – changing her surname to Sugarpova for the two-week duration of the US Open, in honour of her line of sweets.

'The 26-year-old Russian, a former world number one, has asked about a "quickie" name-change through the Supreme Court of Florida, where she has a base, and would revert to Sharapova after the tournament. It is understood also that the striking emblem of

Sugarpova candy, a pair of red lips, will feature somewhere on her attire during the final grand slam of the year.

'It is an extraordinary ruse by Sharapova and IMG, her management company, and there are no legal barriers to stop her. Sources close to the star, who split in Cincinnati last week from her new coach Jimmy Connors after only a single match together, say that she is willing to see whether the change can be made in time.

'Sugarpova, the company, is owned by the athlete, who founded it with an estimated $500,000 of her own money. The sweets come in 15 varieties that have labels like flirty, sassy and smitten. It has been called "the Spice Girls of the candy world" and it is estimated that 1.8 million bags of the confection, which cost $5 a packet, were sold worldwide last year, with special emphasis on Russia, the United States and Europe. There are outlets in Selfridges stores in London, Manchester and Birmingham.

'Should she be able to go through the necessary paperwork, it is understood that she may still need the permission of the grand slam committee. If it agrees, she could be introduced, addressed and have scores called out in favour of Miss Sugarpova for as long as the number three seed remains in the event.'

The rest of the world pooh-poohed the whole thing. US freelance Ben Rothenberg was especially disparaging, as he seemed to be of everything I did. No one could ever disclaim the veracity of the story and though it never actually came to pass, it was a wonderful idea.

* * *

The second and third instalments of my Murray book interviews took place in New York, the last in the back of a tournament Mercedes heading from Central Park South to Flushing Meadows. I could sense that the driver was listening intently to our conversation when he should have been concentrating totally on the treacherous NYC traffic.

As we pulled into the tournament site, he looked back across his shoulder and said that he was getting quite emotional just listening to Andy telling the story of the final against Novak Djokovic. I had to admonish him not to tell anyone anything he'd heard until the book came out. We shook on it (after he'd parked up).

Murray's recall of the final was, indeed, compelling, 'I looked down at my left hand. For the first time I could remember in the middle of a tennis match, it was shaking. Shaking pretty violently. I was in the midst of what was the single game that would change everything in my life.

'I had had three match points already and went to collect the balls to serve again at deuce. You never knew how your body might react in such circumstances but I'd never had a reaction like that before.

'But I steadied myself and managed to give myself a fourth chance. My serve could not have been bettered but Novak got that one back as well, hanging out a racket. I had to get my feet into a position where I could play an off forehand which wasn't one of my best. He took aim with a backhand – and netted it.'

* * *

David Lloyd wanted to be the chief executive of the LTA more than most things in his professional life. In 2013, the position became vacant when Roger Draper departed and Lloyd was scheduled for an interview with the LTA's chairman, David Gregson, on the evening of 13 June, in the middle of the Queen's Club tournament.

That afternoon, in the BBC interview studio at the event, host Sue Barker, commentator Andrew Castle and I discussed in a live broadcast the prospective appointees. Sue asked me who I thought should have the job and my response was an unequivocal backing of someone I'd known for more than 35 years. I said he should have had it before Draper in 2006.

Castle's response was, 'I don't think there's any way you would want David Lloyd in that job now.' I was stunned. What was wrong with his candidature?

'Well there's a difference between him then and now in the way he lives his life and the way … I just don't think it's the right time for him in his personal life. I'm not going to go into detail. I don't think he's the right man for the job now.'

Two days later, Lloyd instructed that legal proceedings should be brought against Castle and the BBC. I was sent a copy of the letter from Lloyd's barrister to Andrew's agents who would be obliged to bring it to their client's attention. In due course the matter was resolved, Castle apologised unreservedly for remarks made in the heat of a TV debate and which he accepted had no foundation. Damages were paid.

Whether or not this had anything to do with Lloyd not making the top six of candidates for the top job in British tennis, I can only speculate. Lloyd was interviewed and was told that the post was for a ten-year period (to which he answered that no job was ever offered with a ten-year timeframe), he was likely too old at 65 to see the role through and that stakeholders and councillors of the LTA didn't like him, which I presumed was a polite way of saying they were scared of him making the waves that British tennis desperately required.

The LTA gave the job to Canadian Michael Downey, who had absolutely no experience of how the sport functioned in Britain and was, in my estimation, deeply unimpressive.

David's elder son Scott became the LTA chief executive in January 2018 and almost everyone from those days remains in position. A job at the LTA really is a job for life.

22
Trouble Ahead

DURING THE Indian Wells tournament in 2014, Mick Desmond, the marketing and media executive at the All England Club, contacted me a couple of times to say he wanted a meeting as soon as possible to talk about the championships. He was unusually persistent.

We arranged to meet on Monday, 31 March. All seemed well as Desmond showed me into his office where Richard Lewis, my old LTA nemesis and now the club's chief executive, was seated with a Wimbledon annual balanced on his knees and a couple more on the table beside him.

The greetings were warm, I was asked how the California trip had gone and I said that, as usual, it was a brilliant tournament. I really had no reason to suspect I'd not be returning there again. The small talk ended there.

Lewis began to quote from the annual. A paragraph or two, maybe more. He then read from an article from *The Guardian* which was word for word that which he'd read from the book. He repeated the process from a different page. Desmond raised his eyes in that 'what's been happening here?' manner.

My mind was in a muddle. I said I surely must have attributed the words to the author, hadn't I? I knew that down the years I had variously written, 'said the *Telegraph*'s Paul Hayward' or 'as Simon Barnes wrote in *The Times*', if I used their words. Yes, I had done that, though Lewis implied several occasions where I'd used match description and not been so scrupulously vigilant.

Retreating from the office, I phoned sports editor Tim Hallissey, who was on another call. Ten minutes later as I sped around the M25, my phone rang. I informed Tim about the Wimbledon meeting, that I'd made some terrible fuck-ups and didn't know what more to expect. There wasn't much he could say.

That evening I wrote an email to Lewis, copied to Desmond, 'I appreciate you seeing me today and, if the circumstances of the meeting were not what I would have wanted, for the frankness with which you dealt with the situation.

'Once again, I wish to apologise to you and to the club for actions on my part which may have brought the good name of Wimbledon into disrepute. I frankly should have checked and double-checked my work more diligently and not rushed what I know is such an important project for the club.'

Less than two hours later, a response from Lewis arrived in my inbox, 'Thank you very much for your follow-up from today's meeting, it is appreciated. I can assure you that there is no animosity whatsoever and today's meeting gave nobody any pleasure or satisfaction at all. We know you are a friend of the club.'

* * *

Within a couple of days of the Wimbledon meeting, the British tennis writing group flew to Naples for a Davis Cup World Group quarter-final tie against Italy and the likelihood of a pulsating three days in a crackling atmosphere.

The British boys were getting closer and closer to a major success in the championship and in Andy Murray and James Ward had a singles selection with the ability to contend with anything the Italians threw at them, be it either verbal or pure sport.

For the first time at such an occasion, my mind was not where it should have been. I was torn between not telling anyone about my meetings at Wimbledon – though that meant no one at the club leaking the fact – or letting my colleagues know what was afoot. I thought it best to come clean.

We were strolling at a gentle pace along the promenade Via Carraciolo on a warm spring evening after dinner on the eve of the tie. I waited for Kevin Mitchell to become detached from the group – like the 2012 fitness test with Andy Murray in Miami – and asked if I could have a quiet word.

As *The Guardian* was the paper Richard Lewis had concentrated on in the previous week's revelations, I presumed I'd lifted some of his work. Kevin took what I said in his stride. I was apologetic and there were no remonstrations; he didn't raise his voice.

As we reached a bar on one of the promenade's curves and decided to have one for the road, I told the other lads who – I seem to remember – were Mike Dickson of the *Mail*, Simon Briggs of the *Telegraph* and Dan King of *The Sun*. They told me not to worry too much about it.

The tie was a corker, the Davis Cup at its disbelieving finest, played out on a court where from the press box end extended a glorious view across the shimmering Bay of Naples and, if you craned your neck to the left, Mount Vesuvius was a majestic testament to our incredible world.

The ancient giant may have rumbled a couple of times across the weekend in light of the brilliance unfurling nearby. Ward lost the first singles to Fabio Fognini and, after a thunderstorm soaked the place, Murray and Andreas Seppi were all square at the back end of their second set, the Wimbledon champion having pocketed the first.

This would mean Murray needing to complete his singles, win in the doubles on Saturday and then another singles on Sunday if Great Britain were to stand an earthly. He managed to fulfil the first two parts of that trilogy and Britain led 2-1 going into the last day.

In Fognini, the Italians had a player who could mess with an opponent's mind when his own appeared to be the consistency of tapioca. I'd seen him have the most self-defeating strops. But this day he was blindingly creative, crafting winners, rousing the fans, drawing the strength out of Murray's limbs. He won in three sets and handed the baton to Seppi to seize the momentum and defeat Ward in straight sets.

I sat in the row behind HRH the Duchess of Gloucester on the flight home. She said something sweet to me at Naples airport but I can't remember what it was. If only she had known the turmoil I was going through.

The sting seemed to go out of my problems as the spring progressed. The 2014 French Open was another of those truly momentous tournaments. Rafa Nadal won the men's singles for the ninth time, his fifth in succession, taking his grand slam tally to 14, level with Pete Sampras. His performance in a five-set final against Novak Djokovic surpassed anything he had produced there before, which was saying something.

Maria Sharapova, gallantly recovering from losing positions throughout the tournament, defeated Romania's Simona Halep in a three-hour, three-set final regarded as the finest the women had produced at the old place since Hingis/Graf/Georgina Clark in 1999.

During Wimbledon I detected rumblings about the seriousness of my situation and made a point of seeking out Jon Wertheim of *Sports Illustrated* as I'd apparently used some of his work for the yearbook. He wasn't happy. I apologised profusely.

Djokovic won the last Wimbledon men's final I would cover and the manner of his victory over Roger Federer was such that, in retrospect, it was a match of the abiding brilliance I would have wanted for a farewell.

My summing-up for *The Times* went, 'Midway through the fifth set of a Wimbledon men's final of true immensity, the mind wandered to how it might be if Novak Djokovic had to walk to the BBC microphone and explain how he had lost his fourth grand slam tournament final in succession. A crackly, crippled voice, perhaps his head back to stem the tears like Andy Murray in 2012, a man utterly crushed. People should know better of him by now.

'A few minutes later, on as pleasant an English afternoon for tennis as is possible, Djokovic was in the arms of his team; the 6-7, 6-4, 7-6, 5-7, 6-4 victor over Roger Federer, for whom the storyline to beat all storylines was dashed from him by an athlete, a fighter, a spirit supreme.

'In the 27-year-old's moment of glory, his mind wandered back to where it had all begun for him in Serbia, and Jelena Genčić, who taught him the rudiments of the sport upon which, thanks to his success at the All England Club, he has returned to the number one ranking.

'Genčić marvelled at this little boy with the neatest tennis bag she had ever seen, everything clean-pressed, folded and ready for play. She never had children of her own, but all those she taught tennis to became her family. She died last spring. Nole [Djokovic] was the head boy, her shining light, her little champion. His love of Tchaikovsky came from listening to her classical collection.

'There was something of the *1812 Overture* about the passions on Centre Court, booming crescendos, subtle changes of melody, big walloping winners and lovely phrasing. It was the perfect match-up, of Federer achieving what had seemed the remote prospect of winning an 18th grand slam tournament in the face of champions far younger than he, and Djokovic concerned that he had lost that certain something that had made him such a titan in finals in 2011 and early 2012. Since then, the phrase "runner-up" had landed next to him with troubling regularity.

'It was then, having seen how Ivan Lendl had turned Murray around, that he decided – in full consultation with his team – to approach Boris Becker and ask him to join the coaching party. In an interview with *The Times* at the Dog & Fox in Wimbledon High Street three days before the Championships, Becker said, "This isn't some ego show and I know it all and I've done it. I'm a different kind of voice, that's why I was called in."

'"My opinion about tennis, the number one ranking, the grand slams is different from anyone else because I speak from my own experience. The choices I've made in my life have not all been perfect but if there's one area I'm better than most, it's tennis."'

* * *

A few days after Wimbledon I was playing golf at our local course, Sand Martins, when a call from media chief Johnny Perkins found me at the halfway hut. Perkins asked if I'd seen an article in the 'Street of Shame' column in the satirical magazine *Private Eye*. I said I hadn't. He said I should. *The Times* got in touch. It had been seen. An investigation was under way.

The family took our regular holiday in Massachusetts. I asked the US Open media department if I was banned from covering the event and they assured me I wasn't. *The Times*, in the shape of managing editor Craig Tregurtha – who'd had a meteoric rise up the journalistic ladder from being a sports sub at the *Sunday Mirror* a few years earlier – ordered me home. I had to attend a disciplinary hearing that stretched to two. Neither went well.

I was told I could have support at the hearings from a chosen *Times* writer who could sit in as a silent witness and see that the proceedings were conducted fairly. The two 'colleagues' – one of whom initially said he'd come – then both declined by which time it was too late to find anyone else. I was on my own. It would be two v one.

The company put a tracer on my work across the previous decade to see if I'd been guilty of the same offence for *The Times*. This was a devastating twist of the knife and they found nothing. I hated them for even suspecting it.

So many stones were being thrown at me, I did have to wonder how many of those without sin were casting the first of them. I was told that at a tennis writers' meeting in New York a British reporter of limited talent said I was 'disgusting'.

I considered hacking dead people's phones was disgusting and taking delight in ruining other people's careers was disgusting, but me? I'd leave that there.

23
Unemployment

THE PHONE rang the morning after the end of my *Times* career, at around eight. It was Paul Hutchins, the former Davis Cup captain. He said he couldn't believe what he'd been told and expressed his support for me, for which I thanked him most sincerely.

A lot more people called, steadfast folk like Alan Jones, Tony Pickard and David Felgate. David Lloyd and John Lloyd were in touch – the Leigh-on-Sea brigade united. It was decent of them all. I was told that colleagues from News International had been warned about speaking to me. To them I was the equivalent of the black spot. What a shit shower.

There were some wonderfully moving emails from those not based in Britain. Edoardo Artaldi, Novak Djokovic's Italian manager, could not have been nicer.

> *Dear Neil,*
>
> *I am very sorry to read about this news and I hope to see you soon at a tennis tournament. Everybody can make mistake and I am sure you did this mistake in good faith and only trying to be ready in timing for the book.*
>
> *Unfortunately, this world is taking care only for bad news and not for the good one.*
>
> *People are envious and are waiting for the first opportunity to attack another person. You are who you are and don't listen*

to a bad voice. I am sure you are at peace with your conscience so stay relax and go ahead as always.

I hope that The Times *will take the right decision and that you can still go ahead with them, you are one of the most important tennis journalists in the world and for us the best!! Stay up and hope to see you soon.*

Big Hug,

Edoardo

None of this was useful for anything other than to assuage a deep hurt. What happened next? I had a family to support, I was 57 years old and had spent 40 of those as a newspaper reporter; some bloody amazing, some incredibly taxing but, for the most part, tremendously rewarding. I had ten good years left in me.

No one was going to hire a writer emitting a bad smell and sneaking towards the official retirement age. I was abject at DIY so painting and decorating wasn't a possibility; I couldn't fix a lightbulb so freelance electrician was out.

I'd never had a car treated by anyone other than a registered mechanic and couldn't discern one end of a jump lead from the other. Since my Railway Tavern days back in the 1970s, I'd always yearned to work behind a bar but no one wanted to take a punt with anyone over the age of 25.

I signed on the dole at the job centre in Bracknell. Each Monday morning I'd amass my attempts at finding work, place them in a folder and be in the queue for the 9am opening. It was soul-destroying but when you'd spent your working life earning a wage and now had nothing, how else did you survive?

I was a writer with a decent track record sat opposite a withering glare explaining my attempts in the past week to try to gain employment. The lady nodded, signed a form and there was another few quid in the bank. The temptation was to look into the sadness on the faces of my fellow jobless and wonder what they had done to deserve such ignominy.

I would never be judgemental and anyway, how in their shoes did I look? I was a number just as they were. After a few weeks I couldn't face the awfulness of being a societal scrounge and stopped going back.

Promises were made about potential business meetings and not kept. Opportunities were raised and dashed. Emails stopped. A dead man walking. At least I still knew who I was.

In the autumn of 2016, I received news that Bryan Webster was in a care home in Stockport, suffering from advanced dementia. All I could think was how random and unfair life was to strip one of the brightest minds I'd met who now couldn't recognise anyone he saw.

His wife Mary had passed away the previous year from a similar illness and whether it was her loss that subconsciously robbed Bryan of his faculties, we could only speculate. I needed to see him at least once more and was pleased in some selfish way that he had no idea what had happened to me professionally.

The nurse in reception said I shouldn't be upset if he walked right past me. I had hoped that as one of those he had worked with so closely over a decent period of time, a spark might form in his eyes, but nothing happened.

I was told that I should make him a cup of tea and just talk about the old days, mention names he might recognise, say 'Doug' as in Doug Weatherall and it might induce a sense of recognition. I thought that on occasions he had understood what I was saying but there wasn't much of a flicker.

I told him about my life, how Maureen and the kids were getting on, though there was nothing to say about work that wasn't soul-destroying and sad. I talked about Sunderland, about the *Mail*, about our days together, how much I loved him. I gave him a hug but his body was limp in response.

After about an hour, the nurse said I shouldn't tire him more and say my goodbyes. I dissolved into tears to which he was totally oblivious.

Bryan passed away in February 2017 and the *Mail* gave the news a miserly two paragraphs on the sports pages he had devoted so much of his life to.

* * *

Hugh Jamieson, a good pal from West Midlands football days who I'd played tennis against and had travelled the world to report on, died from cancer in September 2017. His funeral was held on a beautiful autumnal day at the Our Lady of the Assumption church in Bosham, Hampshire.

The turnout was sparse and a mere four journalists attended. I was the fourth to arrive, finding Barry Flatman of the *Sunday Times*, Steve Howard, chief sportswriter of *The Sun*, and, to my horror, Bryan Cooney in the front couple of pews. I nodded in their direction.

The post-service drinks were to be taken at the Berkeley Arms, directly across the street from the church. I was hesitant about whether to go but Howard was adamant he wanted to buy me a pint.

Cooney strode in and asked if I'd come outside. Flatters gave me an 'are you sure you should?' kind of glance. What was he going to do? Thump me?

To my amazement Cooney spent five minutes profusely apologising for his behaviour at the *Mail*, saying he'd been too hasty to cast me aside and that what happened to me at *The Times* was a travesty. He offered his hand and I took it. I thanked him for his sincerity accepting at face value that he had indeed been sincere.

I'm afraid there is no independent corroboration of my account of the conversation since it was private and Cooney died three years later from prostate cancer, the same disease that killed my father.

* * *

Harry Findlay had invited Maureen and I to his private box at the 2008 running of Royal Ascot. I wouldn't say that Harry was doing all right but our next-door neighbours happened to be Her Majesty The Queen and assorted other members of the royal family.

Harry loved to bet on tennis. At the time, the sport was investing copious hours and money on an exhaustive review into its integrity and Findlay, who risked more on the sport than anyone before or since, did not think much of its remit.

'The police don't know anything about gambling, they [the tennis authorities] might as well appoint a gynaecologist to look at it,' he said. 'If they want to know about gambling, talk to gamblers, talk to me. I'm a legend.'

Harry was that, and still is. He had won and lost more wagering on tennis than Roger Federer, Rafael Nadal and Maria Sharapova had earned in prize money at the time of that royal meeting. 'That's not being flash, that's just the way it is,' he said. 'I love the Fed, he's won me more millions than anyone, he's changed my life.'

In his exclusive corner of Berkshire that afternoon, though, Findlay was in a rage – not the best of moods for a professional gambler who constantly needed to have his wits about him.

'It's time people like me sat down with Etienne de Villiers [president of the ATP] to tell him he doesn't have an inherent problem,' Harry said. 'There's not been a single bent match in grand slam tennis in the past 30 years and I know, because if there had been, I'd be destitute.

'I know there were problems with the (Nikolay) Davydenko-(Martín) Vassallo Argüello match in Poland last August and the naivety of the odds were laughable [Davydenko was the equivalent of 5-1 against when he ought to have been 5-1 on] and something was wrong. But you can't start blaming Davydenko, you just can't.'

Betfair, the world's leading online betting exchange, with whom tennis had a memorandum of understanding, voided all bets on that match. An investigation remained unresolved ten months later; Davydenko and Vassallo Argüello were in a state of limbo.

'It's obscene what's been allowed to happen to these players,' Findlay said. 'We are dealing with a sport and sportsmen who are straighter than most people in business and if they continue to be tarnished, it's unfair. I've heard about supposedly suspect matches but they're in satellite events where no money changes hands.'

Findlay's three great sporting loves were dog racing, horses – he was the joint owner of Denman, the Cheltenham Gold Cup winner the previous March – and tennis. His latest equine purchase was to be named Pearl of Manacor in honour of Rafael Nadal.

'No other sport has made me as much money as tennis and it's getting a lot harder so I don't mind letting some of my secrets out,' he said. 'The biggest financial reward is the switch from clay to grass and the combination of tournaments coming too close to each other.'

His recall of matches was uncanny. 'I had [Paul] Haarhuis to beat [Fernando] Vicente on grass in 1999, I bet ten [thousand] to win one; the opposite would be the case on clay,' he said. 'That is why what Nadal did at Queen's last week [winning the title a week after lifting the French Open] was extraordinary. I had a really good crack at [Ivo] Karlović against Nadal in the quarters. I had six figures on Djokovic in the semis, I put more on when he was 2-0 in the first set and I thought this is it, we're going to get masses today, but did we fuck. Nadal is a monster.

'Do you think I'd be nuts enough to put money like this on if tennis was bent? It's so straight it's unbelievable.'

Harry asked me to write his book in 2017. The pair of us were in need of turning our lives around. He was on his financial uppers; the same was true for me as far as writing was concerned. I had to *do* something.

The adventure began in the town of Clonmel in County Tipperary, Republic of Ireland. You could have written what I knew about hare coursing on the back of a postage stamp. Yet here I was at the Irish National Meeting, completely lost in but mesmerised by the jargon and blarney, betting white against red or the other way around and not knowing what the hell I was doing. In this frenzy of impenetrable accents and ever-changing odds, Harry was in his element.

A dog he owned named Big Fella Thanks had won the Irish Derby in 1999 in a final against Toy Razor that entered coursing legend in the Republic. When Harry walked into Powerston Park, everyone wanted to buy him a drink.

Harry had what passed for his own bookmaking shop in the main stand, accepting money from all and sundry who took his odds. Huge wads of euros were being waved around. 'Evens the red!' 'Two to one the white!'

The essence of the sport was two dogs – one with a red collar, the other white – racing up a relatively steep incline chasing a hare in something called a buckle. The dogs couldn't harm their prey as they wore mouth guards. The first dog to 'turn' the hare, i.e. make it deviate from a straight line, won the race. It was usually over in 20 seconds but provoked mighty adrenalin surges.

Of all the many stories Harry told, that of the Big Fella stood out – a dog that ought to have been too big and laborious to win such a grand title and heroically defied the odds in a come-from-behind final victory. Harry kept the Big Fella as a pet after his racing days were over and cried his eyes out when he succumbed after a long life.

The *Sunday Times*'s sports books review of 2017, written by Nick Pitt, named *Gambling For Life* in its top ten and offered this nugget. 'Most gamblers regale tales of triumph against the odds; the losses are overlooked. Not Findlay, who begins his engaging, rollercoaster memoir with an account of the day a "sure-thing" £2.5m wager went down in flames.

'Findlay knows all the betting angles and calculations, but his winning secret is his rascally character. The choice of collaborator was spot on, for Harman, like Findlay, is fully acquainted with the vicissitudes of life.'

24

Yeah, I'm a Wanderer

THE SENSATION when two large boxes of books arrived on the doorstep was life-changing. I didn't think I would live to feel such emotion again. To pick the one from the top of the pile was akin to the teenage sensation of taking a freshly minted copy of *Evening Echo* when they arrived from the works.

Now I needed something new to aim for. A couple of projects stalled before a fascinating concept stirred. Gareth Ainsworth, the manager of League One Wycombe Wanderers, lived in the next town from me and we would often see each other in Wokingham's coffee shops for a skinny and a chat.

How might Gareth take to the idea of me spending a season with his club, which shared the lowest budget in the division with Accrington Stanley and was tipped to be mired in mediocre results while on financial suicide watch?

Initially reluctant, Wycombe's manager said he'd give the book his blessing so long as the directors – a supporters' trust who were losing the battle to keep the club afloat – were happy to have their competence challenged and that his players were equally content with an intruder in their ranks. There was no open dissent in either case.

I believed absolutely that Wycombe would become a profound story and have reflected almost daily since on the absurdity of the 12 months spent with the Chairboys, who rekindled a joy for football and football people in me I felt I'd lost forever when I walked away from the *Daily Mail* in 1997.

The cast of characters, the way they lived and worked together, a crazy season marked by elements that may never be seen or heard of again, the friendships made, the trials endured, the victories won, the extraordinary finality, all mixed to form a story that blurred the distinction between fiction and non-fiction.

Within two weeks of my introduction to a squad that barely mustered a quorum, a lawyer from Louisiana, Rob Couhig, arrived to offer himself as a sacrificial owner. The 70-year-old agreed to eliminate the debt – paying £1m up front at the first request – and do all he could to underpin a solid, secure enterprise.

Rob required a substantial number of those who supported the club to hand over control to he and his ebullient nephew Pete, who sold himself to waverers by saying he would leave his family in the Deep South at a critical time in his children's educational development to give his full attention to the Wycombe job.

The results flowed. Wycombe went top of League One in September when the story I'd sold the publisher was how they couldn't plausibly escape finishing near the bottom. The lads kept accumulating ridiculous results with ridiculously late goals. There were inevitable setbacks – losses to Portsmouth on Boxing Day 2019 and 4-0 at Sunderland 16 days later to suggest the bandwagon would be derailed but Wycombe hung tough.

They remained in the play-off positions until the start of March when the destiny of the season was to be determined by means far removed from crap refereeing decisions, ill-timed injuries or sudden spirals in individual form. An unseen enemy was casting a shadow across the country, indeed the whole world.

On 7 March, Wycombe were scheduled to have played Bury, a club that went out of business at the start of the season and whose fixtures were thus forfeited. By virtue of the results of those clubs who played that day, Wanderers dropped to eighth, the first time they had been out of the top six.

The Covid-19 signs, foreshadowed by many but missed by more, were now undeniable. The country entered a lockdown with ferocious restrictions on lifestyles and regular patterns as the virus spread like waistlines in the aftermath of Christmas. Football ground to a complete halt.

A debate raged as to how the season should be decided if there was not a ball more to be kicked. One method being discussed was points per game (PPG), by which the calculation of points earned divided by games played would bounce Wycombe to third place and thus – if the season was halted at its current juncture – to a place in the play-offs.

Outrage abounded. Twitter was full of fomenting ferocity mostly directed at Wycombe and what was perceived as their hypocrisy. Peterborough were the club which came off worst if PPG was implemented as they would drop a place from sixth to seventh and miss out on the chance of promotion.

The EFL had to come to a decision one way or another and there were strident views as to how they should use their power. Peterborough's talkative owner Darragh McAnthony issued a statement on 15 May 2020 on behalf of his club and five others: Ipswich, Sunderland, Portsmouth, Oxford and Fleetwood – a self-nominated 'Big Six' of League One. They said they wanted the season completed come what may – the only way the integrity of the sport could be upheld.

Accrington's owner Andy Holt saw it a different way, 'Anyone who puts sporting integrity and football in the same sentence is deluded. It's a financial war, not a sporting battle. It's precisely because there is no sporting integrity that clubs are dying and football is on its arse. We can't waste £640,000 playing the season out and pay for testing just because six clubs want to play on.'

When the vote was taken, 18 clubs wanted to curtail the season, and only four felt the need to play on (not even all of the 'Big Six'). The maligned PPG formula determined the table. Coventry were the champions, Rotherham automatically promoted and by dint of the arithmetic, Wycombe moved up five places and would face Fleetwood in a two-legged play-off semi-final.

Fleetwood's manager Joey Barton and I clinked beer bottles in Ainsworth's office after the Lancashire side's 1-0 league victory in February, at the end of which Barton had been sent off for appalling abuse directed at the referee. That wasn't why our Moretti necks met, more as a hope the sides might meet in a play-off final. Now we'd reacquaint a stage earlier.

Gareth asked me to referee a practice match at Adams Park four days before the first leg. He and assistant Richard 'Dobbo' Dobson wanted to see everyone in action before team selection and tactics were worked out. It was like Manchester United at The Cliff 36 years earlier. And the players were just as testy.

For so long imprisoned by the calamity of Covid, the Wycombe lads lacked their old sharpness, argued among each other and picked on me, even if I was probably a touch rusty myself.

Matt Bloomfield, the club's long-serving captain, asked the manager if he could speak up at half-time and – given his head – he drilled into his players a need for calm and discipline in the approaching storm. 'We've got the play-offs to win and it won't happen if we're having a go at each other and Neil,' he said. 'We are better than this.'

The first leg at Highbury Stadium would be played in a bitter wind and driving rain. Two hours before kick-off, Ainsworth delivered the finest managerial speech I'd heard, 'In the last three months the world has torn itself apart in so many ways. There has been a reset of values, good and bad, people have realised what's important in life. Through this time think about the people you've spoken to. It's been your families, your friends and throughout the whole of lockdown you've been speaking to each other.

'I didn't force you to do it, you did it because you're together. You train together, practice together, work together, win together and hurt together. You've laughed together, cried together and been injured together. You've come back to this season together. You've done that. That's the band of Wycombe brothers I want to see tonight.'

Within 90 seconds of the start, Nnamdi Ofoborh had lashed Wycombe into the lead with the finest left-footed strike of his young life. Fleetwood equalised with a dodgy penalty before Joe Jacobson scored direct from a corner not for the first time in the season, and he then had a penalty saved. David Wheeler made it 3-1, and midway through the second half Alex Samuel swept home a fourth. The second leg would finish a nervy 2-2, Fred Onyedinma settling it with a fabulous late flourish.

Wycombe were in the final to face Oxford United, doughty opponents. Derek Fazackerley, a fine defender I reported on at Blackburn in the 1980s and who became part of the coaching setup under Kenny Dalglish, was now on Oxford's staff. Faz was a lovely bloke I would have wanted to win in any circumstance but this.

In 1964 I was a kid among a full-house Wembley FA Cup Final crowd watching West Ham beat Preston North End. There was no space to be had 32 years later when I was the chief football writer of the *Daily Mail* for the Euro '96 semi-final against Germany and that dreaded penalty shoot-out.

Time had moved on another 23 years and a different Wembley built on the same spot as the beloved Empire Stadium was 99 per cent empty, save for we few fortunate souls in the press boxes and the directors off to our left. It felt wrong but adaptation was vital, especially from the players who had to play the match of their lives with cardboard cut-outs for mute support.

Wycombe took a first-half lead when Anthony Stewart headed in a Jacobson corner at the far post. Oxford responded with a wave of attacks that promised a goal but not one as crushing as the right-wing cross by Mark Sykes that floated in over the head of goalkeeper Ryan 'Rocky' Allsop when he – and everyone else – had expected a conventional delivery.

Rocky made a couple of outstanding saves in the second half to keep his side in the match. Then something crazy happened.

Wycombe appealed for a penalty for handball at one end, but the ball was cleared and just about kept in play by full-back Jack Grimmer who stabbed it towards his own area. Rocky lashed the ball 50 yards downfield – Wycombe didn't much care for the modernist mode of playing it out from the back.

Nine times out of ten, defender Elliott Moore would have headed it away, Onyedinma would have repositioned further to the left and goalkeeper Simon Eastwood would have stayed on his line. Elliott ducked, Onyedinma weaved and Eastwood came rushing out. A clattering of bodies sent Fred to the floor. A clear penalty.

In my book on Wycombe's season, *Close Quarters*, I didn't give Joe Jacobson enough words, recognition or praise. I know he was a bit gutted. So here it is JJ. The penalty you nailed straight down the middle was as good a strike as anyone could have mustered and in the circumstances was phenomenal. It won Wycombe promotion to the Championship for the first time. It sparked joyous celebrations those there will never forget. It changed lives.

The players, management, directors, employees and I went to the Ship Inn in Marlow for a promotion celebration and, quite frankly, I shouldn't have driven home. I was described on one website as 'the luckiest journalist in the world' for choosing to write the Wycombe story. I never much trusted to luck; this was simply being back in the right place at the right time.

Six days later I drove CFO Pete Couhig 500 miles to St Andrews, where he owned a flat and we were going to stay for a few days. We played the New Course that afternoon, the next day a new and glorious links called Dumbarnie and finally, with a five o'clock tee time on a hazy evening, the Old Course, where I'd cut my teeth as a golf reporter over four decades before.

I found the location of the phone box that Jack Statter of *The Sun* had allowed me to use to send my copy to the *Birmingham Evening Mail* during the telecommunications strike of 1978, which may have saved my career. We drank a toast there to old memories and to Wycombe Wanderers.

Almost as importantly, I shot a net 72 off an 18 handicap from the black tees and holed a downhill left-to-right three-foot putt on the 18th green – exactly the one Doug Sanders missed to win the 1970 Open – for a closing par four.

25

Epitaph

EXACTLY A year after my departure from *The Times*, Great Britain won the Davis Cup. I should have been in Ghent because I'd been just about everywhere bloody else. When Andy Murray contrived the final rally to end all rallies I stood and cheered in my living room, on my own. I probably ought to have called someone to congratulate them but they would probably think that was strange.

For years I had seen so much go to waste, Britain failing and falling and then regaining its feet only to stumble again. This was akin to an exorcism for those unhappy years. I was proud as punch and my heart ached for the chance to put the success into my own words. Those days had gone.

In September 2018 I accepted an invitation to deliver the address at the Old Westcliffians' annual dinner in the main hall at Westcliff High School. Before the formalities, I was escorted around and paused at pictures on the walls on which I tried to spot old mates and remember their surnames.

I walked into the hall at the very spot where I had sung the boy soprano solo of the opening verse of 'Once in Royal David's City' in 1969 and Mum, recognising my voice before anyone could see me at the back of the hall, burst into tears. The memories flooded back.

Jim Harrison, the master who had improbably inspired me through Maths as a teenager, was now suffering from dementia and couldn't distinguish names and faces. During my speech I said how much he'd meant to me and Mr Harrison inexplicably rose from his seat, saluted and sat down. This time, I was choking.

The head boy Jonathan Travers toasted the speaker in a manner of such respect for what I had achieved and how I dealt with the end of my career, I had to go across and shake his hand. I had just begun working for the *Evening Echo* at his age. The boy will go far, trust me.

I went further than I ever believed possible. Football was my life for so many years and I lost many companions on the way – dear chums Steve Curry and Alf Smirk, Stuart Jones, David Lacey, Joe Melling, Bob Cass, Jim Lawton, Brian Woolnough, Keith Meadows, Alan Thompson, Derek Wallis, Alec Johnson, Norman Wynne, Don Evans, Martin Leach, Peter Batt, Reg Drury, Ken Montgomery, Bill Mallinson, Glenn Gibbons, Brian Madley, Ian Willars, Mike Gouge, Bob Hall, Jeff Farmer, John Sadler, Mike Beale, Mike Ward, Dave Horridge, Chris James, Mike Ellis, John Bean, Derek Potter, David Meek, Bryon Butler and the best of the best, Ray Matts, Jimmy Armfield and Roy Collins.

In tennis, JP's loss was a savage blow, the redoubtable agency men John Oakley and Bryan Cutress had gone as had Andrew Longmore a predecessor at *The Times* at an untimely age but, as I write, the majority remained this side of heaven including Rex Bellamy, the ultimate tennis writer, in his 90s.

Reflecting on the places and people that cheered a weary traveller, I had always been a (bit of a) singer and so piano bars like Mimi's on Second Avenue in New York, where the unique Hunter Blue (aka Chicken Delicious) was a vocal delicacy and Bill's, home to virtuosos Elliot, Norm and Rick, were wonderfully special places.

There was no singing in Paris but we ate well at Le Lory on Rue Poussin (it's a Lebanese restaurant now) and Le Mouton Blanc. There was the unforgettable Le Bouchon in Coconut Grove where manager George-Eric Farge insisted on playing 'God Save the

Queen' when the British press walked in, swiftly followed by 'La Marseillaise' for diplomatic balance.

No mention of Australia is complete without a tip of the hat to Craig Willis, the best on-court announcer of all, and Victorian newspaper greats Leo Schlink and Bruce Matthews of the *Melbourne Herald Sun*, such supportive mates. I miss their colleague, the late John Thirsk, enormously.

I have been back to the All England Club a couple of time in eight years, first for a drinks' reception after the funeral of Paul Hutchins, the first man to call after my sacking. I chatted to Andy Murray, the Hutchins family were welcoming in their profound grief and when Richard Lewis rose to eulogise Paul and his achievements, I felt nauseous and left.

I doubted I would return to watch the sport itself but in 2022 came the offer of a Centre Court ticket from a member whose name I shan't reveal for fear they may suffer reprisals. I watched Rafael Nadal defeat Taylor Fritz of the US in a phenomenal match decided by a ten-point tie-break in the fifth set, something I never believed would happen. When Rafa had to withdraw from the following round I wondered if I had witnessed his last match at the Club, a relationship turned full circle.

I bumped into Roger Federer's manager Tony Godsick that afternoon who said – without prompting – that the sport missed me which was good for the soul. Then, in September came news of Roger's retirement. Tennis will certainly miss this epitome of grace and grandeur.

* * *

Wycombe Wanderers' first ever season in the Championship was bedevilled by losing their first seven games, the ongoing violations of the Covid pandemic and not possessing the depth of squad to live on equal terms with the massively richer clubs in their new sphere.

Having to play such a compulsive season with not a fan on the terraces was a sickening setback for Wycombe, for their average gates of 6,000 could make the noise of twice that many. They took a couple of poundings at Blackburn and Brentford but were slender losers to Norwich, Bournemouth, Derby and Cardiff, and won four of their last five league games, the first of which was a 2-2 draw at Swansea when Wycombe led 2-0 with ten minutes to go. The club were a point from safety when the campaign ended.

Derby pipped them by that point and then were docked 21 at the outset of the following season for falling into administration and breaking Football League profit and sustainability rules. Had the EFL acted sooner – the case had been dragging on for months – Derby would have been relegated rather than Wycombe.

A return to League One could have knocked the stuffing from them but the resilience Gareth Ainsworth and 'Dobbo' Dobson demanded, a couple of impressive signings in Sam Vokes from Stoke City and Josh Scowen from Sunderland and a composed first few matches raised them into a position to challenge for a top-six place they never squandered. A 12-game unbeaten run at the end of the season took the Chairboys into the play-offs without any need for arithmetical assistance.

The form team were MK Dons who had had an Indian sign over Ainsworth's men but after a 2-0 home victory, their successful deep press at Stadium MK in the face of one goal retrieved and a fiery onslaught would take them back to Wembley, this time to challenge Sunderland, a stirring giant.

There were three starters from the 2020 final: Joe Jacobson, Dominic Gape and Anthony Stewart. From a selection of cardboard cut-outs to the raucous noise of a 72,332 crowd, over 45,000 of them from the north-east and what must have been every inhabitant of High Wycombe. This was a unique bedlam for the Wycombe lads and they never quite overcame it.

Sunderland, who had spent four seasons in League One, led after 12 minutes when Elliot Embleton ran a third of the length of the pitch unchallenged, took a swing and Wycombe goalkeeper David Stockdale – either deceived in flight or underplaying the strength of the shot – helped it into the net.

It was to be one of those afternoons when Wycombe's accuracy of crossing, panache from set pieces and first touch all deserted them. They pressed as much as they could. Vokes had a chance he'd have nailed many times but fluffed and Sunderland were in heaven when Ross Stewart secured promotion for his club with a precise shot ten minutes from time.

The consolations for me were a seat in the Royal Box at Wycombe's invitation, and handshake and hug from two Sunderland stalwarts, Peter Reid and Niall Quinn, about whom I'd written much – mostly from their time at Manchester City – and on a couple of occasions got royally pissed with.

Reid and I once had to be separated by my *Mail* colleague David Walker on the street outside the Portland Hotel in Manchester after a Football Writers' Association awards dinner when he took umbrage to something I'd written about his side.

Big Niall dragged me one Saturday evening into the Ducie Arms in Moss Side, a pub I wouldn't have braved on my own, ordered copious amounts of Guinness and put me up at his lovely home off the Dunham Road after I'd lost the powers of both movement and speech.

Three decades later and we could laugh about it, as it should be.

* * *

I would remain a *Daily Mail* man for all its many blemishes and even if it once preferred someone in charge of sport who manufactured stories rather than allow us to write real ones.

The sports pages in 2022 were bold and bright and the current writing team as good as we had in the 1980s and 90s BC (Before Cooney) and that's saying something. I'm grateful for my 16 years on the paper I always wanted to work for.

The shutters were drawn on the Manchester office in 1986 yet those from the glory days return every Christmas for lunch, a few pints of the finest beer anywhere and fond reminisce. Jack and Oggie were with us last December in their 80s and as waspish as ever. I have to make a speech each year and it's usually a heartfelt re-tread of the truth that in Manchester I enjoyed the greatest time of my journalistic life.

I go alone to the corner of Deansgate and Hardman Street where a characterless, glass-fronted edifice now stands. I can hear creaking passageways, loud Lancastrians, smell fresh barmcakes and something else comes over me – no, I don't mean the rain – that I'll never be able to put into all my own words.